'This carefully-researched book is an important contribution to the scholarship on intelligence. Its focus is leadership, and it provides a theoretical framework for understanding the challenges intelligence leaders will face, broadening the definition of leadership to include ethics, self-awareness and, critically, transformation. Intelligence agencies have not been badly led—I say as someone having led one— but I hope Walsh's book will contribute to a more open debate about how future leaders should be prepared when information multiplies by the second, technology offers dramatic possibilities, both good and bad, and private intelligence providers are both competitors and potential collaborators.'

Gregory F. Treverton, former Chair, U.S.
National Intelligence Council, now Professor
of the Practice of International Relations
and Spatial Sciences, University of Southern
California, USA

'Australian scholar Patrick F. Walsh is one of the most thoughtful contributors to our understanding of how the Intelligence Communities within the Five Eyes nations operate, and how they might improve their performance. In this volume, his third book on intelligence, Professor Walsh impressively lays out important principles of intelligence leadership and governance, then skillfully applies them to the challenge of overcoming the fragmentation that afflicts these organizations. He addresses many other vital leadership problems, too, including the difficulties that accompany the wise integration of Artificial Intelligence and ethical considerations into leadership practices within these unique organizations. The intelligence organizations of the Five Eyes face many institutional obstacles as they confront—separately and together—the many threats that face the world, from terrorism and pandemics to the national security implications of climate change and failing states. Good leadership will be vital and Patrick Walsh lights the way.'

Dr. Loch K. Johnson, Regents Professor
Emeritus, School of Public and International
Affairs, University of Georgia, USA

Intelligence Leadership and Governance

This book explores the challenges leaders in intelligence communities face in an increasingly complex security environment and how to develop future leaders to deal with these issues.

As the security and policy making environment becomes increasingly complicated for decision-makers, the focus on intelligence agencies 'to deliver' more value will increase. This book is the first extensive exploration of contemporary leadership in the context of intelligence agencies, principally in the 'Five Eyes' nations (i.e. Australia, United States, United Kingdom, Canada, and New Zealand). It provides a grounded theoretical approach to building practitioner and researcher understanding of what individual and organisational factors result in better leadership. Using interviews from former senior intelligence leaders and a survey of 208 current and former intelligence leaders, the work explores the key challenges that leaders will likely face in the twenty-first century and how to address these. It also explores what principles are most likely to be important in developing future leaders of intelligence agencies in the future.

This book will be of much interest to students of intelligence studies, strategic studies, leadership studies, security studies, and international relations.

Patrick F. Walsh is an Associate Professor in Intelligence and Security Studies, Charles Sturt University, Australia, and is a former intelligence analyst.

Studies in Intelligence
General Editors: Richard J. Aldrich and Christopher Andrew

Interrogation in War and Conflict
A Comparative and Interdisciplinary Analysis
Edited by Christopher Andrew and Simona Tobia

An International History of the Cuban Missile Crisis
A 50-Year Retrospective
Edited by David Gioe, Len Scott and Christopher Andrew

Ethics and the Future of Spying
Technology, National Security and Intelligence Collection
Edited by Jai Galliott and Warren Reed

Intelligence Governance and Democratisation
A Comparative Analysis of the Limits of Reform
Peter Gill

The CIA and the Congress for Cultural Freedom in the Early Cold War
The Limits of Making Common Cause
Sarah Miller Harris

Understanding Intelligence Failure
Warning, Response and Deterrence
James J. Wirtz

Intelligence Elites and Public Accountability
Relationships of Influence with Civil Society
Vian Bakir

Intelligence Oversight in the Twenty-First Century
Accountability in a Changing World
Edited by Ian Leigh and Njord Wegge

Intelligence Leadership and Governance
Building Effective Intelligence Communities in the 21st Century
Patrick F. Walsh

For more information about this series, please visit: https://www.routledge.com/
Studies-in-Intelligence/book-series/SE0788

Intelligence Leadership and Governance

Building Effective Intelligence Communities in the 21st Century

Patrick F. Walsh

Routledge
Taylor & Francis Group

LONDON AND NEW YORK

First published 2021
by Routledge
2 Park Square, Milton Park, Abingdon, Oxon OX14 4RN

and by Routledge
52 Vanderbilt Avenue, New York, NY 10017

Routledge is an imprint of the Taylor & Francis Group, an informa business

© 2021 Patrick F. Walsh

British Library Cataloguing-in-Publication Data
A catalogue record for this book is available from the British Library

Library of Congress Cataloging-in-Publication Data
A catalog record has been requested for this book

ISBN: 978-1-138-29085-3 (hbk)
ISBN: 978-1-315-26593-3 (ebk)

Typeset in Times New Roman
by Deanta Global Publishing Services, Chennai, India

For all the past, present and future leaders of our intelligence communities

Contents

1 Introduction

Modernization of our intelligence community cannot be slow or timid. Reforms must be undertaken with a sense of urgency. It must be broad, deep and authentic. America's intelligence professionals are capable and dedicated. They often do their jobs in dangerous and difficult circumstances. They **need strong leadership**, a renewed focus on mission, and clear lines of authority and accountability to excel. Structural, organizational, and jurisdictional reforms must be made and will be made. But the goal ultimately is to create an environment and a culture where truth to power is spoken from the bottom to the top.

(Additional Views of Senator Barbara A. Mikulski, cited in Senate Select Report on the US Intelligence Community's Pre War Intelligence Assessments on Iraq, 2004: 509)

The co-ordination that Australia's intelligence agencies require in the twenty-first century is different to that which shaped the establishment of the Office of National Assessments in 1977 and defined its legislative mandate. What is required into the future is an enterprise-based management of the NIC that **provides leadership** and a focus on integration across the full spectrum of Intelligence activities.

(L'Estrange and Merchant, cited in the Australian Independent Intelligence Review, 2017: 56)

We suggest that the government consider establishing a National Intelligence and Security Adviser ('NISA') to oversee and co-ordinate the GCSB, NZSIS and NAB. This would facilitate efficiencies in budgetary and operational matters, and a more effective overview of how the wider NZIC's budget is spent. The NISA could be the principal adviser to the government on matters of intelligence and security. He or she could **provide leadership** and take a whole-of-government view regarding these matters. The NISA could also oversee and direct the implementation of a more flexible budget to ensure the activities of the GCSB, NZSIS, NAB and the wider NZIC are aligned with the government's national security priorities. The government may also wish to consider whether a version of these priorities could be made public.

(Cullen and Reddy, *cited in Report of the First Independent Review of Intelligence and Security in New Zealand, 2016: 62*)

Objectives and overview

The above quotes are a small sample of an ever growing number of political, judicial, and independent inquiries into actual and perceived 'capability short-comings' or 'intelligence failures' across the 'Five Eyes' intelligence communities (ICs). There are many more quotes that could be cited here, but the three above highlight the types of leadership and related organisational deficiencies that have arisen across our intelligence communities since 9/11. While we continue to learn a lot about leadership challenges and failures from public inquiries such as those listed above, there remain however, few academic and publicly available official sources about what leadership means in the intelligence context. After all, if successive inquiries are calling for 'better' or 'new leadership,' it seems critical for scholars and practitioners to reflect more explicitly on what 'IC leadership' is and does.

Additionally, and somewhat more concerning, there is even less reflection on how to address IC leadership shortcomings—the latter of which may potentially lead to intelligence failure. In contrast, there is now a rapidly increasing volume of studies, particularly since 9/11, that have investigated all facets of the analytical role (e.g. tradecraft, education, critical thinking, cognitive bias) and how these impact on effective intelligence processes and outputs that decision-makers value (Walsh 2011; Marrin 2012; George and Bruce 2014; Lahneman and Arcos 2014; Ratcliffe 2009; Walsh 2017a).

Given it is IC leaders of our national security and law enforcement agencies that are meant to set the structures and functions in which intelligence products and processes are delivered, it is surprising that with some limited exceptions (Zegart 2007; Walsh 2017b; Gentry 2008: 133–146; 2015: 637–661; 2016: 154–177; Quarmby and Young 2010; Buckley 2013) the subject of contemporary intelligence leadership remains under-investigated. This is not to suggest that there is not a deep quarry of historical knowledge about intelligence leadership that can be mined. Indeed, Chapter 2 makes the case that understanding contemporary intelligence leadership requires a deep engagement with IC leadership in the twentieth as much as the twenty-first century. Contemporary organisational structures and cultures of ICs have been undeniably shaped by earlier leaders. But this book is not a historical survey of the role played by various leaders on the evolution of intelligence communities in liberal democracies. While current leadership and organisational developments across intelligence agencies have been shaped by post-war, Cold War, and pre-9/11 leaders, what is missing from the literature is a comprehensive understanding of how the cadre of contemporary (since 9/11) leaders have shaped our ICs. What kind of leaders do we now have in our intelligence agencies? Will we need different types of IC leaders in the future than those that ran them during the Cold War or the immediate post-9/11 period and why? What attributes, strategies, and capabilities will IC leaders need to assemble in order to steer intelligence enterprises in directions that allow them to adapt longer term to the ever changing security environment?

All of these questions are important, immense, and no doubt for some largely unanswerable. In part they may seem imponderable because we are not talking about 'leadership' in the private sector—or even leadership in other public agencies such as health or education. After all, intelligence agencies and communities operate largely secretly for obvious operational reasons. Nonetheless, since 9/11 we have seen a greater openness by our intelligence enterprises in liberal democracies to discuss aspects of capability in institutions that once not long ago were impenetrable to any scrutiny. There are many reasons for why a study of contemporary IC leadership is possible now. For one, the various episodes of intelligence failures (9/11, WMD in Iraq)—and efforts by governments to reform aspects of our ICs—has let the light in for intelligence scholars to produce better knowledge about various activities prosecuted by these communities.

The ability to garner more informed insights on the state of ICs has also been assisted by intelligence leaders that have left government employment and entered the academy—particularly in the US. Other episodes such as WikiLeaks and Snowden have also impacted significantly on how our ICs interact with the public and the scholarly community. Indeed, even in times of questions about the legitimacy of ICs and a growing mistrust about their activities, some contemporary IC leaders have chosen not to completely raise the draw bridge. Instead, some have sought as part of their leadership role to engage more publicly about what their agencies do in an attempt to respond—if not always assuage public concerns about IC activities. In summary, from a macro strategic level it is now possible to know more about contemporary IC leadership than would have been possible pre-9/11.

To that end this book seeks answers to four research questions:

1. What is leadership in the contemporary IC context?
2. Is 'intelligence governance' a useful theoretical construct to understand IC leadership; and what are the key governance challenges IC leaders will need to navigate through?
3. How can IC leaders address intelligence governance challenges to improve organisational effectiveness and adaptation?
4. What individual attributes, skills, and capabilities are critical for the next generation of IC leaders to develop, and what principles could underpin leadership development programs?

The four research questions underscore several aspects of 'leadership' in the intelligence context that are not sufficiently understood and the time for scholars and intelligence leaders themselves to address the knowledge gaps are overdue. As discussed in subsequent chapters, we have seen historically and particularly since 9/11 how several leadership-related issues have impacted on ICs—some for the better and others for the worse. Such impacts, whether positive or negative, can significantly influence the adaptability and sustainability of ICs. This can in turn influence both the quality of decision-making support governments can expect—as well as the agility in how these communities grapple with changes in an increasingly complex security environment. Indeed, at the time of writing the existential health security threat posed by COVID-19 is the latest example of how IC leaders will need to demonstrate agility to a changing security environment (Walsh 2020: 586–602). The challenges are likely to include understanding deception by countries seeking to avoid international scrutiny, the dispatch of non-declared human intelligence (HUMINT) missions and the risks that poses, and how ICs can work better with public health agencies (Walsh 2020; 2018). So the stakes are high if researchers and ICs do not make sustained efforts to understand intelligence leadership in all its dimensions.

This study is a clarion call for scholars, policy makers, and both the current and future generation of IC leaders to make greater progress in understanding how to improve leadership in our ICs. As we shall see shortly, leadership in the IC context can be understood during or after a crisis. But a central argument of this study is that learning what makes good leadership solely during intelligence failures is not a sustainable way to build the future generation of IC leaders. As business strategist Michael McQueen suggests, 'if you wait until a crisis unfolds, you will be operating from a position of survival, not strategy' (2018: 85). The book offers an innovative approach to studying contemporary IC leadership by addressing the research questions both from the perspective of *individual leadership attributes* and the *organisational variables* and how the two impact on each other.

Methodological approach

In particular, the book includes four key methodological aspects, which are unique hitherto to any other studies that have examined aspects of IC leadership (Zegart 2007; Walsh 2017; Gentry 2008: 247–270, 2015: 637–661, 2016: 154–177). First, the study is cross-comparative both in intelligence contexts (national security and law enforcement) and countries ('Five Eyes' and other selected liberal democratic countries). The book's exploration of both national security and law enforcement sources across these countries provides a wider understanding of IC leadership; and whether similar or different leadership challenges exist in different contexts and countries.

The second unique aspect to the book's methodological framework is that it explores both the individual and organisational aspect of intelligence leadership using a theoretical model—*the effective intelligence framework* that I developed in 2011 (Walsh 2011: 91–151, 2015: 123–142, 2017b: 441–459). The framework provides researchers and ICs with a tool to 'diagnose' how effective structural and functional aspects of an intelligence agency or entire community are performing. A key argument in my previous work on the model is that 'intelligence governance' is a critical component in the design and implementation of intelligence structures and functions within and across intelligence agencies (Walsh 2011: Ibid, 2015: 123–142, 2017b: 441–459). The framework will be explained in more detail in Chapter 2 (Intelligence and Leadership). In Chapter 10 (Conclusion), we will reflect back on the study's methodological approach and whether 'intelligence governance' is a useful construct in which to understand IC leadership.

A third point of distinction about the book's approach is that it seeks to take a multi-disciplinary perspective when addressing the research questions. The intelligence studies field has grown significantly since 9/11 yet various topics, questions, and issues still remain under-theorised (Walsh 2011: 283–299; Gill, Marrin and Phythian 2008). As noted earlier, there is only a small body of research that may be considered work on 'intelligence leadership;' so bringing in theoretical perspectives from leadership/management, organisational reform/culture, psychology, sociology amongst others will help inform the development of theorising and practice related to IC leadership.

A final (fourth) different aspect to the book's methodological approach is that it adopts a grounded theoretical perspective to addressing the research questions. In other words, a range of qualitative primary and secondary data sources were collected and analysed in order to make some analytical generalisations about IC leadership—from individual attribute and organisational perspectives. Primary data sources included five semi-structured interviews of former IC leaders and a survey of 208 former and current IC leaders.

The survey consisted of 24 questions that asked current and former IC leaders a series of questions about aspects of leadership. Questions included, for example, what leadership attributes they thought were important and why. Others related to what the role of leadership was in various critical IC functions (e.g. collection and analysis), whether they thought intelligence governance was a useful way to think about leadership, and what they saw as the biggest challenges for IC leaders to deal with in the next five years. A total of 210 people responded to the survey with 208 providing complete answers. The survey completion rate was 49 per cent, which was encouraging given most of the questions required IC leaders to provide a text response. In terms of demographics, 74.23 per cent and 24.23 per cent were male and female respectively; with 58.67 per cent in the 40–59 years age range. Respondents came from almost all the agencies across the 'Five Eyes' with the highest number of responses coming from the US Department of Defense and the Australian Federal Police (both n = 18). There was also a large number of respondents (n = 119) who were either from state law enforcement or selected the 'other' option rather than ticking one of the agency names listed in the survey. In some cases, it seems respondents ticked 'other' because they performed related IC leadership roles, such as consultancies or worked in areas that provided technical advice to the IC, but were not currently members of the IC. Another cohort of respondents selected 'other' but under this category listed having worked in agencies that are clearly part of the 'Five Eyes' ICs such as the Australian Secret Intelligence Service (ASIS) in Australia, Office of the Director of National Intelligence (ODNI) and National Geospatial Intelligence Agency (NGA), both in the US, and the

Assessment Secretariat (Canada). The range of IC leadership seniority varied widely (n=196). For example, 2.55 per cent identified as either heads of ICs or agencies, 22.45 per cent retired IC leaders, 10.71 per cent intelligence managers—down to others that indicated they were team leaders (11.73 per cent) or 'other' (14.80 per cent) (e.g. policy makers, consultants, training, and private sector). Finally, in terms of years of experience as an IC leader, 24.16 per cent (n=36) had at least five years but only up to ten years' experience—while 51.68 per cent (n=77) had ten or more years IC leadership experience. The survey responses informed all aspects of the study, but particularly provided insights into the analysis of intelligence governance challenges (Chapter 8 The Future IC Leader and Governance Challenges) and leadership development (Chapter 9 Leadership Development). Secondary data sources included scholarly literature, policy documents, and officially released inquiries.

The audience

This book is primarily for current and future IC leaders—regardless of seniority level within our ICs. If you are already an experienced senior leader, it is hoped that the book provides you with an opportunity to reflect more deeply on the difficult operating environment you are working in, and how you can identify areas for individual and organisational improvement. In particular, though, the book is targeted at the future senior IC leaders, who right now may be in middle management positions. Given the absence of formal leadership programs in many ICs, I seek to provide some scaffolding that can help future leaders better identify the personal attributes and governance challenges they will face should they seek an executive career. I would like the book to also be useful to other areas of our ICs such as human resources, training, and corporate affairs, who may be given the task to develop IC leadership programs in the future. The other audience for the book, I hope, will be scholars who do research in intelligence capability reform issues as well as others outside of the intelligence studies discipline who are interested in leadership theorising and organisational change. Finally, I seek to engage students contemplating higher degrees and encourage them to take up their own research projects on IC leadership.

The book's points of difference

There are several points of difference in this book—some such as the methodological approach (e.g. survey of former and current IC leaders on contemporary leadership issues) have already been mentioned. But in general, I would say, and to the best of my knowledge this is the first larger study publicly available that seeks to understand contemporary leadership in the IC context. As we shall see in the next chapter, there are now many excellent historical studies that traverse important aspects of IC leadership, but this is the first study that I am aware of to comprehensively address both the personal and organisational aspects of contemporary IC leadership.

Book scope and limitations

The small number of interviews and survey responses collected for this study obviously do not constitute either a generalisable sample or complete picture of contemporary leadership in the IC context. I am only too aware of the limitations of doing research into IC capability issues. This is now my third book, which has examined intelligence reform issues—each has involved collecting primary data from IC personnel. As a former intelligence analyst myself, I am acutely aware of the challenges and sensitivities of doing research in this present space. The conclusions made on a range of topics can only be seen as tentative given it is not possible to have completely untethered access or visibility on all leadership-related issues, processes, and initiatives underway across all 'Five Eyes' ICs. There are also always implications in selecting one research strategy and methodological approach over another. In the following chapters, I will come back to some of the specific limitations of the findings as appropriate and their implications—particularly in Chapters 8, 9, and the conclusion (Chapter 10). Finally, before addressing the overall structure, it's worth reminding readers that 'leadership' even in traditional leadership theorising remains empirically and experientially a hotly contested term. It can be hard to quantify the impact and influence of leaders on those who are led in any environment—including in ICs. The survey results help build further theorising about leadership in the IC context. They are sometimes helpful and at times contradictory—much like other theoretical perspectives on leadership. Nonetheless, I have included a range of comments from IC leaders—even some that I may not entirely agree with them all—because along with the secondary data sources they provide a richer tapestry in which to build better knowledge in this area. Finally, in terms of scope, I wish to stress although the book explores ways IC leadership may be improved in the future, I do not want to give the impression that ICs have been mostly or are poorly run. Indeed, over the years I have met many inspiring and competent IC leaders whose leadership has impacted significantly and positively on their organisations. Rather, the central point of the book is how do we prepare our future IC leadership cadre so they and their organisations can better navigate the evolving and uncertain security environment.

Book structure

In order to fully address the four research questions, the book is structured into ten chapters. This chapter introduces the study, including the research questions and overall methodological approach. Chapter 2 (Intelligence and Leadership), examines IC leadership in the national security and law enforcement context. It provides the important multi-disciplinary foundation required to understand aspects of IC leadership in the remaining chapters. It explores how history, leadership, and organisational theory; leadership psychology; and my own theoretical construct of 'intelligence governance' provide the necessary backdrop in which to understand contemporary IC leadership. Chapter 3 (Tasking and Coordination) examines both the external (political) and internal (IC level) dimensions of IC leadership. Using several themes (e.g. organisational structure, information sharing, and politicisation), it explores the tensions between both dimensions and how this impacts on the ability of leaders to effectively task, coordinate, and integrate intelligence.

Chapter 4 (Collection) explores the significance of three major themes (technological; collection and governance; and collection, ethics, and efficacy). The themes are used to assess what intelligence governance challenges will arise for IC leaders related to intelligence collection. Chapter 5 (Analysis) examines a range of analytical techniques—both common and emerging in ICs and the advantages and disadvantages of these in producing more reliable analytical judgements. The discussion again highlights a number of governance challenges arising from the use of various analytical techniques, including how IC leaders can sustain innovation in this vital area of the intelligence enterprise. Chapter 6 (ICT) investigates how artificial intelligence (AI) is being used in various IC applications and explores the extent that IC leaders can reconcile the technological, counter-intelligence, and ethical challenges in its use.

Chapter 7 (Human Resources) explores a series of intelligence governance challenges related to improving workforce planning outcomes. In particular, recruitment, training, education, retention, and attrition challenges are discussed and the critical role IC leaders must play in improving human capability outcomes in the future. Chapter 8 (The Future IC Leader and Governance Challenges) is the first of two chapters (Chapter 9 Leadership Development being the other) that brings together the analysis of key governance challenges—and how IC leaders can begin to better conceptualise solutions to them. After summarising the challenges and potential solutions, Chapter 8 pivots away from the organisational and back to the individual. It asks, given the challenges and opportunities to manage them, what kind of leadership attributes may help in overcoming them. This chapter connects much of the theorising on leadership in earlier parts of the book to several perspectives gathered from the IC leadership survey. Chapter 9 (Leadership Development) draws on the insights of the previous chapter and additional survey results to identify six broad thematic and inter-related areas: *individual behavioural attributes, technical training, strategic and business planning, mentoring, evaluation,* and lastly *training and education strategies*. The chapter argues that these thematic areas should be thought of as five principles that can provide the basis for an IC leadership development framework. The framework is offered as a starting point to discuss how ICs could advance leadership development programs. Chapter 10 (Conclusion) provides a summary of the major themes raised in all sections of the book. It will also evaluate the extent to which the four research questions have been addressed and what the next steps might be in expanding a research agenda on IC leadership.

References

Buckley, J. (2013). *Managing intelligence: A guide for law enforcement professionals.* CRC Press.

Cullen, M., & Reddy, P. (2016). Intelligence and security in a free society. *Report of the first independent review of intelligence and security in New Zealand.* Wellington: New Zealand Government.

Gentry, J. A. (2008). Intelligence failure reframed. *Political Science Quarterly, 123*(2), 247–270.

Gentry, J. A. (2015). Has the ODNI improved U.S. Intelligence analysis? *International Journal of Intelligence and CounterIntelligence, 28*(4), 637–661. doi: 10.1080/08850607.2015.1050937

Gentry, J. A. (2016). Managers of analysts: The other half of intelligence analysis. *Intelligence and National Security, 31*(2), 154–177.

George, R., & Bruce, J. (Eds.) (2014). *Analyzing intelligence national security practitioner's perspectives*. Washington, DC: Georgetown University Press.

Gill, P., Marrin, S., & Phythian, M. (Eds.) (2008). *Intelligence theory: Key questions and debates*. Abingdon, UK: Routledge.

Lahneman, W., & Arcos, R. (Eds.) (2014). *The art of intelligence: Simulations, exercises and games*. Lanham, MD: Rowman and Littlefield.

L'Estrange, M., & Merchant, S. (2017). *Independent intelligence review*. Canberra: Commonwealth of Australia.

Marrin, S. (2011). *Improving intelligence analysis: Bridging the gap between scholarship and practice*. Abingdon, UK: Routledge.

McQueen, M. (2018). *How to prepare now for what's next*. Milton, QLD: John Wiley and Sons.

Quarmby, N., & Young, L. J. (2010). *Managing intelligence: the art of influence*. Federation Press.

Ratcliffe, J. H. (Ed.) (2009). *Strategic thinking in criminal intelligence* (2nd ed.). Sydney: Federation Press.

SSCI (2004). *Report on the US Intelligence Community's Pre war intelligence assessments on Iraq*. Washington, DC: Select Committee on Intelligence. U.S. Senate.

Walsh, P. F. (2011). *Intelligence and intelligence analysis*. Abingdon: UK: Routledge.

Walsh, P. F. (2015). Building better intelligence frameworks through effective governance. *International Journal of Intelligence and CounterIntelligence, 28*(1), 123–142. doi: 10.1080/08850607.2014.924816

Walsh, P. F. (2017a). Teaching intelligence in the twenty-first century: Towards an evidence-based approach for curriculum design. *Intelligence and National Security, 32*(7), 1005–1021. doi: 10.1080/02684527.2017.1328852

Walsh, P. F. (2017b). Making future leaders in the US intelligence community: Challenges and opportunities. *Intelligence and National Security, 32*(4), 441–459. doi: 10.1080/02684527.2016.1253920

Walsh, P. F. (2018). *Intelligence, biosecurity and bioterrorism*. Berlin: Springer.

Walsh, P. F. (2020). Improving 'Five Eyes' health security intelligence capabilities: Leadership and governance challenges. *Intelligence and National Security, 35*(4), 586–602. doi: 10.1080/02684527.2020.1750156

Zegart, A. (2007). 9/11 and the FBI: The organizational roots of failure. *Intelligence and National Security, 22*(2), 165–184. doi: 10.1080/02684520701415123

2 Intelligence and leadership

Introduction

This chapter has four key objectives. First, it provides a thematic and historical (pre-9/11) introduction to the intelligence community (IC) leadership (from individual and organisational perspectives). This is critical to understanding how pre-9/11 leadership has influenced contemporary IC leadership. The first section cannot provide an exhaustive detailed historical analysis of all intelligence leaders nor their actions in each 'Five Eyes' country. This would be an impossible task and is beyond the scope of the book. However, it provides a high-level historical and thematic analysis of leadership in the national security and law enforcement intelligence contexts. Many of these themes will be explored in deeper detail in subsequent chapters as they are relevant to understanding specific aspects of contemporary leadership issues. But the main point made in the first section is that one cannot understand IC leadership today without exploring the broader historical forces that shaped the development of modern intelligence in the early twentieth century.

The second objective (and another unique aspect to the book) is to introduce a cross-disciplinary perspective to contemporary leadership in the intelligence context. The section provides an overview of a range of disciplines (e.g. leadership theory, organisational theory, leadership, and psychology), which provide relevant knowledge and a deeper understanding of leadership in the intelligence context. It argues that understanding leadership—regardless of its context (intelligence/non-intelligence settings) has always been a cross-disciplinary endeavour. The broad-brush stroke discussion of disciplinary perspectives in this chapter and the historical survey of IC leadership will be built on in subsequent chapters. The third objective is to explain the effective intelligence framework, which informs the theoretical foundation and structure for this study. Lastly, the chapter concludes with a working definition of IC leadership.

Historical intelligence leadership dimensions

How can history help us understand what leadership attributes influence IC design and reform, and what organisational factors promote effective contemporary leadership in our ICs? Since the mid-1970s onwards, a growing number of historians and intelligence studies researchers have examined how crises/events, personalities, and organisational change influenced the development of leadership in our intelligence agencies/communities since the early nineteenth century. The two world wars clearly played critical roles in the development of intelligence in each 'Five Eyes' country. Intelligence played an increasingly crucial role on the battlefields of both World War I and II, so it is not surprising that many historians have examined how the military and political leadership of ally countries used and developed intelligence capabilities to fight wars. It is equally of no surprise in the literature to see a focus on World War I and II and how intelligence was used across the military and civilian divide—including assessments about different 'styles' of political leadership and how leaders used intelligence to inform national strategies to prosecute the battles of both wars. An analysis of how the political leadership used intelligence is critical to understanding how this impacted on the development of the ICs that served them.

On the role of the political leadership in World War II, Michael Handel argued that while there may be no 'ideal leader,' the kind of political leader receiving and using the intelligence mattered. Handel provided a loose taxonomy to describe political leaders:

> dogmatic, too open-minded, and distant or too close a relationship to their intelligence services. Personality, experience and the ability for both military and civilian leaders to 'scent out the truth were also all influential attributes' (Handel 1988: 5). Handel and others have argued that 'unquestionably, Churchill could put intelligence to better use than Hitler.' He quips that 'while Hitler was still a runner in the trenches of Flanders, Churchill had already gained extensive experience in intelligence work as the First Lord of the Admiralty'. (1988: 6)

Both President Franklin Roosevelt and UK Prime Minister Churchill were fascinated and fond of intelligence, particularly HUMINT and covert action. Churchill was also an avid reader of both Bletchley Park decrypted intercepts and Joint Intelligence Committee (JIC) reports (Gentry 2018: 5–6; Goodman 2008; Aldrich and Cormac 2016).[1] In contrast, US President Woodrow Wilson had a moral aversion and ignorance of intelligence, as did UK Prime Minister Neville Chamberlain.

Other more contemporary scholars have similarly argued the case (that leadership performance, attitude, personality/psychology, and experience mattered to the ability of intelligence capabilities to reform and adapt), albeit looking more broadly at how intelligence was used in the post-World War II period. For example, Gentry makes the case for how effective political leadership mattered in counter-insurgency operations and leadership preferences and understanding; and interest for certain intelligence sources over others influenced the development of the US IC (Gentry 2010: 50–75; 2018: 1–17).

> From general histories of intelligence we also get assessments of the attributes of political leaders during the Cold War. For example, in the US context,

as Gentry argues: President Eisenhower's extensive experience at the highest levels of staff work also gave him a great appreciation of the positive contribution of intelligence to any decision-making compared to President Nixon, who attributed his narrow defeat in 1960 at least in part to the CIA, which he held responsible for the fact that the 'missile gap' became a campaign issue and was blamed on the Republicans.

(Ibid: 6)

Warner also reminds us that one should not forget the impact of adversarial leaders such as Josef Stalin and Mao Zedong on the development of 'Five Eyes' intelligence communities and those of other western powers (Warner 2014: 216). In summary, historical studies demonstrate that the leader's personality/psychology, experience, and trust with intelligence over time obviously matters (Steinhart and Avramov 2013). Of course, how political leaders use or abuse intelligence continues to be studied avidly by historians and intelligence studies scholars as the misuse of intelligence can result in an overly politicised exploitation of intelligence. In most recent history, the notion of the politicisation of intelligence has been found around the political decision-making that led to the US-led coalition invasion of Iraq in 2003. Though perhaps even more recently concerns remain about how politicisation of the US IC (either from neglect or hostility) by the Trump administration is impacting on that community's ability to provide fully effective decision-making support to the executive. Such actual or potential examples of the politicisation of intelligence are critical to understanding the evolution of intelligence leadership from the twentieth century to the present. This concept will be examined in deeper detail in Chapter 3 (Tasking and Coordination).

In addition to understanding how military and political leaders experience/use intelligence and the impact this had on the development of modern intelligence, various historical sources are also instructive in showing how changes in science and technology were enablers of an increasingly sophisticated intelligence capability. In particular, communications technology that allowed the establishment of code breaking (in Britain, Germany, Italy, and the United States) after World War I only became more integral and sophisticated in World War II and beyond (Kahn 2001: 83). As Warner suggests, 'World War I linked science to intelligence.' 'World War II ensured that science would forever be an element of all aspects of the intelligence field' (Warner 2014: 103). 'Mathematicians and engineers were critical to breaking the axis powers codes and also making sure those of the western allies were impregnable' (Ibid).

This reliance on science and technology clearly increased during the Cold War and by 'the early 1970s the US had become the undisputed world intelligence leader—something it had never been before.' Though, as Warner suggests, 'technology had made American intelligence better but not always smarter' (Warner 2014: 165).

While intelligence historians have now provided a clearer picture of how the two world wars helped develop our understanding of the fault lines that eventually led to the creation of the 'Five Eyes' communities today, other research has explored several other historical case studies from the war years to the present. These have generated knowledge about the role and impact of IC leaders in counter-insurgency, covert action (Scott and Hughes 2006: 653–674), intelligence failure, intelligence and decision-making, efficacy, ethics, and accountability (Wark 1993; Best 2014; Kahn 2001; Warner 2014; Gentry 2016: 154–177). All of these studies provide important knowledge about leadership and how intelligence was used in a variety of different crises between the end of World War II, the Cold War, 9/11, and beyond.

Another key lesson from intelligence historical studies is that ideology— political, economic, and social—have always driven changes in the 'Five Eyes' ICs. Warner refers to how ideologically driven zealotry and violence in the late nineteenth century in various European countries influenced the development of internal policing and security capabilities. This could be seen, for example, in the formation of London's Metropolitan Police and its formation of a Special Irish Branch in 1888 to combat a Fenian bombing campaign (Warner 2014: 26). Additionally, the end of the Cold War in 1991 and the peace dividend that followed was to have significant impacts (many negative) on the capabilities of major intelligence agencies across the 'Five Eyes' alliance.

While there are a vast number of lessons to be learnt from the early nineteenth century and the various major milestones of intelligence history (World Wars, Cold War, Post-Cold War, 9/11, post-9/11) that are important for understanding leadership in the intelligence context, space does not allow a full extrapolation of them all. Instead, in the remaining space I will focus on six broad themes that arose from surveying key historical sources. With each theme, I will explain its relevance to understanding IC leadership. As noted above, this is not the end of the discussion on how history has shaped the 'Five Eyes' intelligence communities and its leaders. As leadership topics are introduced in subsequent chapters, a reflection on historical trends where relevant is included. Additionally, the six themes identified here should not be construed as the only major themes arising from historical sources. There are likely many others, but these ones seem to be commonly found in multiple sources.

The first common theme arising out of multiple historical literature sources is *intelligence failure*. Several historians and intelligence studies scholars have provided cases of intelligence failure and their impact on intelligence capability (Betts 1978; Zegart 2007; Dover and Goodman 2011; Hatlebrekke and Smith 2010). Such works do increase our understanding of how intelligence as an enterprise, process, and product can fail. However, I argue that the phrase is becoming too much of a 'catch all' or shortcut for any event or issue that results in either a minor or catastrophic breakdown such as the failure of warning of the Japanese attack at Pearl Harbor or 9/11. There is a lack of clarity too around the term 'intelligence failure' and it seems in some instances it is used to describe 'something going wrong in the intelligence machinery' which might in fact be more accurately called a policy failure. Is 9/11 and the faulty assessments (provided to governments in the US, UK, and Australia) leading up the coalition invasion of Iraq (2003) more policy than intelligence failures or a bit of both?

On a smaller scale, but nonetheless impactful for the country concerned, did New Zealand's SIGINT agency Government Communications Security Bureau (GCSB) (created in 1955) fail, as Hager suggests, to 'predict' the military coup in Fiji in 1987 or the French sabotage of the Rainbow Warrior ship in Auckland harbour in 1985 (Hager 1996)? Or in both cases were there policy mis-steps taken?

A lack of precision and agreement amongst scholars about intelligence failure can promote sloppy analysis of the real causes why intelligence did not provide warning, reduce uncertainty, or allow sufficient decision-maker support. Nonetheless, examining historical cases of 'intelligence failure' does provide some clarity about the role leadership plays (both political and at IC levels) when things have gone wrong and we will be coming back to examples of intelligence failure in subsequent chapters.

A second theme arising out of historical sources are efforts towards the *integration of people, policy, processes*, functions within intelligence agencies and broader communities. Discussions have included how specific functions might be integrated, such as strategic intelligence and forecasting (Schmidt 2015: 489–511; Michael 2015: 489–511), or how to fuse collection and/or analytical functions across ICs (Walsh 2011a, 2015). Integration was also an important theme arising out of the 9/11 Report and the use of the word has become a bit of a mantra for IC leaders since (2004: 402). The integration theme is linked to another—*organisational design*—discussed later.

The third theme is *liaison*. Any analysis of historical sources will reveal how critical strong liaison was in building cooperation and capability within and across intelligence agencies in each 'Five Eyes' country. Several historical accounts underscore the important role liaison played between the intelligence and political leadership across the 'Five Eyes' ICs in building trust and common capabilities. For example, a profound legacy of World War II was the creation of the vast global SIGINT alliance known as UKUSA—a treaty signed between Britain, US, Canada, Australia, and New Zealand—in 1948, which has deepened significantly since (Aldrich 2010: 89–104; Herman 1996; Andrew 2018: 670–671).

While the UKUSA treaty was a significant stake in the ground in building trust and sharing of intelligence between partner countries, it also had the effect of pushing greater domestic capability building amongst treaty countries—particularly in Australia and New Zealand. For example, in the 1950s both the US Truman and UK Atlee governments were concerned about KGB penetration in Australian politics, bureaucracy, and society. There were leaks of highly sensitive material from the Department of External Affairs in Canberra to the KGB. London sent senior MI5 staff to Australia to pressure the Chifley Government to deal with the security crisis and create their own MI5, later known as the Australian Security Intelligence Organisation (ASIO). Some senior MI5 staff stayed on afterwards in the new ASIO. Similarly, from the NZ Security Intelligence Service (NZSIS) perspective, historical surveys show how the UK was particularly influential in persuading New Zealand to establish the SIS. Sir Percy Sillitoe (Head of MI5) was sent to New Zealand to establish a sister agency there. He was successful in his venture and many original NZSIS staff were British imports from MI5 (Greener-Barcham 2002: 510).

However, any discussion of the role of strong liaison and growing partnership between 'Five Eyes' countries over several decades also needs to balance the periods of success against other historical episodes marked by strain and in a few instances even fraying of bonds. History shows there were occasions where there were real tensions in the alliance, particularly at times when national interests were not aligned. For example, although the Anglo-American partnership became extremely close in the Cold War in monitoring the Soviet Union, it was not close in all places where British and American interests diverged, such as during the 1956 Suez crisis (Warner 2014: 165 and 124). In later decades, as well, there were other examples where the intelligence alliance diverged or was even disrupted temporarily due to differing national interests. For example, New Zealand later became partially blocked from its intelligence sharing arrangements with the US as a result of the NZ Labour Government's (Prime Minister David Lange) nuclear policy that precluded US nuclear powered and/or armed naval ship visits to New Zealand (Hager 1996).

However, despite episodic national interest differences, effective liaison and building partnerships, not just at the most senior political or head of agency level of course, but at working levels between officials, helped paper over more narrow political national interests. Lower working-level contacts helped promote and sustain relations across 'Five Eyes' countries based on 'shared ideals and long-standing transnational connections' (Jeffrey-Jones 2012: 707–721).

A fourth discernible theme is *knowledge management and information sharing*. The historical literature covering the development of intelligence agencies within each 'Five Eyes' ICs periodically refer to both the problems and successes in producing good knowledge management and information sharing practices. How do vast and diverse agencies within the US IC for example bring together knowledge that can benefit the entire community, where historically there remains within all 'Five Eyes' ICs a need to compartmentalise knowledge practice and its management (Desouza 2009: 1219–1267; Lahneman 2004)? A culture of secrecy is critical to the effective and secure operations in all ICs, yet increasingly after 9/11 the mantra of 'need to know' and policies such as the intelligence sharing environment (ISE) have also driven intelligence reform efforts by political and intelligence leaders in each 'Five Eyes' country (Walsh 2011a).

Linked to issues of information sharing and secrecy is the fifth theme—*privacy, transparency, and accountability* in both policing and national security intelligence contexts. Since 2013, intelligence studies scholars have become increasingly focused on the impact the Snowden leaks had on bringing these issues to the public and political consciousness (Walsh 2011a; Walsh and Miller 2016; Miller and Walsh 2016; Walsh 2017a; Omand 2008: 593–607; Omand and Phythian 2018; Patman and Southgate 2016: 871–887; Johnson 2018). However, as significant as the Snowden (and to a lesser extent Wikileaks) episodes were, historical sources provide useful reminders that privacy, transparency, and accountability issues have long been features of the historical landscape, including notably during the Cold War.

It was clear to varying levels of intensity in each 'Five Eyes' country that by the 1960s the tension between secrecy, privacy/liberty, and transparency/account-ability was already fraying between citizens, governments, and the intelligence communities that served them. Following the 1973 Watergate scandal, the *New York Times* ran with a story that the CIA were involved in domestic spying—a violation of the National Security Act of 1947. These revelations led to the Church Committee which 'discovered that the misuse of power by the nation's secret agencies had been far more extensive than suggested by the already eye-popping accounts in the *Times*' (Johnson 2018: 1). The Church Committee also discovered various abuses of power by the FBI in the surveillance and counter-intelligence operations against African-American civil rights activists, anti-war students amongst others (Johnson 2018: 120). The Church Committee heralded in the US the establishment of two congressional intelligence oversight committees (the Senate Select Committee on Intelligence and the House Permanent Select Committee for Intelligence) in the 1970s, which continue to this day to play an important if not always an effective role in promoting oversight and accountability.

In Canada, a series of inquiries, the Mackenzie Commission (1966), the Keable (1977), and the McDonald Commission (1981), also investigated oversight, accountability, and organisational performance issues of the Royal Canadian Mounted Police (RCMP), which up until 1984 had carriage of domestic security intelligence in Canada (Gill 1989; Whitaker 1991, 1992; Sayle 2010: 862–867; Hewitt 2002, 2018). In Hewitt's work (2002, 2018: 67–83), we see how the RCMP Security Service's inability over decades to 'understand the new forces and threats associated with the 1960s—including terrorism or even to qualitatively assess its traditional targets' along with its involvement in illegal and unethical activity in Quebec and elsewhere in Canada resulted (following the McDonald Commission inquiry into the RCMP) in the government creating in July 1984 the Canadian Security Intelligence Service (CSIS) (Hewitt 2002: 166). CSIS then took primary responsibility for domestic security intelligence away from RCMP, including its work on counter-subversion and counter-terrorism to the new agency.

This historical notion of locating the balance between effective security (including secrecy), privacy, and liberty remains an important debate because it impacts on how to preserve the effectiveness of ICs against complex and emerg-ing threats yet also maintains privacy, civil liberties, and trust of citizens in liberal democratic countries. How issues of privacy, transparency, and accountability have been dealt with both by political decision-makers and their intelligence lead-ership cadre are clearly relevant to understanding effective leadership in the cur-rent post-9/11 era (Walsh 2011a, 2016, 2017a, 2017b).

While concerns about privacy, secrecy, transparency, and accountability have often coalesced in historical accounts of unethical, illegal, or over-reach by ICs, there are other dimensions of transparency and accountability that in some respects show a gradual and more positive desire by political and intelligence leaders to be more open about aspects of their operation to the tax payer citizenry. As discussed earlier, it seems clear that one of the impacts of the 2013 Snowden leaks has been efforts made (to varying degrees) by either political or intelligence leaders across 'the Five Eyes' intelligence communities to appear publicly in order to defend and explain in unclassified ways the positive role their agencies play in promoting national security and public safety. For example, in 2014 the then Director General of ASIO, David Irvine, appeared in front of the media to explain the role and need for the new meta data retention laws going through Australia's parliament at the time (Walsh 2017a). Similarly, Loch Johnson's interview with the then Director of National Intelligence Jim Clapper, which was later published in the *Intelligence and National Security* journal, is another example (Johnson 2015: 1–25).

The combined effect from the 'intelligence failures' of 9/11, Iraq, and the Snowden leaks have resulted in the need for intelligence leaders to play a greater public role (sometimes willingly sometimes less so) via media appearances and responding to inquiries. In particular, after Snowden there is now greater public distrust and political and IC leaders have had to come out more publicly and explain the actions of the IC (to the extent they can) in order to sustain or regain trust, legitimacy, and even funding (Walsh and Miller 2016; Johnson *et al.* 2014; Walsh 2017b). The fallout of Snowden also pressured to varying degrees across each 'Five Eyes' country's government to be more responsive to public concerns about unchecked surveillance by ICs. This included efforts to examine intelligence-related legislation that put more 'trip wires' in governing access to warrants and interception, and further efforts by all to review accountability mechanisms (Walsh and Miller 2016).

Importantly though, historical studies focusing on events prior to 9/11 or Snowden also show efforts in some 'Five Eyes' ICs to be less secretive and more transparent. For example, in the UK and Australian intelligence communities a greater openness in the 1990s emerged about the existence of what have been exclusively secret agencies such as MI5/MI6 (in the UK) or Australian Secret Intelligence Service (ASIS), in Australia, and public acknowledgement of their heads. Such a change in the political and policy atmosphere provided further encouragement for the development of intelligence studies. In particular, a move towards greater accountability and transparency across many 'Five Eyes' countries included some historians being granted access to archival records of key intelligence agencies.

Increasingly since the 1990s to the present, much can be learnt about contemporary intelligence leadership from official, semi-official and extensive histories of particular intelligence agencies across the 'Five Eyes' ICs. Official histories are generally authorised by the agency. They may be completed by in-house historians (e.g. Michael Warner's extensive work (e.g. 2001; 2004) on the history of the CIA as part of its history staff) or commissioned by the agency allowing external historians access to restricted archives and staff to interview. Examples of the latter have included Christopher Andrew's *Defence of the Realm* (History of MI5) and Keith Jeffery's 2010 volume *The British Secret Intelligence Service 1909–1949*. In the case of Andrew, it was required that he become an MI5 officer to gain access to material. Others include Michael Goodman's *Official History of Joint Intelligence Committee* (2014). Similarly in Australia, three volumes

chronicling the history of the ASIO—Australia's domestic intelligence agency—
are the result of historians having unrestricted access to ASIO's archival records
for the periods 1949 up until 1989 (see Horner 2014; Blaxland 2015; Blaxland
and Crawley 2017).

Blaxland (2015), like Jeffery's (2010) work on MI6, is also instructive in providing insights into the earlier leadership profiles of ASIO Director Generals and
how they influenced organisational change at the time. Blaxland refers to Charles
Spry as staying too long in the DG position, and his successor Peter Barbour being
too ineffective in managing problems with recruitment of officers and other workforce issues as being partly due to a lack of organisational reform and professional
training in ASIO (2015: Chapter 1).

In contrast to official and authorised histories, much is to be learnt about IC
leadership issues by reading non-official histories, which can provide a comprehensive analysis of material accessed via archives. Examples include Christopher
Andrew's works *The Secret World A History of Intelligence* (2018) and *Her
Majesty's Secret Service* (1987), Richard Aldrich's *GCHQ The Uncensored
Story of Britain's Most Secret Intelligence Agency* (2010), and Frank Cain's
(1994) *The ASIO: An Unofficial History*. Similarly, Jensen's (2008) *Cautious
Beginnings Canadian Foreign Intelligence 1939–51* is a Canadian example of
recently non-official historical studies examining archival material that has not
been reviewed extensively to this point. Additionally, two excellent edited historical volumes have been published focusing on 'spy chiefs' in the US and UK
(Moran *et al.* 2018) and in the Middle East and Asia (Maddrell *et al.* 2018),
respectively.

We will come back to other themes official and non-official histories reveal
about leadership in remaining parts of this chapter, but Section F (after the Cold
War and after 9/11) of Christopher Andrew's *Defence of the Realm* provides a
good example of how political events and leadership interact in ways that from
the 1990s changed MI5 to primary a counter-terrorism rather than counter-espi-
onage agency (Andrew 2009: 771). It also shows how Stella Remington, who
became the first female head of any of the world's leading intelligence or security services in 1992, developed an openness program. The program included
the publication of the first ever booklet on MI5's work with the first official
photo of the DG, increased media engagement, and public lectures—all of which
helped shape a more informed attitude and demystification of the service (Ibid:
776–777).

Both official and non-official histories show not only the bureaucratic development of intelligence agencies and the security environment operating at the time,
but also glimpses of the leader's personalities and how they shaped the future of
their agencies. The ability of intelligence leaders to wield power through their
personalities, and to influence both internally their agency and externally their
political masters, is critical, the latter point being particularly important. No one
can argue the profound impact personalities like J Edgar Hoover had on the development of the FBI or William J Donovan, Allen W Dulles, and William Casey on
the evolution of the CIA.

Similarly in the UK, Jeffery's *The History of the Secret Intelligence Service 1909–1949* explains the role of the first three chiefs: Mansfield Cumming, Hugh Sinclair, and Stewart Menzies in the first 40 years of MI6 were critical to the survival of the new scarcely resourced agency. In the case of Cumming, Jeffery describes him as 'not much more than a one man band who (for the survival and independence of the agency) during World War I had to fend off the predatory attentions of the Admiralty and War Office' (Jeffery 2010: 725). Jeffery also talks about the particular qualities of Sinclair—'his strengths as a leader—charisma, decision and dynamism.' Such qualities according to Jeffery, engendered a fierce loyalty on the part of subordinates, together with his inclination to press ahead with ventures without perhaps fully anticipating all the possible consequences at times led him and SIS into crossing existing Whitehall boundaries and trespassing into the territory of other departments.

(Ibid: 735)

Michael Goodman's work on the history of the Joint Intelligence Committee (JIC) is another good historical analyses on the political, military, and bureaucratic factors that influenced the development of the JIC and the role of leadership in its development (Goodman 2008: 40–56).

Moving beyond the world war years (1945 to the present), and in addition to historical analysis of heads of intelligence agencies completed from archives, there is also much to be learnt from memoirs written by former heads themselves. In the last few decades a steady growth in memoirs show heads are talking more publicly about their own leadership experience, such as former DCI James Woolsey, who believed he had little influence given he had no relationship with President Clinton. In 2005, Admiral Stansfield Turner wrote *Burn Before Reading, Presidents, CIA Directors and Secret Intelligence*, where he provides some useful insights on a range of leadership issues including management of the IC and CIA centralisation, the role of political leadership, and cleaning up after the Church Committee in the late 1970s.

More recently, George Tenet's (2007) memoir *At the Center of the Storm: My Years at the CIA*, Michael Hayden's (2016) *Playing to the Edge: American Intelligence in the Age of Terror*, and Jim Clapper's (2018) *Facts and Fears. Hard Truths from a Life in Intelligence* are also instructive on how leaders present their own leadership skills and the role they play in organisational change. Former CIA Deputy Director Michael Morell's (2015) *The Great War of Our Time. The CIA's Fight Against Terrorism From Al Qa'ida to ISIS* is also a fascinating insight on IC leadership from a senior insider. Tenet's memoir has received mixed reviews, though Sir David Omand, a former UK intelligence leader, suggested the book despite lacking detail was 'essential in understanding how and why the leadership structure of the US IC has taken the form it now has' (Omand, Prados and Jeffreys-Jones 2009: 292).

The sixth historical theme relevant to understanding contemporary leadership is *organisational design*. There are several issues relevant to this theme, including but not limited to organisational structural change, technology, collection and analytical methodologies, and organisational culture. There is insufficient space to assess each of these in detail, however, and like other themes discussed earlier, we will come back to more detailed discussion of these in subsequent chapters. But to provide some contextual understanding of organisational design-related issues, I will briefly mention some key ones here. First, it's clear that intelligence historians and other scholars working in the field show how a combination of factors such as changes in the security environment, political influence, and the leadership within each 'Five Eyes' IC work together to forge changes over time in the organisational design of ICs. In the US, historical studies chart the gradual evolution of centralised and civilian-based intelligence agencies from what in the early 20th century was mainly a function of army and naval intelligence. During World War II, greater efforts were made by the Roosevelt administration for a more centralised intelligence structure with the appointment of William J Donovan, who in 1942 created the Office of Strategic Services (OSS)—the precursor to the CIA (Leary 1984: 3–5).

> The creation of the CIA in 1947 and its historical development is in part a story of organisation design and redesign—with perhaps the first major reorganisation of the agency implemented in 1952 in part influenced by an earlier report (the Dulles, Jackson, and Correa Report to the National Security Council on the CIA and National Organisation for Intelligence released in 1949).
>
> (Ibid)

Later in the post-Cold War period, further changes to the security environment impacted on the organisational structure of 'Five Eyes' ICs, particularly resulting in more centralised and coordinated approaches to all source assessments. Hager paints a picture in New Zealand of a gradual coordination of some intelligence functions away from individual agencies starting in 1975 (mainly assessments) and into the centre of government (1996: 132), but such shifts in approaches to organisational design were also underway in Australia during the 1970s (Walsh 2011a). At the end of the Cold War there is also evidence in MI5 that changes in the security environment resulted in increased strategic planning for the service post-Cold War to be better equipped to handle new and emerging threats such as countering WMD, supporting police against organised crime, protecting the UK's economic wellbeing, and investigating animal rights extremists. The so-called Cold War peace dividend also resulted in budget cuts in MI5, SIS, and Government Communications Headquarters (GCHQ) which undoubtedly had an impact on organisational design and leadership (Andrews 2009: 780; Walsh 2011a).

Earlier discussion also included how catastrophic or significant intelligence failure (Pearl Harbor, Bay of Pigs, 9/11, Iraq) often results in agency or IC-wide organisational redesign. The 9/11 Commission Report in particular referred to the need for IC-wide organisation redesign—including the need for more effective leadership in order to see such change come into reality. The connection between the urgent need for organisational change and leadership can be found in the following two sections:

> modernization of our IC cannot be slow or timid. Reform must be undertaken with a sense of urgency. It must be broad, deep and authentic. America's intelligence professionals are capable and dedicated. They often do their jobs in dangerous and difficult circumstances. They need strong leadership, a renewed focus on mission, and clear lines of authority and accountability to excel.
>
> (2004: 509)

The need for structural reform and leadership are also clear in comments made by Senator Barbara A Mikulski:

> structural, organisational and jurisdictional reforms must be made and will be made. But the goal ultimately is to create an environment and a culture where truth to power is spoken from the bottom to the top.
>
> (Ibid)

But as historical events demonstrate frequently, politically sponsored IC redesign does not always result in 'fit for purpose' architecture. Again, historical studies are helpful in highlighting how the latest attempts to 'fix' intelligence failure— whether they be legislative or policy measures or a combination of both—can arguably make matters worse because some scholars argue the design of some intelligence agencies was flawed from the start. Hammond argues in the case of the organisation of the US IC that the same contributory historical problems from 1947 that led to the creation of the CIA in response to Pearl Harbor have continued post-9/11, with the 2004 creation of the Intelligence Reform and Terrorism Prevention Act (IRTPA) and Office of the Director of National Intelligence (ODNI) and beyond (Hammond 2010; Gentry 2015: 637–661). Of course, other commentators such as Tim Weiner argue that the CIA is so flawed historically by design that it seems there is no 'organisational cure' that can fix design flaws. This is not a helpful end point for thinking about reforming IC organisational design, however, as even if such an agency ceased to exist tomorrow another would need to be created to continue its functions.

Post-9/11, as will be discussed in greater detail in subsequent chapters, the scale and intensity of new emerging transnational threats such as radical Islamic jihadist terrorism groups continues to influence 'Five Eyes' government's implementation of a range of new policy organisational design initiatives in response. In the US, as noted earlier, the Bush administration sought to transform the US IC with the enactment of the IRTPA and the creation of the ODNI and Department of Homeland Security (DHS). In contrast, early policy initiatives in the UK, Canada, and Australia in the initial period after 9/11 (2001–2005) resulted in more gradual reform to the architecture of their ICs. In Australia, both the Flood Report (2004) and Smith Review (2008) came to the conclusion that the fundamental structure of the IC was fit for purpose—though greater coordination was needed along with improved assessment and collection capabilities (Walsh 2011a, 2011b: 109–127). Similarly in New Zealand, the 2009 Murdoch review of the IC 'focused on the ongoing need to integrate the IC and the requirement to govern the intelligence system on behalf of ministers at a cross agency level' (Murdoch 2009: 4; Whibley 2014).

The challenge of course is to build on historical and contemporary sources for intelligence organisational design. How can researchers and IC leaders build on existing sources discussed here that promotes better IC communities (Walsh 2011a, 2015; Omand 2010; Hammond 2010; Brunati 2013) in ways that make them more resilient to 'failure'? As Hammond asks, 'can an alternative design do better?' What is better—centralisation vs decentralisation—particularly in the way intelligence and data is configured (Hammond 2010: 681)? One increasingly common structural configuration for intelligence since 9/11 has been the proliferation of fusion centres (Walsh 2011a, 2015; Lewandowski *et al.* 2017; Taylor and Russell 2012: 184–200). These centres are not of course a post-9/11 'invention,'—coming into existence during World War II. What can a deeper analysis of fusion arrangements in history teach us about similar efforts being made now? In its broadest sense, what should fused organisational designs look like? There is still insufficient research on this point outside of inquiries of intelligence failure (Taylor and Goodman 2004; Walsh 2011a, 2015).

Another issue related to organisational design is how collection technologies and methodologies since World War I to the present have shaped both what 'Five Eyes' ICs do and how they are structured. History shows that the two world wars followed by the Cold War produced a rapid development in technical forms of intelligence collection, particularly SIGINT and geospatial methods (GEOINT). In the post-9/11 era, there has also been a proliferation of technical collection methods such as Unmanned Aerial Vehicles (UAVs) deployed in counter-terrorism intelligence operations (Walsh 2017c). Such technology does shape the structural arrangements of ICs and where investments are made. Intelligence leaders in SIGINT agencies have been successful in arguing for increasing budgetary allocations in technical areas—particularly in the Cold War period. However, other scholars argue that there has been a lack of HUMINT investment across ICs, which has impacted on the organisational design and operations of these agencies. Some have even suggested that the lack of HUMINT has been a recurring problem and led to failures in the twentieth century (Margolis 2013: 43; Hitz 2015). This point seems to be a little over-generalised, though looking across various stages of modern history it does have some accuracy, particularly in the immediate post-Cold War period where there was a reduction in HUMINT investment across 'Five Eyes' ICs (Walsh 2011a).

Leaving aside the need to avoid over-generalising about the relative lack of a collection capability such as HUMINT on the historical development of 'Five Eyes' ICs, it is clear that in some communities the importance or lack thereof placed on HUMINT collection capabilities, particularly foreign intelligence collection, did play a role in shaping the organisational design of certain agencies to this day. For example, the history of the Canadian IC shows evidence in the late

1930s and early Cold War period of how Canadian governments and officials saw value in foreign intelligence (HUMINT) collection, particularly due to concerns about the impact of an atomic war. HUMINT efforts were made by collecting scientific and technical information about the Soviet Union by debriefing Canadians who have travelled abroad or via its embassies (Jensen 2008). However, in the early post-World War II years, Canadian governments did not seem to give any detailed consideration of HUMINT collection internationally, which relied on espionage for secret intelligence. As Anderson suggests, 'the ability to conduct foreign espionage especially to collect HUMINT was not thought to be necessary for the protection of national security' (1994: 465). This was because Ottawa believed it did not have a geopolitical environment, where it faced more immediate threats such as Australia did in the Asia Pacific—and it could rely on its allies to provide this kind of information—as long as Canada continued to make considerable efforts in sharing its SIGINT (Anderson 1994: 464; Rudner 2001). In summary, Canada's approach to foreign clandestine HUMINT collection historically remained different from other 'Five Eyes' partners such as Australia (ASIS), Britain (MI6), and the US (CIA), who saw the need to develop specialised foreign intelligence collection agencies as part of their broader IC design (Anderson 1994: 448–471; Walsh 2011a; Farson and Teeple 2015; Jensen 2004, 2008).

A final thread relevant to our organisational design theme is organisational cultural issues. Our focus in this section has been on the value historical analysis of 'Five Eyes' ICs can bring to understanding the role of leadership in the contemporary post-9/11 world. A critical factor in what can be learnt from history is how events, policies, and intelligence leaders themselves have shaped the culture of the organisations in which they lead. Is it possible, for example, to talk about organisational cultures for the CIA, MI6, or the RCMP? How have they evolved and how do they differ from other agencies within the respective US, UK, and Canadian intelligence community (Bean 2009)? In the case of Canada, the origins of its security service (prior to the establishment of CSIS in 1984) were also entwined as far back as 1914 with the early development of federal police forces (Dominion Police and the Royal Northwest Police) and the establishment of the RCMP in 1920 (Kealey 1992: 179–210), which had the primary responsibility for domestic intelligence and counter-subversion. To what extent did an identifiable police culture impact on the early development of key aspects of the Canadian intelligence community? Additionally, can one discern a particular US IC-wide culture that may differ or indeed be similar for instance to the Australian intelligence community? Historical case studies such as Pearl Harbor, the Cuban Missile Crisis, and 9/11 have all referred to 'organisational cultural' factors explaining intelligence failure. From an organisational cultural perspective, such cases and others show that people in our ICs are subject to confirmation bias whereby as Dan Kahan suggests they 'assign weight to new evidence based on its consistency with what they already believe.' 'This tendency limits the likelihood or speed with which people will revise mistaken beliefs' (Kahan cited in National Academies of Sciences, Engineering and Medicine 2018: 8). Group think or affinity groups within and across intelligence agencies are clearly powerful influences on the evolution of organisational culture. The role leaders have played historically in shaping group think and organisational identity is important in understanding contemporary organisational outlooks in all 'Five Eyes' ICs.

Our discussion on the historical impact of organisational culture so far has focused only on the national security intelligence agencies within 'Five Eyes.' However, as mentioned in the 'introduction' (Chapter 1), one key objective of this book is to look at the nature of IC leadership from both the national security and law enforcement contexts. In this context, one clear historical factor that has shaped how intelligence is integrated into national security vs. law enforcement is that in the latter intelligence is not the core function. In general, as history continues to show, intelligence plays a supportive role to the primary law enforcement functions of investigation and prosecution. This fundamental difference in the priority and purpose intelligence plays in law enforcement compared to national security agencies has had a profound impact on the development of intelligence in broader policing/law enforcement cultures in 'Five Eyes' countries. Space does not allow a detailed exploration of all the law enforcement organisational cultural and leadership factors that have shaped the role of intelligence in such agencies from the twentieth century to the present. There are many factors (such as political, philosophical, fiscal, technological, and training) which need to be considered and these will be explored further where relevant in subsequent chapters (Walsh 2011a, 2007; Ratcliffe 2005). But just restricting our overview here to cultural factors impacting on intelligence in law enforcement agencies from the late 1990s to the present, it's clear how political and policy imperatives (e.g. problem-orientated policing, community policing, zero tolerance policing), public sector budgetary efficiencies, technology, and increased specialisation in law enforcement have all changed the organisational cultural fabric of many law enforcement agencies across the 'Five Eyes'—including leadership beliefs about the role of intelligence.

From the 1990s, starting in the UK but gradually influencing law enforcement intelligence reform in other 'Five Eyes' countries, a new model of intelligence—intelligence-led policing (ILP) swept across law enforcement. For the first time in the history of modern law enforcement, ILP held the potential to influence the organisational culture of law enforcement agencies by giving intelligence a more central role in decision-making about crime reduction. It's clear though that this potential is still to be realised at the national law enforcement level of 'Five Eyes' countries. The rhetoric and efforts to affect cultural change underpinning the ILP philosophy is at best a work in progress (Walsh 2011a; James 2014; Darroch and Mazerolle 2013; Ratcliffe 2016). ILP may be achieving more headway in some serious and organised crime types (e.g. counter-terrorism, child sex exploitation), but it's less clear whether it is having a significant and sustained impact in more high-volume crime areas (Innes *et al.* 2017; Innes and Sheptycki 2004). Attempts to embed ILP models in law enforcement agencies across the 'Five Eyes' countries is in many respects a good case study of how law enforcement leaders and their intelligence leadership subordinates have attempted to transform or resist changes to the dominant investigatory and prosecution culture of law enforcement agencies.

From our brief review earlier of historical sources for IC leadership, it's clear a number of common themes have emerged, which are critical to understanding intelligence leadership in the contemporary post-9/11 world. Not all historical cases of leadership-related issues discussed above (e.g. attributes of certain political and IC leaders or specific security threats) are equally relevant or transferable to understanding leadership in the contemporary setting. But the examination of the six common historical themes shows that issues such as intelligence failure, integration, or organisational design remain relevant regardless of what temporal or spatial characteristics they may have at the particular moment they occur in history. It's the broad relevance of such themes, which will be developed further in the remaining chapters. However, as essential as many historical sources are, they are insufficient on their own in explaining or understanding contemporary IC leadership. Leadership as a concept is inherently cross-disciplinary and a full investigation and understanding of what *intelligence leadership means* in the contemporary setting is not possible without also exploring other cross-disciplinary knowledge areas about leadership. It is to these other cross-disciplinary knowledge perspectives we now turn. In particular, in the following section the focus is on leadership theory. Then the remaining two sections will survey other relevant knowledge areas such as organisational theory and leadership and leadership psychology, which will also likely be useful for ICs and researchers seeking to improve IC leadership knowledge and skills.

Cross-disciplinary perspectives

Leadership theory

If we are to understand intelligence leadership in the contemporary sense, then intelligence studies scholars, in addition to going back to historical sources also need to investigate the broader context of leadership theory (Walsh 2017b: 441–459). Given there is an almost endless array of management and leadership theoretical perspectives, I will restrict discussion here to areas where some empirical work has been conducted. Although one could start this survey of the leadership field by examining Greek and Roman philosophers such as Plato— who wrote about leadership, or Niccolo Machiavelli in the renaissance, who advised his prince on how to rule—our discussion commences in the late 1940s. It was at this time that the early theoretical perspectives now discussed in modern leadership theory began to emerge in the literature (Ibid: 442). Leadership theories are influenced by social and political factors of their day and in the 1940s this was no exception.

World War II showed an oscillation between leadership approaches that were 'scientific' (meaning leaders were the repository of all knowledge to manage workers and costs)—to less normative models—where workers were driven by leaders, who could get them to adhere to a collective organisational vision.

(Ibid)

By the end of the war, theorists began to investigate leadership in the military to assess whether the armed forces may help leadership in other contexts such as industrial organisations (Ibid).

Given the diversity of leadership theoretical perspectives that developed since World War II, I will use three thematic categories (*neo-charismatic theories, follower-centric theories,* and *team leadership theories*) to clump together like-minded theories. But in reality, leadership theories are underpinned by a vast number of different theoretical perspectives—some of which have elements of one or more of the categories that will be discussed. Readers looking for a more comprehensive and global understanding of leadership theory in all its variants can access detailed analyses of these in the following excellent edited volumes and handbooks: Bass and Bass (2008) *The Bass Handbook of Leadership Theory, Research and Managerial Applications,* Nohria and Khurana (eds) (2010) *Hand Book of Leadership Theory and Practice,* Day (2014) *The Oxford Handbook of Leadership Organisations,* and Bryman's (2011) edited volume, *The Sage Handbook of Leadership.* For intelligence studies, scholars, and IC leaders these edited volumes are good places to start if you do not have any background in leadership theory.

Neo-charismatic theories

The most common neo-charismatic theories are transformational leadership, charismatic leadership, and transactional leadership. I will limit the discussion to transformational leadership as it has produced the most empirical work out of neo-charismatic theories. Charismatic and transaction leadership theoretical perspectives cross over significantly with those found in transformational leadership (Walsh 2017b: 443).

Transformational leadership theory has developed over 30 years and as noted above is one of the more empirically successful theories. In an earlier article I wrote on IC leadership, a search of the Scopus data base search from 2000 to 2015 revealed over 2326 articles—which is a good indicator of research activity around this theory (Ibid: 443; House and Antonakis 2013: 3–33). Within transformational theorists there is a great diversity of perspectives that focus on leaders in different contexts (e.g. CEOs of large private sector companies, military leaders, leaders in health and education sectors) (Ibid).

Regardless of the different perspectives transformational theorists have about leaders working in various contexts, most argue that transformational leaders 'share common perspectives that effective leaders transform or change the basic values, beliefs and attitudes of followers so that they are willing to perform beyond the minimum levels specified by the organisation' (Podsakoff *et al.* 1990: 107–142). Many transformational leadership theorists, as noted earlier, adopt an empirical design approach to their research by using quantitative empirical instruments such as the multifactor leadership questionnaire (MLQ) developed by Bernard Bass to measure leadership by assessing a series of behavioural characteristics of leaders and the extent of influence they have on follower's performance (Bass and Avolio 1993; Bass and Riggio 2006).

There has been some empirical success amongst transformational leadership scholars, who have used quantitative metrics like the MLQ, but traditionally there remains a healthy divergence amongst its users on which behavioural characteristics of leaders should be measured and what actual influence these have on follower's performance (Walsh 2017b: 443). In summary, while progress has been made in the quality of empirical research on transformational leadership, theory critiques have identified several deficiencies impacting on the validity of results in transformational studies. First, critiques suggest that transformational leaders give too much credit to the leader and their influence on individual followers rather than other leader influences over groups or organisational processes. Second, criticisms include that most empirical studies are heavily quantitative and psychology driven—with fewer derived from other disciplines such as sociology or qualitative studies. Finally, critiques agree that progress has been made with transformational studies, but argue advancement has been slowed somewhat due to a fragmented research agenda in the field (Ibid).

Follower-centric theories

While the bulk of leadership theories have focused on the leader, there has been another cluster of theories running parallel with neo-charismatic theories like transformational leadership. The work of follower-centric scholars challenge the neo-charismatic adherent's view that leaders are always critical to the leadership processes (Bligh 2011; Hansen *et al.* 2007; Howell and Shamir 2005). Follower-centric theorists argue that understanding leadership dynamics is insufficient if the focus is merely on trying to understand what makes a 'great leader' or what they do. And in the 1990s, follower-centric adherents such as James Meindl began to challenge that leaders and followers are always different actors with distinctive characteristics and behaviours, and that the leadership process was more an interactive relationship between the two (Meindl cited in Bligh 2011: 427). Like transformational leadership theorising, follower-centric researchers also represent a broad church of theoretical perspectives. Bligh argues that research streams tend to fall into three broad categories: (1) *follower attributes* (identity, motivation, follower perceptions, and values); (2) *leader-follower relations* (e.g. how active a role followers play in the leadership process); (3) *follower outcomes* (e.g. how leadership behaviour influences follower performance and creativity (Bligh 2011: 425–436).

There is insufficient space to provide a deep exploration of the follower-centric field; instead the discussion will briefly list three research agendas (*authentic, ethical, and servant leadership*) given these potentially will have more value to understanding leadership in the IC context rather than others such as 'romance of leadership' or 'aesthetic leadership' (Walsh 2017b: 444). Each of these will be briefly defined and like other theoretical perspectives outlined in this chapter, many aspects of these will be discussed in greater detail in the subsequent substantive chapters.

As with most leadership theorising, defining clearly what authentic leadership means is difficult (Ibid: 444–445; Cooper *et al.* 2005: 475–493). In 2003, Luthans and Avolio defined authentic leadership as 'a process that draws from both positive psychological capacities and a highly developed organisational context, which results in greater self-awareness and self-regulated positive behaviours on the part of leaders and associates, fostering self-development' (Luthans and Avolio 2003: 243). Authentic leadership scholars argue that a leader's positive values, beliefs, ethics, and their ability to develop transparency amongst other characteristics impact on whether followers are more likely to adopt such qualities—resulting in a better organisation (Walsh 2017b: 444). Walumbwa *et al.* (2008: 89–126) came up with the authentic leadership questionnaire (ALQ) comprising leader characteristics such as self-awareness, relational transparency, internalised moral perspective, and balanced processing. However, again ongoing difficulties in defining authentic leadership and how authentic leadership behaviour actually and specifically engenders positive emotions in followers remains unclear (Walsh 2017b: 445).

Briefly, the second follower-centric perspective—ethical leadership—is concerned with how the leader's actions result (or not) in ethical outcomes and how these impact on the organisation they lead. This strand of follower-centric leadership is clearly relevant to how IC leaders negotiate the many ethical dilemmas they face in running intelligence agencies. Earlier in the historical sources discussion, we mentioned issues of privacy, transparency, and accountability. In these and many other issues explored in later chapters there is an ethical dimension to the leaders' decision-making and actions that need to be understood. The third example of follower-centric leadership theory is servant leadership. Van Dierendunck (2011: 1228–1261) provides a useful summary of its main theoretical strands. In short it is concerned about how leaders serve others. While it was first introduced in the 1970s, it didn't gain much traction until the early 2000s.

Servant leadership has been applied in different leadership contexts, such as the health and education sectors (Middlehurst 2008: 322–339). Some critiques still question whether it is a distinct, viable, and valuable theory for organisational success (Parris and Peachey 2013: 377–393). Others claim that its empirical assessment instruments are improving—according to some scholars (Ehrhart 2004; Dennis *et al.* 2010: 169–179). For example, Ehrhart's 2004 study developed 14 item scales that make up different categories and dimensions of servant leadership. Ehrhart argued that certain attributes of servant leadership can be shown to have a distinct influence on followers compared to those seen in transformational leadership (Ehrhart 2004: 73).

Team leadership theories

The third and final cluster of leadership theories argue that leadership emerges from the group rather than an individual. Again, like neo-charismatic and follower-centric theories there is a diverse array of theoretical perspectives. These tend to be on a continuum—either focusing on the role of the team leader at one end or the shared, collective, or distributed leadership theories at the other (Walsh 2017b: 445). Distributed leadership is devolved, shared, or dispersed leadership. The empirical base underpinning many of the new ideas or theories in team leadership, including distributed leadership, remain either weak or non-existent (Harris 2007: 315–325). Interpretations vary significantly and there is conceptual ambiguity about units of analysis for empirical studies. For example, how does one define a team, which could be anything from a global to a small functional team, that is part of a bigger organisation (Walsh 2017b: 445)?

Organisational theory and leadership

In the last section, we briefly introduced some of the main leadership theories that seek to define what leaders *are and do* and how they impact on the organisation they lead. The central question from this discussion regardless of what strand of leadership theory one is examining is what is the relationship between leadership and organisational effectiveness. Our earlier review of leadership theory suggests it is difficult to prove empirically (Parry 2011: 54). Parry suggests that leadership impact is 'easier to discern at lower levels of analysis and more difficult to prove at the organisational level' (Ibid: 55). Further, he argues that while 'the links between leadership and organisational outcomes are real, they are complicated and the complexity arises because the links are complicated.' 'Complexity arises because the links are mediated by other aspects of the system such as the performance of subordinates, the teams they compose and the organisation in which they are embedded' (Ibid: 54).

So while understanding the activities and behaviour of the leader are critical, further consideration needs to be given on how leadership at varying levels within an organisation impact collectively on organisational outcomes. A deeper knowledge of organisational theory nonetheless provides another critical dimension for constructing better knowledge about leadership in the IC context. Like leadership theorising, there is no single truth in organisational theory. It has been drawn from many academic disciplines ranging from 'the natural and social sciences to the humanities and arts' (Hatch 2006: 7). It is beyond the scope of this chapter to provide a detailed description of the intellectual pedigree of organisational theory. Hatch's volume provides a good snapshot of the intellectual sources of modern organisational theory for readers looking for more detail (Ibid: 3–59). But suffice it to say, the field has been particularly shaped by influential sociology and political thinkers of the twentieth century: Marx, Durkheim, and Weber. Later in the 1950s, organisations theory became influenced by biologists such as Ludwig von Bertalanffy, who created the general systems theory, which sought to understand how parts of a system or organisation related to each other (Ibid: 38). In the 1960s, organisational theory was influenced by cultural anthropologists such as Clifford Geertz and the German-inspired social construction theory was proposed by sociologists Peter Berger and Thomas Luckman (Ibid: 43). Anthropological perspectives gave organisational theorists an organisational culture to map and social construction approaches provided perspectives on how social activity within a group generates personal and shared realities (Ibid: 44). Finally, social psychologist Karl Weick used social construction to create sense-making theory, which in short is concerned with how individuals within an organisation find meaning from how their environments are socially constructed. It is their construction of meaning in the organisational environment rather than any objective reality of it that is crucial to sense-making theory (Ibid).

Organisational theory can build on leadership theories discussed above by assessing the impact of the leader on organisational variables such as *strategy, technology, change, knowledge management, organisational learning, operations, communications, marketing, and human resources*. For example, how does technological change (see Chapter 6 ICT) within an intelligence agency promote or dissipate closer team cohesiveness both in virtual and physical settings?

In terms of strategy, how do IC leaders improve the value of 'products' to decision-makers? Effective leadership is in part, as we shall see in Chapter 8 (The Future IC Leader and Governance Challenges), having a cohesive strategy—that in turn results in organisational structures and processes that are effective and sustainable. Similarly, and informed by strategy and governance, is knowledge about how the security environment is changing and then how IC leaders need to adapt workforce programs to meet these changes (see Chapter 7 Human Resources). Marketing may at first glance seem more relevant to private sector enterprises than the IC, but organisational theory principles suggest that just like private sector companies, intelligence agencies need to create a successful 'corporate brand.' While governments may set the agenda of what the broad parameters of an intelligence agency's activities are, IC leaders do play a critical role in developing the 'brand identity' and operations of their agencies compared to others in the community. For example, in the United States, one could ask what role IC leaders and managers play in creating successful brands for the FBI compared to the DHS, which in some respects have overlapping functions. Again, many of these organisational variables and how they interact with leadership will be revisited in subsequent chapters.

Leadership and psychology

There is an overlap between our earlier discussion of leadership, organisational theory, and the final broad knowledge area to be discussed in this chapter—leadership and psychology (Leonard *et al.* 2013; Locander and Luechauer 2005). Psychology is a critical dimension to understanding how leadership personality/behavioural attributes impact on organisational performance. Different 'types' of leadership styles/behaviour result in different objectives that determine organisational effectiveness. One of the early works on leader's behaviour was undertaken in 1939 by German-American psychologist Kurt Lewin, who identified three different leadership styles (autocratic, democratic, and laissez-faire) that applied to decision-making (Billig 2015: 703–718; Michael 2015). Autocratic were often speedy decisions made without any consultation with team members. Democratic styles sought input, but may in the end result in slow decision-making; and finally laissez-faire decision-making meant that the leader stood back and allowed the team to make decisions. Other theoretical approaches from social psychology have also built on Lewin's early work to assess the impact of a leader's behaviour. For example, Parry refers to 'change-oriented behaviours include monitoring the environment to identify threats and opportunities, articulating an inspiring vision, building a coalition of supporters for major change and determining how to implement a new initiative or major change' (Parry 2011: 56). Parry also describes two other behavioural styles. Task-oriented behaviours are most useful for improving efficiency and relationship-orientated behaviours are most useful for improving human resources and relations (Ibid).

Other social psychology theories have been more inspired by evolutionary psychology rather than the social context, which may influence the development of various leadership behaviours. For example, Vught and Ronay (2014) apply the principles of evolutionary biology and behavioural psychology to better understand psychology. They argue that the mind and body are products of evolution through natural selection. This means that leadership and followership evolved in humans and in other species to solve ongoing social problems that require coordination such as conflict resolution, punishment, promoting social cohesion, and leading in warfare (Ibid: 76).

Vught and Ronay further contend that there are two principal barriers to improving leadership. One relates to discrepancies between the modern and ancestral environment, and the other involves psychological mechanisms to dominate and exploit other individuals. In summary they suggest that leadership is partly 'heritable' and that further research (survey data, behavioural and neuro-science data) might show if exposure to transformational leaders increases satisfaction and activates ancient reward areas in the brain (Ibid: 82–90). It is a bold supposition that leadership might be partly heritable and by understanding 'the evolved psychological mechanism this may be help us select the right leaders and design more effective organisations' (Ibid: 90). There is no question that such evolutionary leadership theories require a great deal more evidence to demonstrate reliably a connection between biology and the psychological mechanisms that both influence leadership and follower behaviour.

Turning briefly back again to social psychology theories that look at the social rather than biological factors driving leadership behaviour, there have been distinctions made between 'old/traditional' vs 'new psychology' of leadership approaches. The former are similar to the leadership traits we have discussed above in the historical perspectives of both political and intelligence leaders. Old/traditional psychology of leadership approaches emphasise the characteristics of the individual leader and how they influence the situation. In short, traditional approaches leadership is 'treated very much as an "I" thing (Haslam *et al.* 2010: xxi). In contrast, in new psychology of leadership approaches, leadership is a 'we thing' (Ibid: xxii). For new psychology of leadership theorists, 'the we thing' is most important because effective leadership does not come from the leader telling followers what to do in any authoritarian way, but rather in the leader being able to create and participate in a shared social identity in the group. So unlike the heroic leader or, as evolutionary psychologists seem to suggest, one born with innate special qualities that no one else in the group possesses, new psychology of leadership approaches emphasise effective leadership as being one where the leader is skilled in what they call 'identity leadership' (Haslam *et al.* 2010: 197). Identity leadership means leaders need to be seen as one of the group, their actions should be in the interests of the in-group, and finally leaders must 'craft a sense of us' in terms of the group's norms, values, and priorities (Ibid: xxii). This 'identity' concept seems similar to the principle of 'intelligence governance' that we will now turn to.

Effective intelligence framework

In this final section, the aim is to bring together the four leadership knowledge areas discussed earlier (*history*, *leadership theories*, *organisational theory*, and *psychology of leadership*) with my own recent theorising on intelligence leadership and organisational reform.

As argued earlier, historical cases about leadership in the IC context are valuable in understanding contemporary leadership challenges. For example, it's clear from the earlier discussion that in intelligence failure, regardless of whether one looks at historical or contemporary cases, similar variables may be at play. Political failure, failure in adequate collection, analysis, and leadership are all common variables involved in producing intelligence failure through history and into the present. However, exercising care in the extrapolation of lessons learnt from historical cases for the present is warranted given events—whether historical or contemporary—have their own unique characteristics. For one, the leaders involved in these events have their own unique set of attributes and the security environments in which they are operating are different in time and space.

It is for this reason that the other three knowledge areas discussed earlier (leadership theories, organisational theory, leadership and psychology), should also be mined for their potential value in understanding what it means to be an IC leader and how they impact their agencies and communities today (see Chapter 8 The Future IC Leader and Governance Challenges). All three areas offer cross-disciplinary perspectives from non-intelligence contexts that together provide normative, behavioural, and social insights into what leaders do and how this impacts on their organisations.

Again, casting the net wide can only be helpful in understanding more broadly what factors inform effective IC leadership in the contemporary context. What remains missing, however, and is a critical gap that this book seeks to fill, is to what extent the four broad knowledge areas outlined here can improve theorising about leadership in the contemporary intelligence context. Additionally, given the fertile and diverse debates in each of these four knowledge strands, it is not surprising that in the broader theorising on the concept of leadership there are no grand theories to understand reliably leadership. Accordingly, intelligence studies again as it has always done will need to build its own theories about leadership *in the intelligence context*. The four broad knowledge areas of leadership theorising discussed in this chapter will help in this theory building exercise, but this book will also introduce other discipline areas that may be relevant to theorising about leadership in the intelligence context (Walsh 2017b).

The vast array of discipline perspectives, however, which intelligence studies could draw from in constructing its own leadership theorising, do need to be organised in ways to ensure researchers can systematically organise both the data and analysis of knowledge from multiple fields. For this objective, I offer my *effective intelligence framework*—developed originally in 2011, but with further enhancements and applications in later research (Walsh 2011a, 2015: 123–142; 2017b: 441–459, 2018). The effective intelligence framework provides a diagnostic framework for exploring whether an intelligence agency or community is operating effectively—as well as the extent to which it is likely to show signs of positive or negative adaptation and sustainability to the changing security environment. There is insufficient space to provide a full description of the research process that led to the development of the effective intelligence framework. Other sources provide the detail for readers seeking more background (Walsh 2011a, 2015: 123–142). But in brief, the framework was developed by examining five intelligence contexts across the 'Five Eyes' intelligence communities. The research resulted in 61 interviews across the relevant 'Five Eyes' countries and the analysis of common themes (e.g. tasking and coordination, collection, analysis and intelligence production, strengths, and weaknesses). The analysis of the themes resulted in the effective intelligence framework, which incorporated together both the structural and functional aspects of each intelligence context studied (Walsh 2017b: 441–459).

As shown in Figure 2.1, all intelligence contexts regardless of the parameters (national security, law enforcement, military, private sector) are concerned with interpreting threats and risks in the security environment so this central concern is represented in the middle. The framework is then completed with two additional outlays. The inner circle consisting of *tasking and coordination, collection, analysis, production, and evaluation* are the *core intelligence processes*, or the major activities involved in the assembling of intelligence products. The outer circle consisting of *governance, ICT, human resources, legislation and research* are the *key enabling activities* of the intelligence enterprise. These are the structural components of any intelligence framework, which support the core intelligence processes. In short, without the key enabling activities it would be impossible to produce intelligence products. The naming convention of each key enabling activity is mostly self-explanatory. For example, ICT is concerned with all the information architecture and ecology used in the agency/community— and human resources includes recruitment and other activities such as continuing professional development. Full descriptions of each core intelligence processes and key enabling activity can be found in Walsh (2011a, 2015: 123–142).

The most important aspect of the effective intelligence framework is *intelligence governance*, which I define as 'a set of attributes and rules pertaining

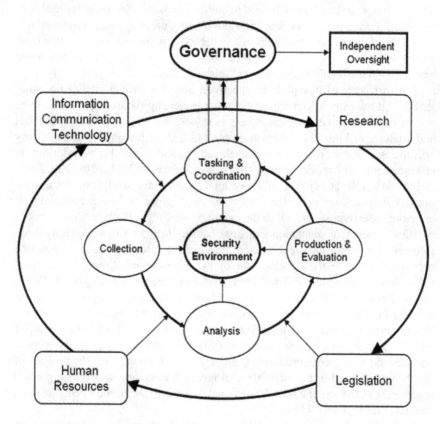

Figure 2.1 Effective Intelligence Framework. Source: Walsh, Intelligence and Intelligence
Analysis, p.148.

to strong leadership, doctrine design, evaluation and effective coordination,
cooperation and integration of intelligence processes' (Walsh 2011a: 135).
Ultimately, effective intelligence governance relies on sound organisational
(and community) leadership that can marshal both an organisation's *core
intelligence processes* and *key enabling activities* in ways that make organisations effective, adaptive, and sustainable as the security environment changes.
Intelligence governance has an external and internal dimension. External governance is that imposed on the intelligence leader by the political leadership.
Internal governance are the activities, policies, processes, and initiatives that the
intelligence leader is able to influence directly. Chapter 8 (The Future IC Leader
and Governance Challenges) will build on discussions here by identifying what
key intelligence governance challenges IC leaders are confronting and how they
may be addressed.

In summary, the effective intelligence framework provides a 'theoretical scaf-
fold' by bringing together multi-disciplinary leadership perspectives discussed

above and assessing their significance to theory building in an IC leadership context. The framework also informs the overall structure of the book.

Conclusion

This chapter provides the broad canvass upon which I argue any conceptualising of IC leadership needs to occur. Understanding contemporary IC leadership, much less any attempts to progress its theorising, will require a deeper understanding of the five perspectives discussed and how they relate to leadership practice in the IC context. These perspectives are historical, leadership theorising, organisational theorising, leadership, and psychology, which are informed by theoretical perspectives like the effective intelligence framework. Combined they allow a multi-disciplinary synthesis of all knowledge areas likely important in progressing our understanding of contemporary IC leadership. Chapter 2 has painted a large canvass. However, I do believe at this very fledgling point in the field of IC leadership theory and practice such a wide terrain is warranted.

While the canvass has been wide in this chapter, in Chapters 3 (Tasking and Coordination), 4 (Collection), and 5 (Analysis) we begin to break it down into areas to better assess the specific challenges IC leaders will be confronted with. You will recall tasking and coordination, collection, and analysis are all core intelligence processes and in all three chapters the objective will be to assess briefly relevant developments and the governance challenges IC leaders are now confronted with.

Starting with Chapter 3 (Tasking and Coordination) and framing the discussion in the post-9/11 contemporary environment, we explore what role IC leaders play in promoting effective tasking and coordination. In particular, what factors (leadership, political, and organisational) influence the ability for leaders to oversee effective tasking and coordination across the 'Five Eyes' intelligence communities? Chapter 3 will demonstrate that the ability of the leader to implement and oversee effective tasking and coordination processes are not just routine bureaucratic processes, but are crucial in providing coherent strategies for the collection, analysis, production, and evaluation of intelligence.

Note

1 The 'JIC' or the UK Joint Intelligence Committee is an inter-agency body responsible for intelligence assessment to assess events and situations relating to external affairs, defence, terrorism, major international criminal activity, scientific, technical and international economic matters, and other transnational issues, drawing on secret intelligence, diplomatic reporting, and open source material.

References

Aldrich, R. (2010). *GCHQ the uncensored story of Britain's most secret intelligence agency*. London: Harper Press.

Aldrich, R., & Cormac, R. (2016). *The black door: Spies, secret intelligence and British prime ministers*. London: William Collins.

Anderson, S. (1994). The evolution of the Canadian intelligence establishment, 1945–1950. *Intelligence and National Security, 9*(3), 448–471. doi: 10.1080/02684529408432261

Andrew, C. (1987). *Her majesty's secret service*. Middlesex, UK: Penguin.

Andrew, C. (2009). *The defence of the realm. The authorized history of MI5*. London: Penguin.

Andrew, C. (2018). *The secret world. A history of intelligence*. London: Allen Lane.

Bass, B., & Bass, R. (2008). *The bass handbook of leadership. Theory, research and managerial implications* (4th ed.). New York: Free Press.

Bass, B., & Riggio, R. (2006). *Transformational leadership* (2nd ed.). Mahwan, NJ: Lawrence Erlbaum Associates.

Bass, B.M., & Avolio, B.J. (1993). Transformational leadership: A response to critiques. In M.M. Chemers & R. Ayman (Eds.), *Leadership theory and Research: Perspectives and directions* (pp. 49–80). San Diego, CA: Academic Press.

Bean, H. (2009). Organizational culture and US intelligence affairs. *Intelligence and National Security, 24*(4), 479–498. doi: 10.1080/02684520903069413

Best, R.A. (2014). Leadership of the U.S. Intelligence Community: From DCI to DNI. *International Journal of Intelligence and Counterintelligence, 27*(2), 253–333. doi: 10.1080/08850607.2014.872533

Betts, R. (1978). Analysis, war and decision: Why intelligence failures are inevitable? *World Politics, 31*(1), 61–89.

Billig, M. (2015). The myth of Kurt Lewin and the rhetoric of collective memory in social psychology textbooks. *Theory and Psychology, 25*(6), 703–718. doi: 10.1177/0959354315594255

Blaxland, J. (2015). *The protest years: The official history of ASIO: 1963–1975* (Vol. 2). Sydney, NSW: Allen and Unwin.

Blaxland, J., & Crawley, R. (2017). *The secret cold war, the official history of ASIO 1975–1989* (Vol. 3). Sydney, NSW: Allen and Unwin.

Bligh, M. (2011). Followership and follower-centres approaches. In A. Bryman, D. Collinson, K. Grint, B. Jackson and M. Uhl-Bien (Eds.), *The Sage handbook of leadership* (pp. 425–436). London: Sage.

Brunatti, A.D. (2013). The architecture of community: Intelligence community management in Australia, Canada and New Zealand. *Public Policy and Administration, 28*(2), 119–143. doi: 10.1177/0952076712458110

Bryman, A. (Ed.). (2011). *The SAGE handbook of leadership*. Sage Publications.

Cain, F. (1994). *The Australian Security Intelligence Organization : an unofficial history*. Richmond, Vic: Spectrum Publications.

Canada, Royal Commission of Inquiry Concerning Certain Activities of the Royal Canadian Mounted Police (McDonald Commission). (1981). Report. (3 vols.). Ottawa: Supply and Services Canada.

Canada, Royal Commission on Security (Mackenzie Commission). (1969). Report. Ottawa: Queen's Printer.

Clapper, J. (2018). *Facts and fears. Hard truths from a life in intelligence*. New York: Viking.

Commission of Inquiry into Police Operations in Quebec; Keable, J.-F.; Quebec (Province). Ministry of Justice. (1981). Report of the Commission of Inquiry into Police Operations in Territory Quebec. Quebec: Ministry of Justice, xv, 451 pp.

Cooper, C.D., Scandura, T.A., & Schriesheim, C.A. (2005). Looking forward but learning from our past: Potential challenges to developing authentic leadership theory and authentic leaders. *The Leadership Quarterly*, *16*(3), 475–493. doi: 10.1016/j. leaqua.2005.03.008

Darroch, S., & Mazerolle, L. (2013). Intelligence-led policing: A comparative analysis of organizational factors influencing innovation uptake. *Police Quarterly*, *16*(1), 3–37. doi: 10.1177/1098611112467411

Day, D. (2014). *The Oxford handbook of leadership and organizations*. New York: Oxford University Press.

Dennis, R.S., Kinzler-Norheim, L., & Bocarnea, M. (2010). Servant leadership theory. In D. van Dierendonck & K. Patterson (Eds.), *Servant leadership: Developments in theory and research* (pp. 169–179). London: Palgrave Macmillan UK.

Desouza, K.C. (2009). Information and knowledge management in public sector networks: The case of the US Intelligence Community. *International Journal of Public Administration*, *32*(14), 1219–1267. doi: 10.1080/01900690903344718

Dover, R., & Goodman, M. (Eds.). (2011). *Learning from the secret past: Cases in British intelligence history*. Washington, DC: Georgetown University Press.

Ehrhart, M.G. (2004). Leadership and procedural justice climate as antecedents of unit-level organizational citizenship behaviour. *Personnel Psychology*, *57*(1), 61–94. doi: 10.1111/j.1744-6570.2004.tb02484.x

Farson, S., & Teeple, N. (2015). Increasing Canada's foreign intelligence capability: Is it a dead issue? *Intelligence and National Security*, *30*(1), 47–76. doi: 10.1080/02684527.2014.961243

Flood, P. (2004). *Report of the inquiry into Australian Intelligence Agencies*. Canberra, ACT: Australian Government Printing Office.

Gentry, J.A. (2010). Intelligence learning and adaptation: Lessons from counterinsurgency wars. *Intelligence and National Security*, *25*(1), 50–75. doi: 10.1080/02684521003588112

Gentry, J.A. (2015). Has the ODNI improved U.S. Intelligence analysis? *International Journal of Intelligence and Counterintelligence*, *28*(4), 637–661. doi: 10.1080/08850607.2015.1050937

Gentry, J.A. (2016). Managers of analysts: The other half of intelligence analysis. *Intelligence and National Security*, *31*(2), 154–177. doi: 10.1080/02684527.2014.961244

Gentry, J.A. (2018). Favourite INTs: How they develop, why they matter. *Intelligence and National Security*, *33*(6), 822–838. doi: 10.1080/02684527.2018.1449371

Gill, P. (1989). Symbolic or real? The impact of the Canadian security intelligence review committee, 1984–88. *Intelligence and National Security*, *4*(3), 550–575. doi: 10.1080/02684528908432016

Goodman, M.S. (2008). Learning to walk: The origins of the UK's Joint Intelligence Committee. *International Journal of Intelligence and Counterintelligence*, *21*(1), 40–56. doi: 10.1080/08850600701649163

Goodman, M.S. (2014). *The official history of Joint Intelligence Committee. Volume 1. From the approach of the second world war to the Suez Crisis*. London: Routledge.

Greener-Barcham, B.K. (2002). Before September: A history of counter-terrorism in New Zealand. *Australian Journal of Political Science*, *37*(3), 509–524. doi: 10.1080/1036114021000026382

Hager, N. (1996). *Secret power: New Zealand's role in the international spy network*. Nelson, New Zealand: Craig Potten.

Hammond, T.H. (2010). Intelligence organizations and the organization of intelligence. *International Journal of Intelligence and Counterintelligence*, *23*(4), 680–724. doi: 10.1080/08850601003780987

Handel, M.I. (1988). Leaders and intelligence. *Intelligence and National Security*, *3*(3), 3–39. doi: 10.1080/02684528808431957

Hansen, H., Ropo, A., & Sauer, E. (2007). Aesthetic leadership. *The Leadership Quarterly*, *18*(6), 544–560.

Harris, A. (2007). Distributed leadership: Conceptual confusion and empirical reticence. *International Journal of Leadership in Education*, *10*(3), 315–325. doi: 10.1080/13603120701257313

Haslam, S.A., Reicher, S.D., & Platow, M.J. (2010). *The new psychology of leadership : Identity, influence and power*. Hove, UK: Taylor & Francis Group.

Hatch, M. (2006). *Organization theory* (2nd ed.). Oxford: Oxford University Press.

Hatlebrekke, K.A., & Smith, M.L.R. (2010). Towards a new theory of intelligence failure? The impact of cognitive closure and discourse failure. *Intelligence and National Security*, *25*(2), 147–182. doi: 10.1080/02684527.2010.489274

Hayden, M. (2016). *Playing to the edge*. New York: Penguin Press.

Herman, M. (1996). *Intelligence power in peace and war/Michael Herman*. Cambridge, UK: Cambridge University Press.

Hewitt, S. (2002). Reforming the Canadian security state: The Royal Canadian Mounted Police security service and the 'Key Sectors' program. *Intelligence and National Security*, *17*(4), 165–184. doi: 10.1080/02684520412331306680

Hewitt, S. (2018). Cold war counter-terrorism: The evolution of international counter-terrorism in the RCMP Security Service, 1972–1984. *Intelligence and National Security*, *33*(1), 67–83. doi: 10.1080/02684527.2017.1323833

Hitz, F. (2015). Human source intelligence. In L. Johnson & J. Wirtz (Eds.), *Intelligence: The secret world of spies* (4th ed., pp. 107–119). New York: Oxford University Press.

Horner, D. (2014). *The spy catchers: The official history of ASIO 1949–1963* (Vol. 1). Sydney, NSW: Allen and Unwin.

House, R.J., & Antonakis, J. (2013). *The full-range leadership theory: The way forward transformational and charismatic leadership: The road ahead 10th anniversary edition* (pp. 3–33). Bingley, UK: Emerald Publishing Group Ltd.

Howell, J., & Shamir, B. (2005). The role of followers in the charismatic leadership process: Relationships and their consequences. *Academy of Management Review*, *30*(1), 96–112.

Innes, M., Roberts, C., & Lowe, T. (2017). A disruptive influence? Preventing problems and counter violent extremism policy in practice. *Law and Society Review*, *51*(2), 252–281.

Innes, M., & Sheptycki, J. (2004). From detection to disruption: Intelligence and the changing logic of police crime control in the UK. *International Criminal Justice Review*, *14*(1), 1–24.

James, A. (2014). Forward to the past: Reinventing intelligence-led policing in Britain. *Police Practice and Research*, *15*(1), 75–88. doi: 10.1080/15614263.2012.754126

Jeffery, K. (2010). *MI6 the history of the Secret Intelligence Service, 1909–1949*. London: Bloomsbury.

Jeffery, K. (2010). *The Secret History of MI6: 1909–1949*. New York: Penguin Books.

Jeffreys-Jones, R. (2012). The end of an exclusive special intelligence relationship: British-American intelligence co-operation before, during and after the 1960s. *Intelligence and National Security*, *27*(5), 707–721. doi: 10.1080/02684527.2012.708523

Jensen, K. (2008). *Cautious beginnings: Canadian foreign intelligence 1939-51*. Vancouver, BC: University of British Columbia.

Jensen, K.F. (2004). Canada's foreign intelligence interview program, 1953–90. *Intelligence and National Security*, *19*(1), 95–104. doi: 10.1080/0268452042000222948

Johnson, L. (2015). A conversation with James R Clapper Jr. the Director of National Intelligence in the United States. *Intelligence and National Security, 30*(1), 1–25.

Johnson, L. (2018). *Spy watching. Intelligence accountability in the United States.* New York: Oxford University Press.

Johnson, L., Aldrich, R.J., Moran, C., Barrett, D.M., Hastedt, G., Jervis, R., … Wark, W.K. (2014). An INS special forum: Implications of the Snowden leaks. *Intelligence and National Security, 29*(6), 793–810.

Kahn, D. (2001). An historical theory of intelligence. *Intelligence and National Security, 16*(3), 79–92. doi: 10.1080/02684520412331306220

Kealey, G.S. (1992). The surveillance state: The origins of domestic intelligence and counter-subversion in Canada, 1914–21. *Intelligence and National Security, 7*(3), 179–210. doi: 10.1080/02684529208432165

Lahneman, W.J. (2004). Knowledge-sharing in the intelligence community after 9/11. *International Journal of Intelligence and Counterintelligence, 17*(4), 614–633. doi: 10.1080/08850600490496425

Leary, W. (Ed.). (1984). *The Central Intelligence Agency history and documents.* Tuscaloosa, AL: University of Alabama Press.

Leonard, H.S., Lewis, R., Freedman, A.M., & Passmore, J. (2013). *The Wiley-Blackwell handbook of the psychology of leadership, change, and organizational development.* New York, UK: John Wiley & Sons, Incorporated.

Lewandowski, C., Carter, J.G., & Campbell, W.L. (2017). The role of people in information-sharing: Perceptions from an analytic unit of a regional fusion center. *Police Practice and Research, 18*(2), 174–193. doi: 10.1080/15614263.2016.1250631

Locander, W., & Luechauer, D. (2005). The psychology of leadership: New perspectives and research. *Academy of Management Review, 30*(3), 641–643. doi: 10.5465/AMR.2005.17293766

Luthans, F., & Avolio, B. (2003). Authentic leadership development. In K. Cameron, J. Dutton & R. Quinn (Eds.), *Positive organizational leadership* (pp. 241–258). San Francisco, CA: Berrett-Koehler.

Maddrell, P., Moran, C., Iordanou, I., & Stout, M. (Eds.). (2018). *Spy chiefs intelligence leaders in Europe, the Middle East, and Asia* (Vol. 2). Washington, DC: Georgetown University Press.

Margolis, G. (2013). The lack of HUMINT: A recurring intelligence problem. *Global Security Studies, 4*(2), 43–60.

Michael, B. (2015). Kurt Lewin's leadership studies and his legacy to social psychology: Is there nothing as practical as a good theory? *Journal for the Theory of Social Behaviour, 45*(4), 440–460. doi: 10.1111/jtsb.12074

Michael, S.J. (2015). Policy, planning, intelligence and foresight in government organizations. *Foresight, 17*(5), 489–511. doi: 10.1108/FS-12-2014-0081

Middlehurst, R. (2008). Not enough science or not enough learning? Exploring the gaps between leadership theory and practice. *Higher Education Quarterly, 62*(4), 322–339. doi: 10.1111/j.1468-2273.2008.00397.x

Miller, S., & Walsh, P.F. (2016). The NSA leaks, Edward Snowden and the ethics and accountability of intelligence collection. In J. Gaillot (Ed.), *Ethics and the future of spying: Technology, intelligence collection and national security* (pp. 193–204). Abingdon: Routledge.

Moran, C., Stout, M., Iordanou, I., & Maddrell, P. (Eds.). (2018). *Spy chiefs. Intelligence leaders in the US and the United Kingdom* (Vol. 1). Washington, DC: Georgetown University Press.

Morell, M. (2015). *The great war of our time: the CIA's fight against terrorism--from al qa'ida to isis*. Twelve. New York: Hachette Book Group.

Murdoch, S. (2009). *Report to the state services commissioner: Intelligence agencies review*. Wellington, New Zealand: New Zealand Government.

National Academies of Sciences, Engineering and Medicine. (2018). *Changing sociocultural dynamics and implications for national security*: Proceedings of a workshop. Washington, DC.

Nohria, N., & Khurana, R. (Eds.). (2010). *Handbook of leadership theory and practice*. Boston, MA: Harvard Business Press.

Omand, D. (2008). Can we have the pleasure of the grin without seeing the cat? Must the effectiveness of secret Agencies Inevitably Fade on Exposure to the light? *Intelligence and National Security*, *23*(5), 593–607. doi: 10.1080/02684520802449476

Omand, D. (2010). Creating intelligence communities. *Public Policy and Administration*, *25*(1), 99–116.

Omand, D., & Phythian, M. (2018). *Principled spying: The ethics of secret intelligence*. Oxford University Press.

Omand, S.D., Prados, J., & Jeffreys-Jones, R. (2009). The embattled helmsman: George Tenet's years at the CIA. *Intelligence and National Security*, *24*(2), 291–302. doi: 10.1080/02684520902826656

Parris, D., & Peachey, J. (2013). A systematic literature review of servant leadership theory in organizational contexts. *Journal of Business Ethics*, *113*(3), 377–393. doi: 10.1007/s10551-012-1322-6

Parry, K. (2011). Leadership and organization theory. In A. Bryman,, D. Collinson, K. Grint, B. Jackson, & M. Uhl-Bien (Eds.), *The Sage handbook of leadership* (pp. 54–70). Thousand Oaks, CA: Sage Publications Limited.

Patman, R.G., & Southgate, L. (2016). National security and surveillance: The public impact of the GCSB Amendment Bill and the Snowden revelations in New Zealand. *Intelligence and National Security*, *31*(6), 871–887. doi: 10.1080/02684527.2015.1095968

Podsakoff, P., Mackenzie, S.B., & Moorman, R.H. (1990). Transformational leader behaviours and the effects on follower's trust in leader, satisfaction, and organizational citizenship behaviours. *The Leadership Quarterly*, *1–2*, 107–142.

Ratcliffe, J. (2005). The effectiveness of police intelligence management: A New Zealand case study. *Police Practice and Research*, *6*(5), 435–451. doi: 10.1080/15614260500433038

Ratcliffe, J. (2016). *Intelligence led policing* (2nd ed.). Abingdon, UK: Routledge.

Rudner, M. (2001). Canada's communications security establishment from Cold War to globalization. *Intelligence and National Security*, *16*(1), 97–128. doi: 10.1080/714002836

Sayle, T.A. (2010). The formative years of Canadian foreign intelligence. *Intelligence and National Security*, *25*(6), 862–867. doi: 10.1080/02684527.2010.537883

Schmidt, J.M. (2015). Policy, planning, intelligence and foresight in government organizations. *Foresight*, *17*(5), 489–511. doi: 10.1108/FS-12-2014-0081

Scott, L., & Hughes, R.G. (2006). Intelligence, crises and security: Lessons from history? *Intelligence and National Security*, *21*(5), 653–674. doi: 10.1080/02684520600957639

Steinhart, A., & Avramov, K. (2013). Is everything personal? Political leaders and intelligence organizations: A typology. *International Journal of Intelligence and Counterintelligence*, *26*(3), 530–549. doi: 10.1080/08850607.2013.780556

Taylor, R.W., & Russell, A.L. (2012). The failure of police 'fusion' centers and the concept of a national intelligence sharing plan. *Police Practice and Research, 13*(2), 184–200. doi: 10.1080/15614263.2011.581448

Taylor, S., & Goldman, D. (2004). Intelligence reform: Will more agencies, money, and personnel help? *Intelligence and National Security, 19*(3), 416–435. doi: 10.1080/0268452042000316223

Tenet, G. (2007). *At the center of the storm: My years at the CIA*. New York: Harper Collins.

The 9/11 Commission Report. (2004). *The 9/11 Commission report. Final report of the National Commission on terrorist attacks upon the United States*. Washington, DC: 9/11 Commission.

Turner, S. (2005). *Burn before reading, presidents, CIA directors and secret intelligence*. New York: Hyperion.

van Dierendonck, D. (2011). *Servant leadership: A review and synthesis* (Vol. 37) (pp. 1228–1261). Los Angeles, CA: SAGE Publications.

Vugt, M., & Ronay, R. (2014). The evolutionary psychology of leadership: Theory, review, and roadmap. *Organizational Psychology Review, 4*(1), 74–95. doi: 10.1177/2041386613493635

Walsh, P.F. (2007). Managing intelligence: Innovation and implications for management. In M. Mitchell & J. Casey (Eds.), *Police leadership and management* (pp. 61–74). Sydney, NSW: Federation Press.

Walsh, P.F. (2011a). *Intelligence and intelligence analysis*. Abingdon, UK: Routledge.

Walsh, P.F. (2011b). Intelligence and national security issues in policing. In P. Birch & V. Herrington (Eds.), *Policing in practice* (pp. 109–127). Sydney, NSW: Palgrave Macmillan.

Walsh, P.F. (2015). Building better intelligence frameworks through effective governance. *International Journal of Intelligence and Counterintelligence, 28*(1), 123–142. doi: 10.1080/08850607.2014.924816

Walsh, P.F. (2016). Australian National Security Intelligence Collection Since 9/11: Policy and Legislative Challenges. In K. Warby (Ed.), *National Security, Surveillance and Terror* (pp. 51-74): Springer International Publishing.

Walsh, P.F. (2017a). Securing state secrets. In R. Dover, H. Dylan & M. Goodman (Eds.), *The Palgrave handbook of security, risk and intelligence* (pp. 177–194). London: Palgrave Macmillan.

Walsh, P.F. (2017b). Making future leaders in the US Intelligence Community: Challenges and opportunities. *Intelligence and National Security, 32*(4), 441–459. doi: 10.1080/02684527.2016.1253920

Walsh, P.F. (2017c). Drone paramilitary operations against suspected global terrorists: US and Australian perspectives. *Intelligence and National Security, 32*(4), 429–433.

Walsh, P.F. (2018). *Intelligence, biosecurity and bioterrorism*. Basingstoke, UK: Palgrave Macmillan.

Walsh, P.F., & Miller, S. (2016). Rethinking 'five eyes' security intelligence collection policies and practice post Snowden. *Intelligence and National Security, 31*(3), 345–368.

Walumbwa, F.O., Avolio, B.J., Gardner, W.L., Wernsing, T.S., & Peterson, S.J. (2008). Authentic leadership: Development and validation of a theory-based measure. *Journal of Management, 34*(1), 89–126. doi: 10.1177/0149206307308913

Wark, W.K. (1993). Introduction: The study of espionage: Past, present, future? *Intelligence and National Security, 8*(3), 1–13. doi: 10.1080/02684529308432211

Warner, M. (Ed.). (2001). *Central intelligence: Origin and evolution*. Washington, DC: CIA History Staff, Center for the Study of Intelligence.

Warner, M. (2004). Intelligence transformation and intelligence liaison. *The SAIS Review of International Affairs*, *24*(1), 77–89.

Warner, M. (2014). *The rise and fall of intelligence*. Washington, DC: Georgetown University Press.

Whibley, J. (2014). One community, many agencies: Administrative developments in New Zealand's intelligence services. *Intelligence and National Security*, *29*(1), 122–135. doi: 10.1080/02684527.2012.746416

Whitaker, R. (1991). The politics of security intelligence policy-making in Canada: I 1970–84. *Intelligence and National Security*, *6*(4), 649–668. doi: 10.1080/02684529108432126

Whitaker, R. (1992). The politics of security intelligence policy-making in Canada: II 1984–91. *Intelligence and National Security*, *7*(2), 53–76. doi: 10.1080/02684529208432156

Zegart, A. (2007). *Spying blind*. Princeton, NJ: Princeton University Press.

3 Tasking and coordination

Introduction

In this chapter, I outline key tasking, coordination, and integration challenges intelligence communities (IC) leaders will be confronted with as the security environment becomes increasingly more complex. More specifically, Chapter 3 is about how leaders, both those external to the IC (i.e. political decision-makers) and internal (IC leaders), navigate through the complexities of tasking, coordination, and integration both at the agency and the entire community level. Tasking and coordination are interrelated functions within intelligence. There can be no intelligence processes or products without a decision-maker tasking our ICs to provide them. Tasking, once initiated, requires the effective coordination of other core intelligence processes (e.g. collection and analytical assets) to ensure the intelligence enterprise has the best chance to support taskers/decision-makers within requested timeframes. In this chapter, therefore, I will refer to tasking and coordination together as both are inextricably linked and rely on each other. We also talk about 'integration' as the chapter progresses as it is linked also to tasking and coordination.

In Chapter 2 (Intelligence and Leadership) we saw how the creation of the modern 'Five Eyes' ICs after World War II developed. The modern history of these ICs, influenced how intelligence was tasked and coordinated, and this in turn over several decades impacted on the strategies, structures, organisational cultures, technology; and workforce development of these communities. Political and IC leaders have both shaped tasking and coordination policies, activities, and processes and this chapter will explore how leaders' interventions have both attempted to improve tasking and coordination as well as how these measures in some cases have fallen short of their intentions. It is not feasible to provide a full assessment on the merits or otherwise of all tasking and coordination activities currently operating across each 'Five Eyes' community. Much of this is classified, but it is possible based on primary (interviews, the IC leadership survey) and secondary sources assembled for this research to provide general insights into how leaders have engaged with tasking and coordination activities and identify where the challenges remain. Our analysis of tasking and coordination across the 'Five Eyes' communities is organised around four broad themes that arose both from primary and secondary research sources. These are: *Theme 1 Intelligence Policy Reform Post-9/11, Theme 2 Risk and Threat Analysis, Theme 3 Role of Science and Technology, and Theme 4 Strategic Intelligence, Tasking, and Coordination.* I will briefly discuss the role of leaders in each and their impact on tasking and coordination activities after which some general implications will be made in the conclusion. In Chapter 8 (The Future IC Leader and Governance) we will come back to how IC leaders will deal with the most critical tasking and coordination issues raised here.

Theme 1 Intelligence policy reform post-9/11

Theme 1 surveys the broader policy, operational, organisational, and cultural issues that impact on effective tasking and coordination across 'Five Eyes' intelligence communities from 9/11 to the present. All of these issues continue to play a role to varying degrees in how intelligence is tasked and coordinated. The impact of such issues—good or bad—goes beyond how effectively intelligence is tasked and coordinated. Poor tasking and coordination can have broader knock-on effects, such as wasting limited collection and analytical resources—or the failure by governments and their ICs to fully identify the likelihood and consequences of emerging risks in the security environment.

In the remaining discussion here, we first refer to some broader policy, organisational, and cultural issues as they relate to *external factors* of tasking and coordination. External dimensions refer to how the political leadership in each 'Five Eyes' country drives tasking and coordination of intelligence and how they have sought since 9/11 to reform issues that relate to or impact on tasking and coordination. Secondly, we will explore the *internal factors* of tasking and coordination to see how IC leaders have sought to improve such activities. In each case, the aim is to examine the most important key broad policy, operational, and cultural factors and how they continue to impact on tasking and coordination processes and outputs.

External factors

Chapter 2 described how since the end of World War II (with varying levels of intensity and success) 'Five Eyes' governments have orchestrated policy, organisational, and legislative initiatives to bring greater integration, centralisation, and coordination of intelligence. Indeed, as far back as the Truman administration successive US governments have expressed the desire to see better intelligence coordination (Best 2014: 254). In the United States alone, at least 14 IC studies have been conducted over the years and despite each recommending reforms, few resulted in significant changes. Only the Dulles Report (1949), Schlesinger Report (1971), Church Committee Report (1976), and 9/11 Commission Report (2004) achieved any substantial change (Warner and McDonald 2005). Additionally, and more recently, just on the issue of terrorism and intelligence performance alone 'there was 12 major bipartisan commission, governmental studies and think tank task forces that examined the US IC and its counterterrorism efforts' (Zegart 2007: 27).

The objective here is not to provide a detailed assessment of pre-9/11 policy reform efforts in each 'Five Eyes' country. Some of these were highlighted in Chapter 2 and although many pre-9/11 policy reform efforts were influential in the development of 'Five Eyes' ICs, the focus here will be on how 'Five Eyes' countries responded to 9/11 and post-9/11 failures. Turning to the United States first, a large volume of sources document the concerns that drove the Bush administration, reluctantly at first (Goodman 2003: 60), and Congress to implement an intelligence reform policy agenda post-9/11. Detailed analysis of how the US political leadership understood the causes of 9/11 as an intelligence failure and what the policy remedies might be can be found in several sources (The 9/11 Commission Report 2004; Zegart 2007; Goodman 2003: 60; Marrin 2011: 182–202; Posner 2005; Best 2014: 253–333). Amongst these sources there are a range of perspectives on the main drivers of intelligence failure leading up to the events of 9/11, including but not limited to the FBI and CIA not sharing information sufficiently, coordination issues, policy failures, intelligence collection failures, and analytical deficiencies. Furthermore, even a cursory review of the Bush administration and Congressional statements demonstrate what many politicians in Washington, DC thought were the main causes in the failure of intelligence around the events of 9/11. For example, members of the legislative branch referred frequently to a fragmented, uncoordinated response by the IC pre-9/11, which required both a strategy and structure that would facilitate a more integrated approach by the IC against Al Qaeda and other threats moving forward. In the 2002 *Report of the Joint Inquiry of the House Permanent Select Committee on Intelligence and the Senate Select Committee into Intelligence Community Activities Before and After the Terrorist Attacks of September 11*, there were several references underscoring views that radical changes to the IC was required. For example, the inquiry reported the Director of Central Intelligence (DCI) had failed to integrate resources from across the IC against al Qaida, which

> suggests a fragmented intelligence community that was operating without a comprehensive strategy for combating the threat posed by Bin Laden, and a DCI without the ability to enforce consistent priorities at all levels throughout the community.
>
> (HPSCI 2002: 40)

Language used by senior political leaders such as a 'fragmented intelligence community,' 'no comprehensive strategy,' and a 'lack of integration' amongst agencies in the US IC highlighted that both effective tasking and coordination, particularly as it related to bringing together domestic and foreign intelligence, was not effective (HPSCI 2002; The 9/11 Commission Report 2004: 402; Walsh 2011a, 2011b, 2015). The Bush administration's policy response to a lack of coordination and integration was legislative with the creation first of the Homeland Security Act of 2002 designed to link the national intelligence community with domestic state and local law enforcement. This led to the establishment of the Department of Homeland Security (DHS). Two years later, the administration enacted the Intelligence Reform and Terrorism Prevention Act (IRTPA). The full Act is accessible in the ODNI's 2009 published legal guide reference (ODNI 2009).

The IRTPA created a new over-arching coordination agency, the Office of the Director of National Intelligence (ODNI), to be led by a new Director of National Intelligence who was meant to be the leader of the entire US IC. It also created the Information Sharing Environment (ISE) and other measures for improving analytical capabilities (see Chapter 5 Analysis). However, our discussion here will be restricted to an assessment of the type of authority invested in the new DNI role by the IRTPA and whether this newly legislated position has improved tasking and coordination. I will come back to another important aspect of the IRTPA—the ISE in the next heading, 'internal factors.' While the ISE was initially a politically driven initiative in the IRTPA, its implementation by the US IC also demonstrates well how IC cultural issues within have at times impeded externally and politically driven structural change to the IC.

Turning back to the discussion of the role of the DNI, as outlined under the IRTPA, the DNI was meant to establish objectives and priorities for the IC and manage and direct tasking of collection, analysis, production, and dissemination of national intelligence. The Act also detailed the role of the DNI in developing personnel policies and programs to enhance the capacity for joint operation and facilitate staffing of IC management functions (in consultation with the heads of the other agencies or elements of the IC). The spirit of the act envisioned a DNI who would accomplish major structural reforms, including how intelligence was tasked, coordinated, and integrated. However, while some progress has been made this overall vision has not materialised. The end result on the tasking, coordination, and integration front has been more mixed. Successive DNIs have made some progress in producing more integrated intelligence missions. However, the IRTPA did not provide this new 'head of the US IC' with sufficient power to implement structural reforms originally foreseen as necessary by the Bush administration (Gentry 2015; Johnson 2015b, 2017; Allen 2013). As Harknett and Stever argue, 'schisms between the legislature and the executive also hampered reforms' (Harknett and Stever 2011: 705).

Despite the early limitations placed on the DNI position, DNIs have attempted to implement initiatives and processes that would better set intelligence tasking priorities, coordination, and integration. For example, the first DNI John Negroponte started the process and developed in October 2005 a national intelligence strategy to prioritise what information to collect and analyse (Lowenthal 2012: 32). More recently, efforts to improve the alignment of the IC's resources and capabilities continued under former DNI James Clapper (Johnson 2015a).

In a 2019 interview with Director Clapper, he elaborated on some of the ways he tried to improve tasking, coordination, and integration. In particular, on integration he said:

> I used the considerable budget and programmatic authority the DNI has to induce the desired behavior among the IC components. Other tools included

IC ITE and joint duty. I stayed in weekly contact—by email—with all 16 components, as well as the ODNI staff. Very time-consuming, but being informed about what was going on all over the IC is almost mandatory if you are going to lead it, and promote integration. Also, visits to each component periodically (which often included a Town hall with the respective work force also afforded me the opportunity to push integration directly to the rank and file. As well, I focused on ICD's (Intelligence Community Directives) to push policies. I had a lot to do, of course, with picking component leaders, another way to foster integration. In sum, no one silver bullet—rather, a series of things both big and small.[1]

At the time of writing (during the Trump administration), it is less clear how successive DNIs (Dan Coats) and the current DNI John Ratcliffe have built on Clapper's reforms to better integrate whole IC approaches, including improving tasking and coordination processes. Indeed, increasingly since commencement of the Trump administration in January 2017, the President has expressed varying attitudes to the IC at best tolerance, though often neglect, suspicion, and even hostility. Outgoing senior US IC leaders such as John Brennan (CIA) and DNI Jim Clapper have periodically raised concerns that the President has not only played down the role Russia took in interfering in the 2016 US elections, but that the President fails to see the broader threat from cyber in Russia, Eastern Europe, and Syria. Also concerning is reports that President Trump early in his presidency rejected a regular written or orally delivered presidents daily brief (PDB). This was delegated to others—reducing the IC's direct access to the President and their ability to provide assessments to him. This can have the effect of not in return receiving back coherent and consistent executive-level intelligence tasking (Strategic Comments 2017).

Although efforts have been made, particularly under Clapper's time as DNI, to produce a comprehensive IC strategy and articulated strategic priorities, these initiatives have not yet achieved the desired unity of effort throughout the enterprise (Johnson 2015b; Harknett and Stever 2011). In the end, rather than provide a single point of authority within the US IC, the IRTPA created another layer of bureaucracy with the DNI given little more power than the former DCI had over the US IC to affect alignment of resources and mission across the IC. The DNI by political and bureaucratic design could not be entirely a single point of authority to ensure a whole of IC tasking and coordination approach could be achieved across the community.

In contrast to the United States, structural reform initiatives of other 'Five Eyes' intelligence countries, the IRTPA represented 'major surgery' compared to what governments in Australia, the UK, Canada, and New Zealand implemented after 9/11. In Australia, the Flood Review may have been the earliest substantial review of the IC since 9/11 commissioned by an Australian government. However, its focus was not on how to restructure the Australian intelligence community after 9/11—rather its central remit was to examine intelligence assessments made in the lead up to the coalition invasion of Iraq (Walsh 2011a: 16; Flood 2004b; Jones

2018). In Australia, the UK, Canada, and New Zealand, the immediate post-9/11 policy reform response was more legislative—reviewing definitions of terrorism offences and giving ICs greater and proactive surveillance and collection powers than setting up new standalone bureaucratic structures within their ICs (Walsh 2011a: 218–227). In short, in the non-US 'Five Eyes' countries, the political and policy response was not to affect large-scale structural reform of their intelligence communities right away but to achieve improved integration via legislative reforms. In Australia, the evolving complexity of transnational threats such as Al Qaeda sparked the implementation of several pieces of legislation to improve the collection of intelligence. From 11 September 2001 to 11 September 2011, the Australian Parliament passed 54 pieces of anti-terrorism legislation—much more than Canada, New Zealand, and the UK (Walsh 2016: 51–74; Williams 2011: 1144). Australia's key anti-terrorism laws are enshrined in Division 100 of the Criminal Code Act 1995 (*Cth*), which has been amended several times. Sections 100–105 deal with: definition of terrorism; receiving and providing training (Australian Government, Criminal Code Act 1995, p. 137). Other new amendments to the Criminal Code included terrorist financing offences (Division 103), speech offences (i.e. urging violence) (Part 5.1), as well as new powers to allow the Attorney General to prescribe a terrorist organisation (Division 102).

The other significant intelligence collection and counter-terrorism response during the early post-9/11 years (during the Howard conservative government) were control and preventative detention orders. Division 104 of the Criminal Code now allowed control orders against individuals not suspected of any criminal offence that may be subjected to restrictions (equivalent to house arrest). These measures were thought by government to be reasonably necessary to protect the public from terrorism. Views on the need for control orders varied at the time these reforms were introduced (see for example, McDonald 2007: 106; White 2012; White 2007: 116–25). The preventative detention measures under Division 105 of the Criminal Code allowed for an individual to be detained for up to 48 hours if there was a reasonable expectation this would prevent imminent terrorist acts or assist in preserving evidence relating to a recent terrorist act. The initial 48-hour period could be further extended under state law by 14 days (Walsh 2016: 51–74). A more detailed survey of Australian and Canadian counter-terrorism and intelligence legislation can be found in Walsh (2016: 51–74).

Similar to the United Kingdom's Terrorism Act 2000, Australia also separated terrorism laws from other criminal offences, while the criminal law was expanded to deal with association with terror groups and participation in a terrorist act (Misra 2018: 108). Immediately after 9/11 in the UK, the Anti-Terrorism, Crime and Security Act was passed, described by one expert as 'surely the most draconian legislation Parliament has passed in peacetime in over a century' (Phythian 2005: 668). Controversially, this legislation introduced a system of indefinite detention without trial for immigrants and asylum-seekers, who could not be deported, but were certified by the Home Secretary, on the basis of intelligence, to be a 'suspected international terrorist' and so a threat to national security. Hence, a politician, not a judge, would rule on indefinite detentions.

Similarly in Canada, the most immediate and widely recognisable response to 9/11 was the introduction of Bill C-36, the Anti-Terrorism Act. An omnibus piece of legislation, Bill C-36 provided a three-pronged response to terrorist threats facing Canada: it enacted a legal definition of terrorism and related activities as criminal offences; it provided for the public designation and outlawing of terrorist groups; and it instituted measures to better facilitate the identification, prosecution, conviction, and punishment of terrorist operatives and co-conspirators (Shore 2006: 457).

Additionally, efforts were made in all countries (just as the US had done) to establish counter-terrorism fusion centres: the National Threat Assessment Centre (NTAC-Australia), the Joint Terrorism Analysis Centre (JTAC-UK), the Integrated Terrorism Assessment Center (ITAC-Canada), and the Combined Threat Assessment Group (CTAG-New Zealand). The function of each is to better coordinate and integrate in one location counter-terrorism intelligence collection and analytical priorities across their ICs (Walsh 2011a). Other initiatives sought to strengthen existing intelligence coordination institutions at the centre of governments in the Prime Minister and Cabinet offices of Australia, Canada, New Zealand, and the UK. None of these measures were, at least initially after 9/11, wholesale attempts by the political leadership to refashion their ICs. For example, in Australia several smaller-scale reviews in addition to the legislation changes described above were carried out such as the 2004 Flood Report, the 2005 Taylor Review into ASIO's technical and proficiency gaps, and in 2008 the Smith Review (Misra 2018). The Smith Review was significant not for any major surgical reinvention of the IC, but more for what it rejected than recommended. The review recommended against a new homeland security super agency to coordinate Australia's IC. It suggested instead better coordination of existing arrangements by the Department of Prime Minister and Cabinet and the creation of a new national security advisor (Walsh 2011a, 2011b). However, in December 2017 the Department of Home Affairs (Home Affairs) was finally created—though there remains a lack of compelling independent evidence for the need of this kind of super-coordinating agency.

It remains difficult to assess with accuracy whether the more 'micro-surgical' interventions by non-US 'Five Eyes' countries resulted in better tasking and coordination of intelligence. Providing a full assessment will not be possible until further details of reform outcomes become unclassified, which could be decades away. However, subsequent inquiries in all 'Five Eyes' countries suggest that the ability for political leaders to affect via post-9/11 legislation and policy measures effective and consistent improvement in a range of intelligence capability areas (including tasking and coordination) remain works in progress.

In Australia, since the 2004 Flood Report, which was an independent review of Australia's intelligence capabilities, there have been periodic reviews (every five to seven years) of IC capability. These are the 2011 Independent Review of the Intelligence Community by Rufus Black and Robert Cornall and the most recent— the 2017 Independent Intelligence Review of the Intelligence Community by Michael L'Estrange AO and Stephen Merchant PSM (L'Estrange and Merchant

2017). In each review, suggestions have been made on how to strengthen the coordination and integration of the IC, which also serves to improve the efficient tasking of intelligence. The Flood Report referred to the need for the community to bolster effectiveness, communications, and interoperability. It recommended a strengthened coordination role for the Office of National Assessments (now called ONI) and suggested the creation of a foreign intelligence coordination committee.[2] The Committee would be chaired by DG ONA and have representations of all IC heads to discuss coordination, capability, and intelligence policy (Flood 2004: 60). The 2017 L'Estrange and Merchant report did not specifically identify any major improvements in tasking and coordination required by the AIC. The report indicated that:

> over recent years, the AIC has worked collaboratively in specific areas to deliver more focused and timely intelligence, particularly for operational decision makers. Through enhanced co-ordination initiatives and fusion centres, agencies have addressed particular areas of interaction that reflect the changing nature of Australia's national security environment. L'Estrange and Merchant added that an important feature has been the growth in 'mission approaches' to tackle complex issues through whole-of-government operational and policy responses.
>
> (2017: 42)

However, the reviewers recognised managing the ongoing challenges in effective coordination of the AIC is both necessary and desirable in the pursuit of a range of critically important objectives. These include the provision of IC leadership and broad strategic direction-setting for intelligence as a national enterprise; the clear identification of national intelligence priorities in support of the policy priorities of the government of the day; effective cross-agency implementation of those priorities, maximising the efficiency of resource allocation (particularly in terms of the impact of the accelerating pace of technological change); and the robust evaluation of individual agency and broad-based AIC performance. Effective coordination also requires the development of relevant joint capabilities and assets across the AIC, a strategic focus on AIC workforce planning requirements, and accountability to the Prime Minister and other Ministers for the AIC's output and performance (Ibid).

Given all the challenges identified above, L'Estrange and Merchant concluded that in their 'view across all these benchmarks of effective AIC co-ordination more can be achieved. In particular, they argued that the IC leadership is impeded by the absence of an appropriate explicit remit, by the nature of the current deeply 'federated' intelligence structure, and by an insufficient number of individuals with comprehensive cross-agency appreciation of the full range of Australian intelligence capabilities, activities and potential synergies' (Ibid: 44). The L'Estrange and Merchant 2017 review of the AIC is the most significant completed in several decades and its 23 recommendations (at time of writing) are still being implemented. The 2017 Independent Intelligence Review throws up other intelligence governance challenges, not just in the areas of tasking, coordination, and integration. We will come back to these in Chapter 8 (The Future IC Leader and Governance Challenges).

Similarly, in the UK the Butler Inquiry identified areas in the UK IC where there could be better coordination of counter-proliferation activity:

> we consider that it would be helpful through day-to-day processes and the use of new information systems to create a 'virtual' network bringing together the various sources of expertise in Government on proliferation and on activity to tackle it, who would be known to each other and could consult each other easily.
>
> (Butler 2004: 158)

In Canada, in the aftermath of 9/11 and in addition to legislative changes, the government invested more significantly in the capabilities of foreign intelligence capabilities of Communications Security Establishment (CSE) and CSIS as well as the Royal Canadian Mounted Police (RCMP).[3] The government set up a new cabinet committee on security, public health, and emergencies to better manage national security and intelligence matters and 'to better coordinate a government wide response to all emergencies' (Shore 2006: 459).

The government also created the Minister of Public Safety and Emergency Preparedness Canada (PSEP), which brought together national security, policing, border and emergency management under the one department—allowing for an optimised coordination of national security and intelligence resources (Ibid). Also, although a much smaller community compared to the US or even Australia, the government of New Zealand's first independent review of its IC—the 2016 Cullen and Reddy review remarked that despite colocation of the Government Communications Security Bureau (GCSB), the New Zealand Security Intelligence Service (NZSIS) and the National Assessments Bureau (NAB) into a single building in Wellington, products don't always meet needs of decision-makers—intelligence priorities can be inadequately defined and there is a lack of understanding of the needs and priorities of decision-makers (Cullen and Reddy 2016: 62).[4]

Cullen and Reddy made a series of recommendations to oversee and coordinate GCSB, NZSIS, and NAB including the establishment of a national intelligence and security advisor (NISA). The NISA would become the principal advisor to government on intelligence and security matters (Ibid). Post the review, New Zealand governments thus far seemed to have opted for strengthened oversight of priority setting and coordination within the national security group of the Department of Prime Minister and Cabinet rather than appointing a NISA.

The final externally driven factor impacting on effective tasking and coordination is the politicisation of intelligence. Like the policy-driven structural reform agenda of 'Five Eyes' governments discussed above, politicisation also has its historical precedents. Chapter 2 showed how politicisation of intelligence in all its forms extends back in history before the modern evolution of intelligence in the 20th century. For the purposes of this section, which is to explain how external policy factors impact·on effective tasking and coordination, I will not embark on a full discussion of how various types of politicisation have revealed themselves across the historical record since 1945. There are other good sources which provide detailed analysis of historical cases of politicisation (Hastedt 2013: 5–31; Rovner 2013: 55–67; Lucas 2011: 203–227). Instead I will briefly explain the main types of politicisation since 9/11 and how they have impacted on building better tasking, coordination, and integration. As the literature shows, politicisation (of intelligence) remains a vague and contestable term, but there is at least some agreement that it can come in a range of forms—some clearly more obvious while others are more subtle (Walsh 2011a: 204–210; Treverton 2008: 91–106; Marrin 2013: 32–54; Rovner 2013: 55–67; Lucas 2011: 203–227). For example, there can be pressure or interference by policy makers directly in the intelligence assessment process to change, amend, and leave out relevant information. Politicisation can also be more subtle such as political leaders self-selecting or cherry picking 'bits' of intelligence to support policy objectives. Hastedt has provided a framework for studying politicisation of intelligence analysis by introducing soft vs hard politicisation. A historical or contemporary case can be studied by examining its context for how soft and hard politicisation might impact on intelligence analysis (Hastedt 2013: 6). Soft politicisation is defined as 'deliberate attempts to alter the assumptions underlying an analysis, the decision rules by which an analysis moves forward and institutional setting within which these deliberations are made' (Ibid: 10). In contrast, hard politicisation involves the use of coercion to eliminate options and if need be impose an outcome. In this case, there are deliberate attempts to coerce analysts into adopting a certain set of assumptions, conclusion, or in the extreme overruling analysts imposing a conclusion on the analysis (Ibid). As was seen with the various announcements made by senior officials in London and Washington about the imminent threat posed by Saddam Hussein and his WMD—a flurry of political announcements about every single piece of intelligence found (reliable or otherwise) resulted in a hyper-sensitised IC analytical processes.

> Despite all that has been written about the intelligence assessments into WMD of Iraq and whether they resulted in political directed amendments to assessments *per se*, it seems clear enough that this highly politicised environment gradually saw an evolution of political judgements that eventually either matched or supported the policy makers perceptions of the threat.
>
> (Walsh 2011a: 206)

Jervis suggests in situations such as the Iraq WMD assessments, the evolution of analytical judgements to match political judgements creates a motivated bias 'where the analyst seeks to avoid the painful value-trade-off between pleasing policy makers and following professional standards' (Jervis 2009: 212). In essence, they are motivated in favour of producing assessments that support or at least do not undermine policy (Ibid). The many public pronouncements by senior members of the Bush administration, particularly Vice President Dick Chaney, about the links between Iraq and Al Qaeda and that Saddam Hussein had WMD underscore the politicised environment in which intelligence was being produced and used (Walsh 2011a: 206). The various public announcements about what the intelligence was saying about WMD in Iraq as noted earlier produced a politicised environment and the administration's cherry picking of intelligence are examples of Hastedt's hard politicisation (Hastedt 2013: 10, 26–27).

While the political leadership can ignore intelligence assessments and make decisions based on other information or their own world view, this can be a dangerous situation in some circumstances, for example, if political leaders in doing so still refer to aspects of the intelligence to justify their preferred course of action out of context or spin the significance of a threat or risk that the intelligence community has still not made a final assessment on. These actions can subvert the proper tasking of collection and analytical assets based on spurious political belief—thereby wasting resources and possibly lives and producing damage to the IC reputation and further policy failure.

Another type of intelligence politicisation is bureaucratic politicisation, which has an impact on the normal running of tasking and coordination processes particularly when political leaders actively seek to obtain intelligence from either not the usual appropriate suppliers of that information in the IC—or receive raw intelligence that has not yet been processed. In the US we saw how the Pentagon shortly after 9/11 established an Office of Special Plans (OSP), which utilised raw intelligence from the field. The intelligence was fed into the offices of Secretary Rumsfeld, Paul Wolfowitz (Deputy-Secretary Defense), and the Vice President's Office. The information was not filtered or vetted by other member agencies of the IC, who would normally assess its reliability against other sources. The OSP underscored a battle within the IC between the CIA and DIA versus the Pentagon for control over US foreign policy on the WMD in Iraq issue (Walsh 2011a: 207–208). The net effect of the OSP case was that some unreliable sources from certain Iraqi opposition groups (e.g. the Iraqi National Congress) were being used to make policy, whereas they had been discounted by the CIA earlier. The OSP raw intelligence was stove piped to the highest ranking cabinet level, while other processed intelligence was blocked or ignored by the Pentagon. Blocking the filter of all source intelligence assessments on as many issues as possible might have helped certain figures in the Bush administration continue their agenda over WMD in Iraq—but it also meant other senior cabinet leaders including the President were not getting good quality or reliable intelligence in which to task correctly foreign, military, and intelligence assets (Walsh 2011a: 208). The OSP establishment might well be a case of Hastedt's soft politicisation as it was non-coercive, but it did set out to 'alter the assumptions and institutional settings within which analytical deliberations occurred' (Hastedt 2013: 10, 26–27).

I do not want to skew arguments about the impact of the politicisation of intelligence on IC processes, including tasking and coordination. Clearly in liberal democracies, IC activities should be at arms lengths from political decision-makers (or the hand that feeds them). But intelligence is by definition a politicised process. While intelligence assessments should not from a good practice perspective be written around policy dilemmas or specific outcomes, they nonetheless need to be aware of the policy issues decision-makers are grappling with to ensure they assess priority issues in ways that can inform the policy making process. Nonetheless, since 9/11 there is sufficient evidence to suggest that at times the arm's length gap between the political leadership and the IC is closing (e.g. Iraq 2003; Afghanistan, the Trump administration, and Russian collusion in elections and over the nature of the Russian threat). In the United States, the intelligence/policy gap is closing in perhaps ways yet to be fully understood—through the interference with the way normal cabinet-level decisions about intelligence tasking of top priorities are made but also by pressuring senior intelligence officials to paint a rosier picture of current operational activity—or worse still the Trump administration's downplaying (for personal political reasons) of the growing malignant threat posed by Russia to American electoral systems and other critical infrastructure. At the January 2016 briefing of President-elect Trump at Trump Tower, DNI Jim Clapper, Director CIA John Brennan, and FBI Director James Comey briefed the incoming President about the strong intelligence confirming Russian influence operation in the recent presidential election. Clapper, in his 2018 memoir *Facts and Fears. Hard Truths from a Life in Intelligence*, records that the President-elect accepted initially this intelligence, but was seeking confirmation that the interference did not have any effect on the outcome of the election. Clapper replied that 'we had neither the authority nor capabilities to assess what impact—if any—the Russian operation had' (Clapper 2018: 375). As Clapper and his team began to leave Trump Tower, he overheard some of the President-elect's staff get to work on a press briefing saying aloud 'the IC assessed that the Russian interference did not change the outcome of the election—which he says was very different from our acknowledgement that we hadn't and couldn't assess its impact' (Ibid: 376). The Trump administration was starting to cherry pick the intelligence even before taking office.

In addition, we have seen in the Trump administration the public disrespect, denigration, and even hostile comments about the 'trustworthiness' of the IC over the extent of Russian involvement in US internal affairs and in contrast the willingness to trust Vladimir Putin over the President's own IC. The President also accused the FBI of wire-tapping Trump Towers just before his victory as well as the firing of James Comey, the FBI director, in May 2017, which again underscores a distrust and hostility to the IC. Former intelligence leaders such as John Brennan, Jim Clapper, and Michael Hayden amongst others have since come out in the media and in print to criticise President Trump's ongoing politicisation of intelligence. In summary, all of these developments are yet additional layers of the politicisation of intelligence, which potentially can significantly damage the relationship between the number one 'intelligence tasker'—the US President and the IC. They can also have an effect on the democratic institutions of the US if the truth to power that the IC seeks is dismissed by the political leadership as 'fake news' (Hayden 2018).

What can intelligence leaders do about different forms of politicisation is difficult to know. Different circumstances may require varied approaches, which suggests there is no magic off the shelf panacea to politicisation in all its forms. There are all the usual things managers and IC leaders should do related to quality control of products and assigning the most 'accurate' probability of certainties around collection sources and analytical judgements. We will come back to these issues in subsequent chapters. There is no doubt also that leaders of ICs and the agencies therein need to continue to publish whole of IC assessments on issues not just at the strategic level, but where possible at the operational level as well. Of course you want to avoid political decision-makers receiving a bland lowest common denominator product that every agency will agree on. There still needs to be contestability in products, but with some major political decisions, particularly around whether the country will go to war, robust whole of IC products that don't gloss over the uncertainties may still in some instances guard against politicisation. If the political leadership sees that the IC speaks with one voice on an important issue this can be compelling for at least some politicians (though not all as the Trump administration has shown) to deal with the assessment provided whether politically advantageous or not. Agencies can still provide appendix notes if they disagree on a judgement of other IC member agencies. Accountability mechanisms are also important ways to diagnose and treat politicisation of intelligence in 'Five Eyes' countries. We will briefly return to the subject of politicisation and the ways IC leaders may deal with it in the future in Chapter 8 (The Future IC Leader and Governance Challenges).

Internal factors

The types of politically sponsored major redesign of the US IC post-9/11 and the initially less dramatic policy and legislative reform measures to achieve better coordination across the other 'Five Eyes' countries has no doubt improved tasking and coordination across ICs in some areas. The growing complexity of many threats, both state and non-state variants, in a way is bringing IC agencies within and across 'Five Eyes' countries to share resources, identify priorities, and take more a mission approach to specific threats (Walsh 2011b). How political and policy-driven reform measures discussed above are implemented within ICs is of course largely in the hands of senior leadership. In this section, we briefly explore how 'Five Eyes' IC leaders have sought to implement the broader policy and legislative measures constructed by their political leadership post-9/11 and how these have impacted on the tasking and coordination of intelligence. As with the earlier discussion of external factors, this section provides only a short summary of three inter-related issues: *organisational structure*, *information sharing*, and *cultural matters* as these continue to influence how effectively intelligence is being tasked, coordinated, and integrated post-9/11.

If the clarion call (to varying degrees) from political leaders since 9/11 has been for more centralised, coordinated, and integrated intelligence processes within and across IC agencies, senior leaders have had a large leeway on how to achieve such policy and legislative directives. One of the key leadership-driven internal organisational reform responses since 9/11 has been the proliferation of fusion centres. This has been one way that IC leaders can demonstrate to the political leadership their broader concerns about organisational structure, information sharing, and effective intelligence support to decision-makers are being addressed. Of course, as noted in Chapter 2, fusion centres are not new. In their modern manifestation they appeared on a more regular basis during World War II and continued their expansion on during the Cold War—both in the national security and law enforcement contexts. But there is no doubt after 9/11 there has been an even greater proliferation of fusion centres. As noted above, particularly in the counter-terrorism area in the United States after 9/11, but also the other 'Five Eyes' countries' political decision-makers funded large fusion centres like the NCTC (US), NTAC (Australia), ITAC (Canada), CTAG (NZ), and JTAC (UK) were established to better coordinate the tasking, analysis, coordination, and integration of all intelligence across government relating to terrorism and counter-terrorism.

Post-9/11, fusion centres became a kind of 'insurance policy' for both the political and IC leadership that there was now, at least in theory, a much more coordinated, integrated approach to collection, analysis, and operational activity. Fusion centres again theoretically would fill in the silos identified by the 9/11 Commission as well as deconflict effort across entire ICs. With the potential benefits in mind there has been a further proliferation of fusion centres in the US. There are now over 72 across the United States in metro and regional areas that seek to fill another important gap between federal government intelligence and intelligence extracted at the state and local level largely by law enforcement agencies (Masse and Rollins 2008). While there are less fusion centre operations in the other 'Five Eyes' countries, fused arrangements have emerged across Australia, UK, Canada, and New Zealand in national security and law enforcement priority areas in counter-terrorism, anti-money laundering and terrorism financing, border protection, and organised crime amongst others. However, how IC leaders have established and managed a range of fusion centres since 9/11 shows that not all function as intended for a range of reasons. Arguably chief among these has been poor governance (i.e. the coordination of resourcing, business rules, the establishment of a communal identity and issues related to making collective decisions). Governance issues in turn impact on whether intelligence is tasked and coordinated in ways that can maximise the results of many agencies being co-located physically or virtually. Of course I am mindful not to over-generalise the governance issues to the point of inaccuracy. Not all centres have poor governance issues or are racked with other performance challenges (Carter and Carter 2009: 1323–1339).

For example, Van Puyvelde explored the El Paso Intelligence Center (EPIC) in EL Paso, Texas—a 30-year-old fusion centre of federal and local authorities focused on countering drug trafficking (Van Puyvelde 2016: 888–902). His article demonstrates that fusion centres can be an effective force multiplier for more effective tasking and coordination of intelligence beyond what might be achieved if these agencies were working exclusively out of their own headquarters. However, my own research, which included visits to two very different fusion centres back in 2009 (the JRIC and the ROIC), show how diverse such centres can be. Both these centres differed in several factors including how they were led as well as how leaders navigated intelligence governance issues. These factors impacted on the ability for the fusion centres to identify tasking priorities and support robust coordination of intelligence collection, analytical and operational action once priorities have been tasked (Walsh 2011a, 2015: 123–142). More recent evidence showed that many fused arrangements in the US have not necessarily resulted in identification of tasking, collection, analytical, or operational priorities because of leadership and governance issues, limited resourcing, or poor training. In late 2012, the US Senate's Homeland Security and Governmental Affairs Permanent Subcommittee on Investigations released an uncomplimentary assessment of US fusion centres that provided further evidence about the challenges they face—particularly on a range of governance issues. For example, the Senate report found poor leadership efforts on improving information sharing, funding oversight (at the fusion centres and in the DHS headquarters), and questions about the 'value added' that fusion centres intelligence was providing from an analytical perspective (US Senate Committee on Homeland Security and Governmental Affairs 2012). These issues have also been identified by other researchers along with concerns about privacy, security, and the implications of a greater number of agencies—particularly local law enforcement having access to national security intelligence (Carter and Carter 2009; Newkirk 2010: 43–60). Additionally, it is less clear how fusion centres build effective partnerships between the centre and local agencies. In particular, in the case of law enforcement fusion centres there are questions about how they facilitate actionable intelligence products that can result in intelligence-led and data-driven policing strategies (Lewandowski *et al.* 2018: 177–193).

In addition to how IC leaders have developed organisational structures such as fusion centres for better tasking and coordination of intelligence, a big factor in their proliferation since 9/11 has been to provide an integrated or fused intelligence picture for decision-makers. This relies on having the right type and volume of intelligence collected, and making sure in order to create that fused picture all intelligence has been shared across the fusion centre or broader IC to all that need to see it as quickly as possible. Optimal intelligence sharing is a function of many factors including types and capabilities of various collection methodologies (Chapter 4) and the supporting ICT architecture (Chapter 6). For the purposes of our discussion here though, we will restrict our discussion to cultural barriers, which can restrict adequate information sharing. The knock-on effect of cultural barriers can be decision-makers making less informed tasking decisions or an uncoordinated and insufficient response to intelligence collection and analysis.

There are several cultural factors that impact on information sharing across 'Five Eyes' ICs including in fused arrangements or joint task forces that were set up to improve information sharing. Some, as noted earlier, relate to the mandates of different agencies, bureaucratic history (e.g. national security vs law enforcement organisational and cultural identities), funding, and leadership dynamics (Cotter 2017: 173–187; Catano and Gauger 2017: 17–34; De

Castro Garcia *et al.* 2017: 736; Herman 2003: 50–52). As seen with inclusion of the ISE in the IRTPA, cultural issues cannot be legislated easily away in any prescriptive sense in the short term given the longstanding bureaucratic priorities and cultural differences between agencies across the US IC. The wording within the IRTPA outline both the intent, attributes, and steps required for the enactment of the ISE across the US IC. For example, in terms of the attributes of the ISE:

> the President shall, through the structures described in subparagraphs (B) and (C) of paragraph (1), ensure that the ISE provides and facilitates the means for sharing terrorism information among all appropriate Federal, State, local, and tribal entities, and the private sector through the use of policy guidelines and technologies. The President shall, to the greatest extent practicable, ensure that the ISE provides the functional equivalent of, or otherwise supports, a decentralized, distributed, and coordinated environment that...
>
> (ODNI 2009: 152)

While extensive progress has been made on information sharing, it still remains difficult to overcome the cultural organisational barriers across the US IC that would allow the fullest expression of ISE sentiments expressed in the IRTPA. Since 9/11 and across the 'Five Eyes' there are a number of other examples of how organisational cultural issues impact on information sharing. Tromblay's survey of the FBI's IT development process, for example, highlights the implementation of several IT capabilities such as the case management system Sentinel in 2012, and how these are indicators of larger cultural problems across the organisation. In his words, 'information systems have been historically cobbled together in an uncoordinated fashion' (Tromblay 2017: 828).

Information sharing problems that demonstrate cultural issues have been raised in Australia and Canada as well. In Australia, a 2012 Parliamentary Inquiry, which I provided testimony to and identified a number of IT architectural and cultural impediments, prevented the sharing of criminal intelligence across Australia's law enforcement agencies (Walsh 2012). In Canada, a 2012 externally funded government report suggested that 'support requests that specific organizations receive from consumers are also often not shared with other organizations and potentially several agencies might be tasked to produce intelligence on the same "hot" topic' (Adams *et al.* 2012: 18). This suggests that information sharing may not be as sufficient in some instances as it needs to be. On the point of information sharing, the report pointed out that:

> the Canadian intelligence community, having a relatively small size, is particularly prone to the problem of overextending its resources, and that unclear or overlapping mandates among organizations can create unnecessary redundancy. IC members participating in the research noted that having more clear delineation of roles and responsibilities, promoting more of a cross community view, endorsing joint projects within the community as

well as developing better information sharing mechanisms could facilitate a higher level of coordination.

(Ibid)

Another dimension on information sharing across 'Five Eyes' ICs is how cultural issues play out in the broader homeland security and law enforcement communities. As noted earlier, since 9/11 in each 'Five Eyes' country, governments have enacted policy and legislative reforms aimed at broadening the corporate identity of IC communities beyond the traditional national security and defence agencies involved in national intelligence to include a broader church of agencies such as those responsible for border protection, immigration, financial intelligence, organised crime, and to some extent state and even local law enforcement. The ISE, fusion centres, ODNI, and DHS all represent efforts by successive US administrations to not only restructure the US IC architecture, but provide frameworks that allow a larger number of agencies, particularly state, regional, and local law enforcement, to potentially play a greater role in a broader reconceptualising of the national intelligence community. Similar efforts have been made incrementally by governments in Australia and Canada as well to create more whole of government ministerial and policy responses to intelligence, national security, and law enforcement issues (Walsh 2011b: 109–127; Shore 2006: 456–479).

It is hard to argue at least against the policy efforts of 'Five Eyes' governments that try to engender a broader IC enterprise that includes increasingly at least at the margins more law enforcement agencies, who are often best placed to collect and operationalise intelligence about threats in local settings that may have national or even international importance. Having therefore structures, systems, and cultural customs in place that facilitate the sharing of intelligence in both directions between the traditional IC agencies in each 'Five Eyes' country with their law enforcement counterparts is critical. Yet, as discussed earlier, one policy solution to facilitate intelligence and information sharing—the creation of fusion centres have not always been an exemplary approach for the promotion of information sharing, even when agency representatives may be co-located in the same physical space. Federal, state, and local agencies have their own legislative, resourcing, and management issues, which influences how intelligence and information sharing takes place. There are also, in many cases, a diverse array of historical and organisational cultural issues which can constrain sharing. Lambert's study on the sharing of homeland security information outlines some of the obstacles to information sharing at the state and local levels, including inter-agency and intra-agency issues that arise for police agencies. Lambert explores the complexities of information sharing across highly decentralised policing systems in the US. Many police departments lack a formal intelligence function that limits their ability to share information (Lambert 2019). There have been several other studies which have examined the various constraints for optimal information sharing including organisational cultural factors (Best 2011; Walsh 2011a; Maras 2017: 187–197; Jones 2007: 384–401). While in all 'Five Eyes' ICs, efforts have been made from a digital information and ICT network perspective to address information sharing issues, research shows that the role of improving trust in social networks amongst intelligence agencies is as important as ICT technology solutions (Cotter 2017: 173–187).

Finally, as outlined in Chapter 2, we saw from the 1990s onward how intelligence led policing models have influenced the broader organisational cultures of 'Five Eyes' law enforcement communities, particularly how intelligence is tasked and coordinated through the broader non-intelligence parts of law enforcement. As noted, efforts by intelligence leaders in various law enforcement agencies to use intelligence-led policing strategies aimed at putting intelligence more front of centre of the 'policing business' continues to be largely a work in progress. Right from the early implementation of intelligence led policing strategies such as the national intelligence model in the UK, efforts were being made by heads of intelligence functions within law enforcement agencies to integrate intelligence into all aspects of the policing business—particularly in how intelligence was tasked and coordinated with and by other non-intelligence functions of policing such as investigations (Sheyptycki 2004: 307–332). It was clear though that there were challenges in getting new ILP inspired tasking and coordination processes off the ground in UK policing (John and Maguire 2004; Flood 2004a: 37–52; Bullock 2012: 1–20). In the UK and in other 'Five Eyes' countries such as Australia, Canada, and the United States, the implementation of intelligence-led policing models that can inform better tasking and coordination of intelligence across law enforcement agencies have also met with their challenges. These have included senior and non-intelligence law enforcement staff not knowing how to—or not wanting to maximise strategic, operational, or tactical tasking and coordination meetings and processes to direct resources in more proactive ways to reduce crime (Walsh 2011a; Crous 2012: 3–16; Ratcliffe 2008, 2016; James 2014; Burcher and Whelan 2018: 1–22; Darroch and Mazzerole 2013: 3–37). Again, care needs should be exercised in avoiding over-generalising to the point of inaccuracy the many challenges 'Five Eyes' countries have experienced in the implementation of ILP strategies. However, many studies examining the implementation of intelligence-led policing in these countries show that one critical challenge remains building in sustainable ways tasking and coordination processes. Sustainable tasking and coordination mean placing intelligence capabilities at the centre of law enforcement decision-making rather than exclusively relying on input solely by investigators. The inability in many cases to develop viable intelligence-led tasking and coordination processes is linked to law enforcement leadership cultures. These are in turn linked to how intelligence has been viewed as a supportive function compared to law enforcement's main functions of investigations.

Theme 2 Risk and threat assessment

The ability of IC leaders to oversee the development of better risk and threat methodologies also has an impact on effective tasking and coordination across 'Five Eyes' ICs. While it can be difficult to assess risk and threats in an increasingly complex threat environment (particularly emerging threats), ICs still need to allocate resources to do so. Risk and threat assessment clearly remain critical tools for political decision-makers in apportioning resources in managing threat and risks. In addition to apportioning resources for policy interventions, decision-makers will use risk and threat assessment methodologies for tasking ICs and their collection, analytical, and operational assets. Likewise, IC leaders and other managers in their agencies will also rely, at least partially, on risk and threat assessments to determine internal tasking priorities.

This section will not provide a detailed analysis of the range of threat-and-risk methodologies used across 'Five Eyes' countries. There are too many to examine adequately in this book and many are classified. Instead, the objective here is to discuss in a general and unclassified sense some of the problems that have been identified in the application of threat-and-risk assessment methodologies both in the national security and law enforcement contexts and the impact these have on how intelligence is tasked, coordinated, and integrated. A second objective is to then reflect on what some of the consequences of these challenges are for contemporary IC leaders.

Since 9/11 in particular, a greater understanding of methodologies, which might be useful for assessing both threat and risk, has emerged (Meloy and Hoffman 2014; Monahan 2012; Otto and Douglas 2010; Strang 2005; Kebbell and Porter 2011). Both threat and risk are interrelated with threat focused on the actor(s) intentions and capabilities. In other words, how likely and capable are they to conduct a criminal or terrorist act? Risk assessment is focused on the consequences, harm, or impact of the threat being carried out against a range of factors, including political, economic, physical, psychological, and environmental interests of a nation, community, or individual. However, across and within each 'Five Eyes' country, several threat-and-risk methodologies have developed resulting in a lack of consistent approaches to 'measuring' threat and risks of both simple high volume crimes and more complex ones such as terrorism and organised crime. In both national security and law enforcement agencies, some threat-and-risk methodologies have demonstrated more durability, reliability, and validity than others. For example, Project Sleipnir, developed by Stephen Strang and colleagues at Canada's RCMP to assess threats posed by different organised crime groups (Strang 2005), has been one methodology that has gained traction over the years in several 'Five Eyes' countries though others remain either flawed or works in progress. For example, the FBI's Threat Review and Prioritisation Process (TRP) seems to focus on disrupting reactively 'here and now' threats rather than providing a methodology for the Bureau to collect intelligence systematically against the US's National Intelligence Priorities Framework (NIPF). A more systematic intelligence collection driven approach would help the FBI ensure its strategic and operational work is aligned to national priorities in a way that can identify threats that are priorities before they coalesce (Tromblay 2016: 769). Using risk and threat methodologies to drive intelligence priority setting also become difficult when threats and risk involve an understanding of the significance of particular variables such as technology—and how it may facilitate or inhibit the realisation of emerging threats and risks. For example, in complex and emerging threat areas such as cyber and biotechnology the ability of ICs to develop robust threat-and-risk methodologies can be hampered by technological determinism and a failure to sufficiently reach out to outside experts in the research community and private sector—who may have a better understanding of particular technologically enabled threats and risks (Walsh 2018).

Of course in some cases, reaching outside the IC to external experts may not result in better understandings of threat and risk. For instance, in the areas of violence and radicalisation, researcher contributions have been picked up by parts of the IC and law enforcement agencies, but the validity and reliability of their methodologies vary considerably. Some methodologies have solely relied on clinical assessments or actuarial approaches, which have resulted in false positives and an inability to assess whether an individual is at high risk of becoming an offender or terrorist (Dean 2014: 1–2). More recently though, other structured clinical judgement approaches (SPJ), which are a combination of empirical knowledge and clinical professional judgement, have been used with some success to assess high-risk violence in adult, forensic populations (Ibid: 3). For example, the Violent Extremism Risk Assessment (VERA) has been developed to assess the risk of violent political extremism. However,

> it is not clear if VERA can discriminate between all of the individuals identified through its set of defined risk factors with a risk score indicative of future terrorism from those more likely to go to actively engage in terrorist actions.
>
> (Ibid: 6)

Threat-and-risk terminology can also be poorly understood within the IC, which can contribute to a lack of rigour around assessing risk and threat. Other researchers have pointed to threat assessment methodologies, where a diverse number of threat actor categories have been blurred—potentially over or under measuring the significance of actual or potential threats. For example, leading up to the Vancouver Olympics in 2010, Canada's terrorism fusion center ITAC (mentioned earlier) created a classifier multi-issue extremism matrix (MIE), which in addition to jihadi terrorism included other social dissenting movements (Monaghan and Walby 2012: 147).

Since 9/11, threat-and-risk assessments have also fallen down due to the lack of information flows within agencies, across the community, and even outside the IC. As Cormac suggests, analysis of threats has often been incremental rather than a broader picture being developed and disseminated to decision-makers (Cormac 2013: 488). Another potential issue with some threat-and-risk methodologies that can be promoted, however unintentionally, is via a kind of racial profile or random selection data collection process rather than an approach which is the result of evidence-based choices (Kebbell and Porter 2011). It's clear that leaders need to sponsor the development of better risk and threat assessments, particularly in areas of emerging threats and risks such as cyber and biosecurity. Finally, assessment methodologies also need a greater focus on measuring the harms associated with threat actors and risks across the entire national security and crime continuum (Sherman *et al.* 2016: 171–183; Ratcliffe 2015: 164–182).

Theme 3 Role of science and technology

As discussed in Chapter 2, science and technology have always under-written the development of 'Five Eyes' intelligence capabilities and this has only become more so from the Cold War onwards (Warner 2014: 165). In this book, across all chapters, we will talk a lot about science and technology and how IC leaders work with it to improve outcomes for decision-makers. But for the purposes of this chapter, and for this section, I will focus on how the use of science and technology by ICs impacts specifically on intelligence tasking and also its influence on how core intelligence processes are coordinated.

The best way to illustrate the role of science and technology on intelligence tasking and coordination is by exploring case studies. Given the pervasiveness of technologically enabled threats such as cyber and the ongoing and rapid uptake of new science and technology to improve intelligence capabilities there is potentially an infinite number of case studies that could be explored. For example, the explosion in telecommunications, and digital communications in particular, is just one area where decision-makers can task ICs to extract threat information in order to better understand threats and risks. Digital communications provides a suite of technologies for interception of threat actor's communications (Walsh 2011a; Walsh and Miller 2016: 345–368; Sims and Gerber 2005: xi). Data mining and knowledge discovery is another cluster in the science and technology area where decision-makers can task ICs to extract threat/risk information from an ever increasing volume of data. As discussed in more detail in Chapter 6 (ICT), for at least the last three decades ICs have been investing heavily in more advanced knowledge discovery techniques, knowledge, and infrastructure to better classify threat patterns and hopefully in some threat/risk types attempt to 'predict' future events (Walsh 2011a: 246–253; Skillicorn 2009).

All these areas have consequences for intelligence tasking and coordination and their management is a leadership responsibility for ICs mainly. Governments may fund new science and technology capability for ICs or be interested in how the same technology facilitates the reduction of risk and targeting of threat actors. However, it is the IC leadership that are ultimately responsible for understanding technologically enabled threats and the incorporation of science and technologies into current capabilities to deal with them. In this short section we focus on forensic science and technologies as a case study. First, from a threat actor perspective, it remains less clear how aspects of forensic science are being exploited to commit simple and complex crimes. A better understanding of how offenders may exploit forensics used by the IC and the broader law enforcement community to avoid detection or facilitate illicit activity will improve the processes under which intelligence tasking of collection and analytical assets take place across a range of national security and law enforcement threats and risks.

Secondly, how forensics sciences and technology are incorporated into the IC and law enforcement communities' existing capabilities can both facilitate or inhibit core intelligence processes. If used well with other intelligence processes, forensics can strengthen IC outcomes. However, if poorly used, coordinated, or integrated into mainstream IC activities, then this can have negative consequences on how tasking and coordination occur within and across ICs on a range of threat-and-risk issues, where the inclusion of forensic knowledge is crucial for better decision-maker support.

For the purposes of this chapter, when discussing forensic science and technology I am referring to a diverse array of techniques and knowledge such as matching fingerprints, DNA profiling, chemical, biological analysis, ballistics, digital images, footprints, and other environmental factors which generate data that can reveal patterns of criminal activity and can augment other intelligence sources in the investigation of crimes. In addition to the development in forensic techniques and knowledge, over the last two decades there has also been a flourishing of the field of forensic intelligence. Forensic intelligence as defined by Oliver Ribaux

> is the accurate, timely and useful product of logically processing forensic case data. Of importance is the implication of an additional level of consideration, where collectively (across numerous investigations or various disciplines) the outcomes of forensic analysis become the source of intelligence.
>
> (Ribaux cited in Milne 2012: 1–2)

Forensic intelligence to varying degrees across each 'Five Eyes' country has moved both the practice of intelligence and investigations beyond merely analysing a substance forensically for the evidence it alone contains. Rather, the objective now is to go beyond the single specimen or forensic data to assess how it can be examined holistically against a range of other forensic data and then to use the evidence gained with other sources of intelligence (HUMINT, SIGINT, open source) to build a stronger case for prosecution or disruption. Forensic intelligence is also concerned with how various forensic data sources can be used to 'reveal patterns of criminal activity and the production of intelligence products for action' (Milne 2012: 2–3). It is beyond the scope of this section to provide an analytical breakdown of the reliability and validity of various forensic techniques and knowledge that may be applied across the full spectrum of crime—from simple high volume crimes such as burglaries to more complex variants such as terrorism and cyber hacking. What can be said in a general sense is that there are two issues with the application of forensic science, knowledge and intelligence, that impact on how it is used across ICs and law enforcement agencies. Both of these broad issues impact on how intelligence is tasked (if forensic intelligence is used or not) and how its capability is coordinated across the IC.

First there are a general set of issues and debates about forensic methods, their characteristics, and how reliable and valid they are. Related to this is how to optimise the use of forensics in an intelligence and investigative context, and what barriers prevent the optimal exploitation of forensic data, particularly as another intelligence source. In terms of the first issue, the 'CSI (crime scene investigation) factor' now for several decades has become glamorised by several television shows—sometimes over-selling the capabilities of various forensic techniques. Even with now well-established forensic techniques such as DNA profiling, false positives can occur in crime scenes or in cases where DNA may have been planted at a scene to implicate an innocent person rather than the offender. Similarly, the field of digital forensics, which has been in existence for 30 years, while producing great benefits in the investigations of complex digital crime, has increasingly caused concern amongst political leaders, ICs, and law enforcement agencies as the growing use of encrypted technologies have facilitated terrorist attacks and other criminal offences. For example, in 2015 MI5 Head Andrew Parker said individuals were engaging now in computer acts which were beyond the control of authorities (Horsman 2017: 449). Other senior intelligence officials such as former director CIA Michael Morrell have raised concerns that one of the implications of media sensationalism in response to Edward Snowden has been the development of a security and privacy-conscious public and this allows terrorists to communicate without detection (Ibid). Additionally, in the microbial forensics field, which has increasingly developed after 9/11 to attribute the origin of various dangerous pathogens in actual or potential bioterrorism events, there is still a great deal of refinement required in various forensic techniques (Walsh 2018: 113–114).

The second issue outlined above is how forensics sciences and technology are incorporated into the IC and law enforcement communities along with other capabilities and how this can either facilitate or inhibit core intelligence processes such as effective collection and analysis. There are many issues that could be discussed here, but for the sake of brevity the main issue is one of organisational integration of forensic capabilities into the broader collection and analytical structures and functions of ICs and law enforcement agencies. There are examples in the literature that show how some agencies have done a good job of integrating forensic intelligence along with other criminal or national security intelligence. Rossy and colleagues refer to efforts by six states in the western part of Switzerland in sharing a common data base for the analysis of forensic data (e.g. DNA, shoe marks, images) and criminal intelligence in high volume crimes (Rossy *et al.* 2013: 137–146). Similarly, in the national security context the FBI's Terrorist Explosive Device Analysis Center (TEDAC)—an international inter-agency collaboration coordinating effort by law enforcement, intelligence, and the military to gather and share intelligence about explosives and their role in regional insurgencies and domestic intelligence—has made progress in aligning forensic intelligence with criminal intelligence sources (Walsh 2018: 253).

But there remains for many 'Five Eyes' IC agencies limitations in how forensic intelligence is integrated into the broader intelligence collection and analytical enterprise. While there may be good reasons to integrate forensic intelligence into broader intelligence databases in allowing a greater and more explicit collaborative approach between forensic specialists, intelligence analysts, and investigators, there remain in many agencies structural impediments to allow this to occur. Both forensic specialists and intelligence analysts can be siloed in their practice. A forensic specialist in fingerprints is more likely to see themselves as a fingerprint analyst rather than part of a broader identity specialist or a forensic intelligence analyst (Walsh 2018: 249). A more siloed linear approach by forensic scientists does not make collaboration with the broader intelligence enterprise easy particularly if this is also imbued with other professional attributes of forensic specialists, who traditionally see themselves as conservative and evidence orientated (Ibid).

However, the complexity of the most serious threats and risk in the post-9/11 environment as noted earlier can no longer just rely on a pathway to prosecution. All 'Five Eyes' ICs now need to look for opportunities for disruption and harm reduction and forensic specialists are increasingly relied upon at early stages of intelligence operations and investigations. This will require still a cultural shift for both forensic specialists and intelligence analysts, who have tended to connect on a more ad hoc basis—mainly at the end of an intelligence operation or investigation at the prosecution stage. The challenge for leaders is how to build organisational structures within and across the IC that integrates forensic intelligence more seamlessly into other national security and criminal intelligence collection and analysis. This integration is not just an ICT architecture problem, but also a training, legislative, and cultural issue.

Finally, how can intelligence leaders better anticipate strategically what forensic and other science and technology capabilities will be required to manage both the known and unknown threats and risks (Walsh 2018: 253)? Arguably, it may well be this last point that will impact on how well forensics and other science and technology capabilities can improve the effectiveness of tasking and coordination of intelligence over the next several decades. If leaders are able to better anticipate what kinds of threats and risks may emerge and what science and technology capabilities will be needed to collect and analyse these threats—political leaders and ICs themselves will have a better understanding of how to task, coordinate, and integrate the intelligence enterprise to work these threats/risks.

Theme 4 Strategic intelligence, tasking and coordination

Strategic intelligence has periodically played an important role in how 'Five Eyes' ICs task and coordinate intelligence priorities and processes from the end of World War II onwards. Several authors illustrate the origins of strategic/estimative and early warning intelligence in the US, which included the establishment of the Office of National Estimates (O/NE) by DCI Walter Bedell Smith in October 1950 at the CIA. Later, Sherman Kent, a former Yale University history professor, took over as chief of the O/NE from 1952 to 1967 (Gentry and Gordon 2019: 73–74; Walsh 2017: 548–562; Fingar 2011; Marrin 2017: 725–742; Johnson 2015).

In his 1949 book *Strategic Intelligence for American World Policy*, Kent clearly states the importance of strategic intelligence for decision-makers.

He says amongst other things; 'to begin with knowledge which strategic intelligence must produce deserves a more forbidding adjective than "useful." You should call it the knowledge *vital for national survival,* and as such it takes on sombreness and stature.' (Kent 1949: vii)

Strategic intelligence also became widely used in Australia, the UK, Canada, and New Zealand, with each IC establishing agencies and/or committees to bring together all source-strategic assessments on emerging threats and risks (Walsh 2011a; Walsh 2017). However, the role of strategic intelligence across the 'Five Eyes' ICs has been a story of mixed success—with arguably even less success across their law enforcement agencies. There are a range of policy maker, academic, and practitioner opinions on why strategic intelligence has not played an optimal role in decision-maker support (Gentry and Gordon 2019). In the US context and to some extent in the UK and Australia, strategic assessments have been either fairly or unfairly associated with historical intelligence failures. Earlier in the chapter, mention was made of the 9/11 and WMD Iraq intelligence failures and it's clear in both that policy makers believed some of the analytical deficiencies attributable to either absent or poor strategic analysis.

According to the 9/11 Commission report, the September 11 attacks exposed the inability of analysts and agents to perform strategic analysis. Aligned with this was the conclusion that 'no agency in the IC could imagine a terrorist operation conducted inside the United States, using commercial airplanes as weapons, although Al-Qaeda had planned such operations in the mid-1990s in Europe and Asia' (Goodman 2003: 62). A 'failure of imagination' became one of the catch phrases from the 9/11 Commission report. Implicit in such a phrase is that perhaps strategic intelligence analysis is about analysts improving their imagination, which does seem a little absurd given the trajectory of many emerging threats are beyond the confines of either analytical probability or plausibility. This does not negate that improvements in analysis were not possible or desirable after 9/11, but linking a failure of imagination to strategic intelligence practice does not lay out a valuable direction or metric for improvement.

Others have suggested additional factors behind specific intelligence failure events like 9/11 and WMD in Iraq. In the case of 9/11, others have accused Commission investigators of misrepresenting the IC's strategic intelligence capability, which had been strong at the time (Pillar 2006: 1022–1044), and that policy failures were the main breakdown pre-9/11 rather than strategic intelligence (Marrin 2011: 182–202). In between historical cases of intelligence failures, where perhaps a more forensic examination of the strengths and limitations of strategic intelligence can be made, senior intelligence leaders, scholars, and practitioners have raised several other issues, which may explain the varying utilisation of strategic intelligence assessments, particularly in the national security space across 'Five Eyes' countries. Marrin raises a number of issues which are also documented by others. These range from the irrelevance many decision-makers see in using strategic assessments to make 'the big policy decisions' such as war and peace. He argues that intelligence analysis at that most senior policy level is seen as a duplicate step in the policy process—it 'supplements but does not supplant policy assessment' (Marrin 2017: 727). Having strategic intelligence as a 'nice to have add on' to the main policy assessment process is itself due to a number of factors—some of which have already been raised earlier and in Chapter 2. Political leaders have confidence in their world view. They have their own biases, agendas, and political calculations, which are independent and often more compelling (for them) than any intelligence assessment they may receive. Decision-makers at the executive cabinet level have an entire policy and bureaucratic support structure around them in addition to the service provided by the IC. This support structure often reads the raw intelligence itself and will bring in other information sources that the IC may or may not possess, which can challenge strategic intelligence assessments. All of these factors impact on how and when strategic intelligence is tasked and coordinated across the IC.

Marrin suggests that perhaps the value of strategic intelligence may come at the lower bureaucratic working level, where policy is fashioned 'by giving government an aggregate picture enabling the government to learn about threats and problems over time' (Ibid: 732).

There are several other issues too that have contributed to the mixed success of improving the tasking and uptake of strategic intelligence across 'Five Eyes' ICs over several decades. Probability, training, and organisational support have also been identified as issues. Given strategic intelligence relies on making key analytical judgements about evolving threat-and-risk factors, assessments are typically based on probabilities given the body of evidence tends to be less robust or clear compared to operational and tactical assessments. In the intelligence studies literature there is an ongoing debate about how to more accurately 'measure' probability attached to levels of certainty for both analysts and decision-makers. Across ICs up to recently, there has been a diverse set of probability criteria used by various agencies to convey probability levels, which can confuse decision-makers (Rosenberg 2008: 139–152; Barnes 2016: 327–344; Dhami 2018: 257–272). These debates are ongoing and unresolved, but it is clear that more refinement in quantitative and qualitative descriptors of probability are required. Another issue is the value of structured analytical techniques that have been the bedrock of a lot of strategic analysis, and horizon scanning work completed in ICs over several decades. More recently, a few studies in the United States and United Kingdom have emerged questioning the value of these techniques in strategic analysis and other non-strategic products (Coulthart 2016: 933–948; Whitesmith 2020: 1–20). A further set of issues relate to the extent and quality of strategic analytical training offered across each 'Five Eyes' country. From my own experience of teaching strategic intelligence in Australia and other 'Five Eyes' countries, some intelligence agencies offer better training than others and this impacts on the quality of key judgements. In particular, sound training and experience are critical to whether analysts are able to go beyond the descriptive summary of information to answer clearly 'the so what question' and whether the judgements can provide a firm bridge between policy and operational action (Walsh 2011a; Walsh 2017: 548–562; Walsh and Ratcliffe 2005). Establishing in the organisational structure of IC agencies a strategic intelligence capability also takes consistent focus by the leadership and even in agencies where there has been a long tradition of a strategic analytical capability such as the CIA and INR (US), JIO (UK), ONI (Australia), IAS (Canada), and NAB (New Zealand), these capabilities need to be constantly strengthened and demonstrate their value against the greater demands and pull of current or 'here and now' intelligence (Gentry and Gordon 2019; Gustafson 2010: 589–610).

Generally speaking, strategic intelligence has played a less central role in the allocation of strategic or operational priorities in law enforcement (Walsh 2011a). In many respects the reasons for this are similar to those discussed above for national security intelligence agencies. In particular, the impediments are linked to organisational cultural issues in many law enforcement agencies, which as seen earlier are historically linked to attitudes about the role of intelligence. As discussed under Theme 1, efforts to reset the traditionally peripheral and supportive role of intelligence in law enforcement to one where it is more central and proactive has been constrained by a range of factors including the value placed by law enforcement leaders on their intelligence functions compared to other law enforcement disciplines such as investigations. What strategic intelligence capability that has developed in 'Five Eyes' countries has failed to be consistently supported by law enforcement leadership. This is because it hasn't been invested in consistently in terms of analytical training—or if training has been provided law enforcement leaders have not understood how to engage with the product. Even in cases where law enforcement leaders have engaged with strategic analysis, the products have not been easily transferable into setting operational priorities. In cultures, where the value of intelligence itself in some agencies is still being questioned it is difficult for strategic intelligence to play a fully effective role in setting strategic tasking and coordination within law enforcement agencies let alone operational priorities—the latter of which tend to drive the business of law enforcement. The 'here and now' of most law enforcement work continues to create a tactical drag where there may be periodically good intentions to invest in strategic intelligence capabilities yet analytical staff find themselves re-tasked on tactical and operational investigations. This creates a failure point for many law enforcement agencies if they are not able to build up a sustainable strategic intelligence capability that can help law enforcement and political leaders identify early and emerging threats and risks.

The above issues related to the implementation and nurturing of a strategic analytical capability beg the question what role can strategic intelligence and horizon scanning play in improving decision-maker tasking for strategic, operational, and even tactical action. Can strategic intelligence improve coordination of intelligence at these lower levels? Can political decision-makers and IC leaders see more value in the future by investing in and improving strategic intelligence and horizon scanning?

Conclusion

Since all 'Five Eyes' ICs operate in an external environment filled increasingly with volatility, uncertainty, complexity, and ambiguity (VUCA), it is critical that they can align key organisational processes such as tasking and coordination with other core intelligence processes (collection, analysis) and key enabling activities. As shown in the discussion of all four themes (*policy reform, science and technology, risk and threat,* and *strategic intelligence*), the tasking and coordination process may have improved in some respects after 9/11. But the analysis of issues here show that broader IC initiatives to improve tasking and coordination in many cases are works in progress. Further integration, collaboration, and sharing is still required. Improving tasking and coordination structures and processes within ICs will likely never reach a state of perfection. The volatile and uncertain security environment will conspire against it. Perfection is not a realistic objective, but IC leaders can and will need to do more to improve tasking and coordination structures, processes, and initiatives in the future. In Chapter 8 (The Future IC Leader and Governance Challenges), we will come back to the key intelligence governance challenges raised as they relate to tasking and coordination and how IC leaders may begin to address them. The following chapter (Chapter 4 Collection) explores some of the key challenges IC leaders face in optimising the vital role intelligence collection plays in improving intelligence outcomes for decision-makers.

Notes

1 The IC ITE, or the Intelligence Community, Information Technology Enterprise (IC ITE), was created by the ONDI in 2012. It is a digital platform for the IC to store, process, analyse, and share intelligence of all forms.
2 The ONI was established in 2018 and was the key recommendation of the 2017 Independent Intelligence Review.
3 CSE is Canada's national cryptologic agency. It provides the Government of Canada with information technology security (IT Security) and foreign signals intelligence (SIGINT) services. CSE also provides technical and operational assistance to federal law enforcement and security agencies. CSIS or the Canadian Security Intelligence Service is Canada's security and intelligence service. Its role is to investigate activities suspected of constituting threats to the security of Canada and to report these to the Government of Canada. CSIS collects and assesses threat-related information, which is typically disseminated to government partners through intelligence reports and other intelligence products. Key threats include terrorism, the proliferation of weapons of mass destruction, espionage, foreign interference, and cyber-tampering affecting critical infrastructure. The RCMP, or the Royal Canadian Mounted Police, is Canada's federal policing agency.
4 GCSB, NZSIS, and NAB are New Zealand's SIGINT, security intelligence and assessments agencies, respectively.

References

9/11 Commission. (2004). *The 9/11 commission report: Final report of the National Commission on terrorist attacks upon the United States.* Washington, DC: 9/11 Commission.
Adams, B., Thomson, M.H., Derbentseva, N., & Mandel, D.R. (2012). *Capability challenges in the human domain for intelligence analysis: Report on community wide discussions with Canadian intelligence professionals.* Guelph, ON: Humansytems Incorporated.

Allen, M. (2013). *Blinking red: Crisis and compromise in American intelligence after 9/11.* Washington, DC: Potomac Books.

Barnes, A. (2016). Making intelligence analysis more intelligent: Using numeric probabilities. *Intelligence and National Security, 31*(3), 327–344. doi: 10.1080/02684527.2014.994955

Best, R.A. (2011). *Intelligence Information: Need-to-Know vs. Need-to-Share.* Darby, PA: DIANE Publishing.

Best, R.A. (2014). Leadership of the U.S. Intelligence Community: From DCI to DNI. *International Journal of Intelligence and Counterintelligence, 27*(2), 253–333. doi: 10.1080/08850607.2014.872533

Bullock, K. (2012). Community, intelligence-led policing and crime control. *Policing and Society, 23*(2), 1–20. doi: 10.1080/10439463.2012.671822

Burcher, M., & Whelan, C. (2018). Intelligence-led policing in practice: Reflections from intelligence analysts. *Police Quarterly, 22,* 139–160. doi: 10.1177/1098611118796890

Butler, R. (2004). *Review on weapons of mass destruction. Report of a Committee of Privy Counsellors.* London: The Stationary Office.

Carter, D.L., & Carter, J.G. (2009). The intelligence fusion process for state, local, and tribal law enforcement. *Criminal Justice and Behaviour, 36*(12), 1323–1339. doi: 10.1177/0093854809345674

Catano, V., & Gauger, J. (2017). Information fusion: Intelligence centers and intelligence analysis. In I. Goldenberg, J. Soeters & W.H. Dean (Eds.), *Information sharing in military operations* (pp. 17–34). Cham: Springer International Publishing.

Clapper, J. (2018). *Facts and fears. Hard truths from a life in intelligence.* New York: Viking Press.

Cormac, R. (2013). Much ado about nothing: Terrorism, intelligence, and the mechanics of threat exaggeration. *Terrorism and Political Violence, 25*(3), 476–493. doi: 10.1080/09546553.2012.667018

Cotter, R.S. (2017). Police intelligence: Connecting-the-dots in a network society. *Policing and Society, 27*(2), 173–187. doi: 10.1080/10439463.2015.1040794

Coulthart, S. (2016). Why do analysts use structured analytic techniques? An in-depth study of an American intelligence agency. *Intelligence and National Security, 31*(7), 933–948. doi: 10.1080/02684527.2016.1140327

Crous, C. (2011). Policing with intelligence: Leading a paradigm change. *Journal of the Australian Institute of Professional Intelligence Officers, 19*(1), 13.

Cullen, M., & Reddy, P. (2016). *Intelligence and security in a free society. Report of the first independent review of intelligence and security in New Zealand.* Wellington: New Zealand Government .

Darroch, S., & Mazerolle, L. (2013). Intelligence-led policing: A comparative analysis of organizational factors influencing innovation uptake. *Police Quarterly, 16*(1), 3–37. doi: 10.1177/1098611112467411

De Castro Garcia, A., Matei, F.C., & Bruneau, T.C. (2017). Combatting terrorism through fusion centers: Useful lessons from other experiences? *International Journal of Intelligence and Counterintelligence, 30*(4), 723–742. doi: 10.1080/08850607.2017.1297119

Dean, G. (2014). *Neurocognitive risk assessment for the early detection of violent extremists.* Cham: Springer.

Dhami, M.K. (2018). Towards an evidence-based approach to communicating uncertainty in intelligence analysis. *Intelligence and National Security, 33*(2), 257–272. doi: 10.1080/02684527.2017.1394252

Dulles, A. W., Jackson, W. H., & Correa, M. (1949). *The Central Intelligence Agency and the National Organization for Intelligence*. Report to the National Security Council, Washington DC.

Fingar, T. (2011). *Reducing uncertainty*. Stanford, CA: Stanford University Press.

Flood, B. (2004a). Strategic aspect of the UK national intelligence model. In Ratcliffe, J.H. (Ed.), *Strategic thinking in criminal intelligence* (pp. 37–52). Sydney, NSW: Federation Press.

Flood, P. (2004b). *Report of the inquiry into Australian Intelligence Agencies*. Canberra, ACT: Australian Government Printing Office.

Gentry, J. (2015). Has the ODNI improved US intelligence analysis? *International Journal of Intelligence and Counterintelligence, 28*(4), 637–661.

Gentry, J.A., & Gordon, J.S. (2019). *Strategic warning intelligence: History, challenges, and prospects*. Washington, DC: Georgetown University Press.

Goodman, M. (2003). The failure of strategic intelligence. *Intelligence and National Security, 9/11*(4), 59–71. doi: 10.1080/02684520310001688871

Gustafson, K. (2010). Strategic horizons: Futures forecasting and the British Intelligence Community. *Intelligence and National Security, 25*(5), 589–610. doi: 10.1080/02684527.2010.537118

Harknett, R.J., & Stever, J.A. (2011). The struggle to reform intelligence after 9/11. *Public Administration Review, 71*(5), 700–706. doi: 10.1111/j.1540-6210.2011.02409.x

Hastedt, G. (2013). The politics of intelligence and the politicization of intelligence: The American experience. *Intelligence and National Security, 28*(1), 5–31. doi: 10.1080/02684527.2012.749062

Hayden, M. (2018). *The assault on intelligence. American national security in an age of lies*. New York: Penguin Press.

Herman, M. (2003). Counter-terrorism, information technology and intelligence change. *Intelligence and National Security, 18*(4), 40–58. doi: 10.1080/02684520310001693181

Horsman, G. (2017). Can we continue to effectively police digital crime? *Science and Justice, 57*(6), 448–454. doi: 10.1016/j.scijus.2017.06.001

HPSCI. (2002). *Report of the joint inquiry of the House Permanent Select Committee on Intelligence and the Senate Select Committee into Intelligence Community Activities before and after the terrorist attacks of September 11*. Washington, DC: US Congress.

James, A. (2014). Forward to the past: Reinventing intelligence-led policing in *Britain. Police Practice and Research, 15*(1), 75–88. doi: 10.1080/15614263.2012.754126

Jervis, R. (2009). Reports, politics and intelligence failures. In C. Andrew, R. Aldrich & W. Wark (Eds.), *Secret intelligence* (pp. 93–22). New York: Routledge.

John, T., & Maguire, M. (2004). *The national intelligence model: Early implementation experience in three police force areas*. Cardiff: Cardiff University.

Johnson, L. (2015a). A conversation with James R Clapper Jr. the Director of National Intelligence in the United States. *Intelligence and National Security, 30*(1), 1–25.

Johnson, L. (Ed.). (2015b). *Essentials of strategic intelligence*. Santa Barbara, CA: Praeger.

Johnson, L. (2017). *National security intelligence*. Cambridge, MA: Polity Press.

Jones, C. (2007). Intelligence reform: The logic of information sharing. *Intelligence and National Security, 22*(3), 384–401. doi: 10.1080/02684520701415214

Jones, D.M. (2018). Intelligence and the management of national security: The post 9/11 evolution of an Australian National Security Community. *Intelligence and National Security, 33*(1), 1–20. doi: 10.1080/02684527.2016.1259796

Kebbell, M., & Porter, L. (2011). An intelligence assessment framework for identifying individuals at risk of committing acts of violent extremism against the West. *Security Journal*, *25*(3), 212.

Kent, S. (1949). *Strategic intelligence for American world policy*. Princeton, NJ: Princeton University Press.

Lambert, D.E.(2019). Addressing challenges to homeland security information sharing in American policing: Using Kotter's leading change model. *Criminal Justice Policy Review*, *30*(8), 1250–1278. doi: 10.1177/0887403418786555

Lawrence et al 2016" Sherman, L., Neyroud, P. W., & Neyroud, E. (2016). The Cambridge crime harm index: measuring total harm from crime based on sentencing guidelines. *Policing: A Journal of Policy and Practice*, *10*(3), 171–183. doi: 10.1093/police/paw003

L'Estrange, M., & Merchant, S. (2017). *Independent intelligence review*. Canberra, ACT: Commonwealth of Australia.

Lewandowski, C., Carter, J.G., & Campbell, W.L. (2018). The utility of fusion Centres to enhance intelligence-led policing: An exploration of end-users. *Policing: A Journal of Policy and Practice*, *12*(2), 177–193. doi: 10.1093/police/pax005

Lowenthal, M. (2012). *Intelligence from secrets to policy*. Thousand Oaks, CA: Sage Publications.

Lucas, S. (2011). Recognising politicization: The CIA and the path to the 2003 war in Iraq. *Intelligence and National Security*, *26*(2–3), 203–227. doi: 10.1080/02684527.2011.559141

Maras, M.-H. (2017). Overcoming the intelligence-sharing paradox: Improving information sharing through change in organizational culture. *Comparative Strategy*, *36*(3), 187–197. doi: 10.1080/01495933.2017.1338477

Marrin, S. (2011). The 9/11 terrorist attacks: A failure of policy not strategic intelligence analysis. *Intelligence and National Security*, *26*(2–3), 182–202. doi: 10.1080/02684527.2011.559140

Marrin, S. (2013). Rethinking analytic politicization. *Intelligence and National Security*, *28*(1), 32–54. doi: 10.1080/02684527.2012.749064

Marrin, S. (2017). Why strategic intelligence analysis has limited influence on American foreign policy. *Intelligence and National Security*, *32*(6), 725–742. doi: 10.1080/02684527.2016.1275139

McDonald, G. (2007). Control orders and preventative detention-why alarm is misguided. In A. Lynch, E. MacDonald, & G. Williams (Eds.), *Law and liberty in the war on terror* (pp. 106–115). Annandale: The Federation Press.

Masse, T., & Rollins, J. (2008). *Information and intelligence (including terrorism) fusion centers*. New York: Nova Science Publishers.

Milne, R. (2012). *Forensic intelligence*. Boca Raton, FL: CRC Press.

Misra, A. (2018). Australia's counter-terrorism policies since September 11, 2001: Harmonising national security, independent oversight and individual liberties. *Strategic Analysis*, *42*(2), 103–118. doi: 10.1080/09700161.2018.1439325

Monaghan, J., & Walby, K. (2012). Making up 'terror identities': Security intelligence, Canada's Integrated Threat Assessment Centre and social movement suppression. *Policing and Society*, *22*(2), 133. doi: 10.1080/10439463.2011.605131

Monahan, J. (2012). *Violence risk assessment. Handbook of Psychology*, second edition, 11. Hoboken, NJ: John Wiley and Sons, Inc

Newkirk, A. (2010). The rise of the fusion-intelligence complex: A critique of political surveillance after 9/11. *Surveillance and Society*, *8*(1), 43–60.

ODNI. (2009). *ODNI intelligence community legal reference book*. Washington, DC: ODNI.

Otto, R., & Douglas, K. (Eds.). (2010). *Handbook of violence risk analysis*. New York: Routledge.

Phythian, M. (2005). Still a matter of trust: Post–9/11 British intelligence and political culture. *International Journal of Intelligence and CounterIntelligence, 18*(4), 653–681. doi: 10.1080/08850600500177127

Pillar, P.R. (2006). Good literature and bad history: The 9/11 commission's tale of strategic intelligence. *Intelligence and National Security, 21*(6), 1022–1044. doi: 10.1080/02684520601046366

Posner, R.A. (2005). *Preventing surprise attacks: Intelligence reform in the wake of 9/11*. Lanham, MD: Rowman & Littlefield.

Ratcliffe, J.H. (2015). Towards an index for harm-focused policing. *Policing: A Journal of Policy and Practice, 9*(2), 164–182. doi: 10.1093/police/pau032

Ratcliffe, J. H. (2016). *Intelligence-led policing*: Abingdon, UK: Routledge.

Ratcliffe J.H., & Ray, G. (2008). State police investigative structure and the adoption of intelligence-led policing. *Policing: An International Journal, 31*(1), 109–128. doi: 10.1108/13639510810852602

Rosenberg, J. (2008). The interpretation of probability in intelligence estimation and strategic assessment. *Intelligence and National Security, 23*(2), 139–152. doi: 10.1080/02684520801977238

Rossy, Q., Ioset, S., Dessimoz, D., & Ribaux, O. (2013). Integrating forensic information in a crime intelligence database. *Forensic Science International, 230*(1–3), 137–146. doi: 10.1016/j.forsciint.2012.10.010

Rovner, J. (2013). Is politicization ever a good thing? *Intelligence and National Security, 28*(1), 55–67. doi: 10.1080/02684527.2012.749065

Schlesinger, J. (1971). *The Schlesinger Report. A Review of the Intelligence Community*. Washington, DC: White House Office of Management and Budget.

Sheptycki, J. (2004). Organizational pathologies in police intelligence systems: Some contributions to the lexicon of intelligence-led policing. *European Journal of Criminology, 1*(3), 307–332. doi: 10.1177/1477370804044005

Shore, J.J.M. (2006). Intelligence review and oversight in post-9/11 Canada. *International Journal of Intelligence and Counterintelligence, 19*(3), 456–479. doi: 10.1080/08850600600656350

Sims, J., & Gerber, B. (Eds.). (2005). *Transforming U.S. Intelligence*. Washington, DC: Georgetown University Press.

Skillicorn, D. (2009). *Knowledge discovery for counterterrorism and law enforcement*. Boca Raton, FL: CRC Press.

Strang, S. (2005). *Project SLEIPNIR: An analytic technique for operational priority setting*. Ottawa: Royal Canadian Mounted Police.

Strategic Comments. (2017). Trump and the US intelligence community. *Strategic Comments, 23*(1), i–iii. doi: 10.1080/13567888.2017.1288898

Treverton, G. (2008). Intelligence analysis: Between politicisation and irrelevance. In George, R.Z., & Bruce, J.B. (Eds.), *Analyzing intelligence: Origins, obstacles, and innovations* (pp. 91–106). Washington, DC: Georgetown University Press.

Tromblay, D.E. (2016). The threat review and prioritisation trap: How the FBI's new threat and prioritisation process compounds the bureau's oldest problems. *Intelligence and National Security, 31*(5), 762–770.

Tromblay, D. E. (2017). Information Technology (IT) woes and intelligence agency failures: the Federal Bureau of Investigation's troubled IT evolution as a microcosm of a dysfunctional corporate culture. *Intelligence and National Security, 32*(6), 817–832. doi: 10.1080/02684527.2017.1296947

U.S Senate Committee on Homeland Security and Governmental Affairs. (2012). *U.S. Senate Permanent Sub-Committee on investigations, federal support for the involvement in state and local fusion centers (majority and minority staff report)* Washington, DC: Senate Committee on Homeland Security and Governmental Affairs.

Van Puyvelde, D. (2016). Fusing drug enforcement: A study of the El Paso Intelligence Center. *Intelligence and National Security, 31*(6), 888–902. doi: 10.1080/02684527.2015.1100373

Walsh, P.F. (2011a). *Intelligence and intelligence analysis*. Abingdon, UK: Routledge.

Walsh, P.F. (2011b). Intelligence and national security issues in policing. In P. Birch & V. Herrington (Eds.), *Policing in practice* (pp. 109–127). Sydney, NSW: Palgrave Macmillan.

Walsh, P.F. (2012). Submission and testimony to inquiry into the use of criminal intelligence, by Joint Parliamentary on Law Enforcement, Australian Parliament, Canberra. Retrieved from www.aph.gov.au/parliamentary_business/Committees/S enate_Committees?url=le_ctte/criminal_intelligence/submission.htm

Walsh, P.F. (2015). Building better intelligence frameworks through effective governance. *International Journal of Intelligence and Counterintelligence, 28*(1), 123–142. doi: 10.1080/08850607.2014.924816

Walsh, P.F. (2016). Australian national security intelligence collection since 9/11: Policy and legislative challenges. In Warby, K. (Ed.), *National security, surveillance and terror* (pp. 51–74). Cham, Switzerland: Springer International Publishing.

Walsh, P.F. (2017). Improving strategic intelligence analytical practice through qualitative social research. *Intelligence and National Security, 32*(5), 548–562. doi: 10.1080/02684527.2017.1310948

Walsh, P.F. (2018). *Intelligence, biosecurity and bioterrorism*. London: Palgrave Macmillan.

Walsh, P.F., & Miller, S. (2016). Rethinking 'five eyes' security intelligence collection policies and practice post Snowden. *Intelligence and National Security, 31*(3), 345–368. doi: 10.1080/02684527.2014.998436

Walsh, P.F., & Ratcliffe, J.H. (2005). Strategic criminal intelligence education: A collaborative approach. *IALEIA Journal, 16*(2), 152–166.

Walsh, S.J. (2018). Australasian forensic science summit 2016: The external future context and the case for change. *Australian Journal of Forensic Sciences, 50*(3), 245–258. doi: 10.1080/00450618.2017.1383572

Warner, M. (2014). *The rise and fall of intelligence*. Washington, DC: Georgetown University Press.

Warner, M., & McDonald, J. K. (2005). *US Intelligence Community reform studies since 1947*. Washington, DC: Center for the Study of Intelligence.

White, M. (2012). A judicial perspective–the making of preventative detention orders. In A. Lynch, E. MacDonald & G. Williams (Eds.), *Law and liberty in the war on terror* (pp. 116–127). Annandale: The Federation Press.

Whitesmith, M. (2020). Experimental research in reducing the risk of cognitive bias in intelligence analysis. *International Journal of Intelligence and Counterintelligence, 33*(2), 380–405. doi: 10.1080/08850607.2019.1690329

Williams, G. (2011). A decade of Australian anti-terror laws. *Melbourne University Law Review, 35*, 1137–1151.

Zegart, A. (2007). *Spying blind*. Princeton, NJ: Princeton University Press.

4   Collection

Introduction

Intelligence collection is the second critical node of intelligence production. Effective leadership over collection processes, both within agencies and across intelligence communities (ICs), has always been vital to good intelligence outcomes—at tactical, operational, or strategic levels. However, since 9/11 the challenges for maintaining and improving collection platforms and processes are increasing. These include how leaders navigate technological issues that can both facilitate and inhibit collection efforts against increasingly technologically nimble threat actors. Other challenges include the impact of IC history and culture and how both influence efforts for effective coordination and integration of information and collection platforms. Notably as well, perhaps the Snowden episode has like no previous leaks exacerbated the dilemmas for IC leaders between enhancing proactive collection capabilities and attempting to reconcile this with the public's increasing questioning of what should be legitimate secrets and the impact of collection on privacy.

In order to understand the myriad of collection challenges, I have organised this chapter into three broad thematic areas: *technological and methodological, intelligence collection and governance*, and *intelligence collection ethics and efficacy* challenges. The analysis of both primary and secondary data sources in this study underscores how these three themes remain critical for IC leaders to understand if they wish to continue to deploy effective collection strategies against the evolving security environment. In the conclusion, I summarise briefly the general implications of all three thematic areas. However, as mentioned earlier, a more detailed discussion of how leaders may address collection challenges will be explored in Chapter 8 (The Future IC Leader and Governance Challenges).

A final note before we begin discussing the three themes. This book is pitched primarily at the IC leader, so a certain level of knowledge about collection platforms and methodologies is assumed. However, if you are new to the world of intelligence collection, there are several good sources which explain both the historical development of collection, technologies, platforms and methodologies and how they are used (e.g. Lowenthal 2012; Clark 2014; Gill and Phythian 2018; Higgins 2009: 85–107; Johnson and Wirtz 2015; Shulsky and Schmitt 2002).

Technological and methodological challenges

As discussed in Chapter 2 (Intelligence and Leadership), the history of each modern 'Five Eyes' IC is entwined with the technological developments that marked the decades following World War II (Warner 2012: 137–138). Advances and investment in larger-scale technological collection platforms started in World War II. The wartime 'British codebreaking enterprise, which penetrated Enigma resulted in more than 30,000 decrypts a month at the beginning of 1943 and nearly 90,000 a month by the end of that same year' (Brantly 2018: 564–565). As Brantly points out:

> the scale and complexity of communications globally at the end of the war were significant, though the coming expansion of communications mediums and the diversity of their use and applications were set to grow substantially in the decades following the war.
>
> (Ibid)

Brantly provides a good overview of later technological developments and how they impacted on intelligence capabilities during the Cold War, such as 'the first electric programmable computers Colossus Mark 1 and later Mark 2 demonstrated high levels of efficiency well in excess of their human computational counterparts' (2018: 564–565). The use of computers to process large volumes of data was of critical importance in the early Cold War period for intercepting communications as well as predicting how Soviet nuclear weapons would perform (Ibid). But while the development of larger more capable computers for collection during the Cold War period is fascinating, our focus here is on the technological and methodological challenges of post-9/11 intelligence collection.

In the remaining discussion, therefore, we will focus on several collection methodologies, which grew in prominence towards the end of the Cold War and into the current post-9/11 period. We will briefly discuss data mining and machine learning, social media, the internet of things (IoT), and the dark web, including the challenges that surround each of these collection platforms and associated methodologies. You will recall in Chapter 3 (Tasking and Coordination), under the sub-heading 'Theme 3 Role of science and technology,' that some of these (e.g. data mining) were discussed. However, that discussion focused on how various technology platforms influence the identification of intelligence priorities and shape how decision-makers task the IC. In contrast, the emphasis here is not on how collection priorities are set at the policy level, but rather the discussion below is an exploration of what benefits and problems different technologically enabled collection platforms present to IC leaders.

Before we begin, it's worthwhile keeping in mind that the collection platforms explored in this chapter are not isolated pieces of technology; and their individual significance should be understood as part of a bigger narrative—perhaps best captured as part of the digital revolution which emerged towards the late twentieth century. If the Industrial Revolution provided mechanical power, the digital revolution has provided humans with computer power. Starting in 1995, more powerful and faster computers have provided all sectors of the global economy with technologies that have replaced or supplemented the mundane mental processes humans had to do (Seel 2012; Lamarre 1998). The digital revolution is particularly marked by the invention of the internet and smaller, cheaper, speedier computer and communication devices such as smart phones. The explosion in the uptake of the internet has naturally recast the way IC collection takes place, as we shall see in the following sub-sections.

Big data and machine learning

As noted in Chapter 3 (Tasking and Coordination), big data and machine learning capabilities do play a role in shaping how decision-makers understand intelligence priorities and gaps. As a set of collection capabilities, big data and machine learning has been an operational feature of ICs for over two decades, though its adoption remains comparatively more recent in many law enforcement agencies. Importantly, as mentioned earlier, large data sets in the intelligence collection context are nothing new—going back before the end of World War II. However, during the digital revolution 'big data' has become associated with very large volumes, velocity, and variety of data (i.e. unstructured and structured) that can be stored and whose value and 'meaning' can potentially be more quickly extracted than was ever possible in the early Cold War years. As Lim notes,

> the key vector for the rise of Big Data is the digitization of information. In 2000, only a quarter of the world's stored information was digital. In 2013, this figure rose to over 98 per cent of the approximately 1200 Exabyte (1 Exabyte equalling 1 billion gigabytes) of information stored worldwide in all forms.
>
> (Lim 2016: 622)

It's hard to not think of an economic sector particularly in transport, commerce, medicine, business/finance and communications that has not been shaped in the last two decades by big data and machine learning. The advantages to business are well documented in the ability to correlate data sets to maximise profits in tightly competitive markets where strategic edge is everything. Big data can link goods associated with purchaser sentiment across different demographics and/or geographic locations to detect patterns and opportunities for increased market share over competitors. A more recent extension of big data capability of course has been the explosion of social media. We will come back shortly to a more detailed discussion of social media, but it too has demonstrated enormous capabilities to correlate google queries or Facebook, Twitter, and Amazon likes/dislikes and networks—all providing opportunities for companies to identify patterns of human behaviour to better target products. In many of these cases, 'big data can infer the "probabilistic associations" of future events by relying on a variant of inductive

(Bayesian) reasoning and repeated historical patterns (historical corpora)' (Lim 2016: 623).

There are now several sources surveying how big data and machine learning techniques have been incorporated over the last three decades into IC and law enforcement collection capabilities. There is insufficient space to provide a detailed analysis of the various techniques employed and the contexts in which they are used. Suffice it to say, there are sources which the reader can refer to that describe in detail the range of techniques used such as link analysis, text mining, social network analysis, neural networks, and machine learning (e.g. Skillicorn 2009; Pramanik *et al.* 2017; Van der Hulst 2009: 101–121; Masys 2014; NRC 2013; Olson and Delan 2008). There is also an increasing volume of unclassified sources on how big data and machine learning techniques are deployed in particular threat and risk contexts such as terrorism (Zijuan and Shuai 2017: 320–322; Ding *et al.* 2017; Skillicorn and Reid 2014: 1–16), and in a range of organised crime and crime prevention issues (Purda and Skillicorn 2015: 1193–1223).

In general, big data has allowed ICs and law enforcement agencies to do three things according to Lim (Lim 2016: 627). First, big data collection and then analysis has acted as a kind of 'applied grounded theory'—allowing the data to speak for itself, which in turn facilitates analysis of possible general trends and anomalies. Second, Lim suggests that the application of big data in the IC and law enforcement contexts allows the generation of hypotheses about what might happen. Finally, and related to generating hypotheses: big data analytics 'allow the intelligence analyst to cut through the overwhelming morass of supporting facts in order to adduce those with refutative value.' In Lim's words,

> the benefit of big data being—the search for that one black swan also being naturally far more defined than for the thousandth white one—and this possibly in real-time, is an invaluable advantage in intelligence work.
>
> (Ibid)

Of course, finding that black swan or outlier in many threat contexts remains very difficult for reasons we will turn to shortly. It's clear that big data has increasingly facilitated the automatic and manual collection of volumes of data particularly in sensing, communication, and information processing systems. It frees up the time spent on analysis and sense-making in relation to collection—providing of course analysts are able to make sense of the data—a point we come back to in the following chapter (Chapter 5 Analysis). Bigger more capable computers to rapidly 'do the collection' can potentially identify anomalies in anything from energy usage, vehicle number plates, social media, and bank records, which may indicate actual or potential criminal activities. However, a downside to big data, which continues to be a problem for ICs and law enforcement agencies, is to efficiently analyse these data sets (see Chapter 5). Pavlin encapsulates the challenge, arguing 'the problem remains how more rapidly and accurately ICs can "decode" threat behaviour patterns consisting from ever increasing volumes of heterogeneous types of data generated at different locations and points in time' (Pavlin 2013:

137–146). The impressive inroads in being able to collect ever large volumes of big data has resulted in what Lim describes a kind of 'data asphyxiation and decision paralysis' (Lim 2016: 628). He gives the examples of the US National Security Agency (NSA), where SIGINT technology far outpaces the organisation's human analytical capabilities. Even the US Navy, he suggests, in order to track the movement of seagoing vessels worldwide, alone collects 200 terabytes of data approximately every 48 hours (Ibid).

Despite this data deluge, all technical intelligence forms (SIGINT, MASINT, and IMINT (now GEOINT) and other emerging fields of CYBINT and SOCMINT (Social Media Intelligence) are expanding at near exponential rates, according to Brantley. This means that 'the signal to noise ratio within this data is very low, and vast collections of data make analysis extremely difficult' (Brantly 2018: 566).

This is not to suggest that big data analytics has not improved and found meaningful correlations between data sets leading to preventing or disrupting threats. Certainly in areas such as money laundering, fraud, and high volume crimes (e.g. burglaries), gains have been made—but in more serious organised crime or terrorism—correlation much less causation can be more difficult to find. Equally too, the notion of 'predictive analytics,' which has worked well in some commercial settings such as marketing, are currently less able to show threat actor intent or the planning of serious crimes such as terrorist attacks without of course other intelligence (HUMINT) and investigative sources being thrown into the mix.

Nonetheless, given the diversity, volume, and speed of big data compared to other intelligence feeds (e.g. HUMINT), one key strength is that it 'often can provide more value in its exhaust (data captured as a residual) than in its deliberate data collections.' 'This exhaust can (still) prove useful to future analysis efforts. In particular, as Brantly suggests in addressing questions not yet formulated by a given client' (2018: 566).

Perhaps, as Lim argues, big data analytics might be particularly useful for 'surveillance and warning against unlikely but nonetheless high-impact events or "black swans," as they are now referred to in the popular literature' (Lim 2016: 629). We have seen how for decades big data analytics has helped provide surveillance for a range of diseases in public health and biosecurity—but even in these contexts the systems are not perfect or necessarily 'predictive' (Walsh 2018). I expect/hope though that after the global COVID-19 pandemic even greater improvements can be made in big data-driven health security surveillance systems to improve early warning on further novel catastrophic infections (Ibid).

While it might become possible in some complex threat contexts to more quickly correlate patterns in a variety of data sources that could indicate potential threat pathways such as planning of a terrorist event, I remain sceptical whether big data analytics can reliably on its own lead IC agencies to sufficient predictive or early warning in such complex threat contexts. In contrast, Lim is of the view that big data analytics can take on this strategic/predictive role—arguing it might be 'best suited in discerning long-term developments, including generating intelligence hypotheses, and adduce refuting facts' (Ibid: 619). However, I think Lim's point remains contestable.

The 'predictive power' of big data analytics applied to complex threats is hampered by data sets that are usually historic and/or incomplete. While patterns in historical data may infer the existence of a pattern of threat behaviour, terrorism and organised crime behaviour are complex and historical patterns are not necessarily a judge of future ones in a correlational let alone causational sense. In addition to not easily inferring or explaining the future potential of threat actor groups, generating hypotheses from historical data may just reinforce 'noise' in already overwhelmed data systems in our ICs. In addition, there is a problem in data analytics algorithms resulting in false positives. Advancements in machine learning have also resulted in biases within algorithms. These biases can be self-reinforcing and result in even less accurate analysis. The role of a human analyst therefore remains critical in correcting bias generated by automated learning algorithms and making the necessary adjustments to reduce the significance of error.

So for the moment, algorithms alone cannot replace other collection methodologies. Human subject matter experts, SIGINT, GEOINT, and Open-source intelligence (OSINT) all offer opportunities to triangulate the validity and reliability of big data analytics. This is not to marginalise the importance big data analytics has played in our IC and law enforcement agencies over the last two decades in particular. However, IC leaders need to see big data as merely another tool in the collection toolbox. An important tool perhaps in many contexts but nonetheless just another tool. Each tool, technology, and technique have potential utility but they also each have their own limitations. How they are applied depends on the threat context.

Efforts continue in ICs to improve the anticipatory and predictive reliability of big data analytics that assess events and information. While much of this is classified, some of the Intelligence Advanced Research Projects Activity's (IARPA's) work is illustrative of what is being done to improve 'forecasting' of big data analytics used in ICs. IARPA funds a variety of research initiatives. Just two of many examples include the Aggregate Contingent Estimation (ACE) and Forecasting Science and Technology (ForeST) (Brantly 2018: 567). ACE was 'designed to focus on probabilistic assessments for contingent events, the aggregation of events by multiple human analysts and the representation of these forecasts and their distributions' (Ibid). ForeST was 'designed to fund projects that could accurately forecast significant advances or milestones in science and technology' (Ibid). There have been several other projects as well to improve the collection and automated analysis of publicly available data to better anticipate events, as we shall see below in the discussion on social media.

Regardless of these research improvement efforts, the sheer volume of big data and enhanced technologies to improve the speed of which it can be collected and analysed still makes a lot of big data analytics 'reactive' rather than properly getting to the intention, causes, and prediction of threats. Our ICs will still struggle to make sense of the relentless data feeds (Pannerselvam *et al.* 2015) in ways that allow them to understand intention and causes better. As discussed in Chapter 6 (ICT), artificial intelligence (AI) advancements could be used to exploit the power of machine learning to even higher levels, thereby automating or speeding up the analytical capability of current machine learning capability. This point was echoed by one IC leader surveyed, who said: 'the use of big data, deep learning and eventually artificial intelligence will help to speed up the processing of unstructured data (video/audio) for analysis' (survey respondent reference 30).

And despite the volume of data, which will impact on the ability to efficiently analyse it, machine learning technologies, techniques, and methods (leaving aside some of their shortcomings) will be increasingly relied upon to assist intelligence analysts to exploit more efficiently patterns in massive data sets. In addition to efforts being made by government-funded research agencies such as IARPA, the IC and private sector are also looking at other ways of meeting some of the challenges the intelligence agencies have with extracting more sense-making and forecasting capability out of big data. But what other approaches are being developed and will they help ICs analyse the volumes, velocity, and variety of data? A US National Academies of Science workshop report on big data suggested three approaches would be useful in improving IC analytical capability, including for the remote detection of weapons of mass destruction and improved methods of cyber command and control (NRC 2013: 39). Their report suggests that

> first, streaming algorithms that can process data in one pass with limited memory are clearly important. Second, for data at rest, transactional databases are generally not needed, but highly usable systems for hosting and querying massive data, including data distributed across multiple sites will be essential. Third, the NRC report argued that better visualization tools are also needed to conserve the scarce and valuable time of human analysts.
>
> (Ibid)

Additionally, big data techniques may be increasingly deployed to exploit data from the internet of things (IoT) as other communications 'go dark' to the ICs. However, it's less clear how the explosion of data available from the IoT will be captured in a way that can allow it to be analysed in real time or integrated perhaps with other intelligence collection sources. As Brantly says, 'what is more remarkable is not the number of users going online, but rather the increase in the number of internet-enabled devices that received Internet Protocol (IP) addresses.' 'Cisco estimated that between 2008 and 2009 the Internet of Things (IoT) first exceeded the number of human beings on the planet' (Brantly 2018: 563). 'Cisco continues to estimate that by 2020 the number of internet-enabled devices will reach approximately 50 billion' (Ibid). IoT sensing, processing data aggregation systems in people's homes, cars, personal devices, private sector, and government systems could all potentially be sources of collection. However, the development in IoT is far outstripping SIGINT and other IC agency's ability to target them— leaving aside for the moment the privacy issues (Jani and Soni 2018: 183–203; Kaul *et al.* 2018).

New innovations in improving big data analytics will increasingly rely on cross-disciplinary approaches (computer science, engineering, statistics, and even social sciences) in order to provide intelligence analysts and ICs more broadly with even better designed systems for massive data analysis that can operate more reliably in real time. Computer scientists need a better understanding of statistical ideas and improving their understanding of risk when designing algorithms and statisticians need a better understanding of computational ideas (NRC 2013: 39).

Clearly one major task for the future IC leader will not necessarily be to reengineer themselves as data scientists—though in some contexts that might be required. But regardless of where they sit in the IC, they will need a better understanding of data science than the current generation of leaders—as machine learning and AI will likely loom ever larger in the twenty-first century 'Five Eyes' ICs (see Chapter 6 ICT). Additionally, leaders will need to make better evidence-informed decisions about what mix of data scientist capabilities (in-house vs external contractors) they need. In other words, in addition to having the right kind of training in computational and statistical skills data, scientists will need relevant domain knowledge and apply their knowledge flexibly to adapt solutions to data analytics problems as the threat environment changes. In the future, as the data sets continue to grow, the future cadre of 'whizz kid data scientists' will need to demonstrate clearly to the IC leadership opportunities and limitations for improving the inferential accuracy of data sets in the IC—particularly relating to more high risk and complex threats. What other challenges future intelligence leaders will face in the broader data, information communications, and technology areas will be discussed in Chapter 6 (ICT). Additionally, in Chapter 8 (The Future IC Leader and Governance Challenges) we will come back to an assessment of the collection challenges future IC leaders will face and what can be done about them.

Social media

Social media data sources are increasingly providing our ICs with a range of information that can be integrated with other data sources on a person or group. Lim provides a useful description of the variety and utility of social media for ICs:

> Twitter, Facebook, YouTube, Instagram, LinkedIn and sundry social media applications have melded into a 'vast digital social commons' capable of facilitating complex analyses of sentiments, semantics, clusters and networks, for instance, in the effort to map, among other things, global Jihadist activity.
> (2016: 629)

In particular, over the last two decades, social media sources or social media intelligence (SOCMINT) has seen an explosion in development as well as users facilitated by breakthroughs in smart phone and tablet technology. Not counting all the diverse social media platforms and applications that seem to emerge on an almost daily basis, just two of the major social networking sites (Facebook and Twitter) are estimated to have reached a worldwide user number of 2.5 billion people (Hayes and Luther 2018: 9). Facebook alone has an active user number of over 1.5 billion people (Ibid). Social media provides several platforms for people to communicate for personal and commercial reasons.

There is insufficient space to provide examples of all the contexts in which SOCMINT may be a useful collection source for ICs. Here we will summarise some instances where SOCMINT has been used, but as with earlier discussion in this chapter the focus is on what challenges SOCMINT presents to IC leaders in the future. We will come back to the challenges shortly, but one obvious advantage of SOCMINT's various platforms (e.g. Facebook and Twitter) is that many provide real-time crowd-sourcing information. In crisis situations such as natural disasters or fast-moving security environments such as pandemics, riots, radicalisation, or a terrorist attack, citizens can take on the role of journalists—quickly relaying information in real time or near real time that can provide emergency responders, police, and the IC situational awareness (Stottlemyre 2015: 578–589; Richey and Binz 2015: 347–364). For example, in late April 2020 the Australian government launched its COVIDSafe app designed for the public to receive alerts about whether people in their vicinity have been exposed to COVID-19. The app speeds up the contacting and tracing process carried out by health authorities and within the first two days of its release two million Australians downloaded the non-mandatory app onto their smart phones. Such a real-time social media application can (and leaving aside the privacy issues) allow for better operational and tactical responses by ICs and emergency responders. As Omand *et al.* suggest,

> the rise in use of social media, together with the rapid development of analytics approaches, now provides a new opportunity for law enforcement to generate operational intelligence that could help identify criminal activity, indicate early warning of outbreaks of disorder, provide information and intelligence about groups and individuals, and help understand and respond to public concerns.
>
> (Omand *et al.* 2012: 805)

It is not just the variety of SOCMINT in real time that is potentially of interest to the police and ICs, it is also that many social media platforms work with geolocation capabilities that bring together a potential behaviour of concern and a map of areas where such behaviours might be of greatest concern.

The IC's ability to access SOCMINT varies. Open source information from Twitter feeds for example are public and therefore easily accessed, while other platforms require legal authorisation to remove privacy settings and encryption. As we shall see in our later discussion of intelligence collection, ethics, and efficacy, the ability of ICs to override privacy settings and encryption has increasingly become a strident policy and community debate exacerbated further after the Snowden leaks in 2013.

Despite the increasing exploitation of social media for intelligence purposes, SOCMINT technology uptake and analysis continue to present ongoing challenges for IC leaders and the agencies or communities they manage. Examples can be seen in the last decade when ICs were struggling to keep up with the massive Facebook and Twitter feeds emanating from North Africa and the Middle East during the 'Arab Spring' in 2011–2012 (Rovner 2013: 260–271; Newham and Bell 2012: 36–50). While harvesting an ever greater volume of SOCMINT has increasingly become a mainstay of IC collection strategies, Omand and colleague's seminal SOCMINT article plainly outlines the two major challenges with its application. The first is methodological. In other words, does the social media source 'rest on solid methodological bedrock of collection, evidence, verification, understanding and application' (2012: 801). Second, 'can the moral hazard it entails be legitimately managed'? Again, we will come back to the second point shortly.

On point one, it's clear that a great deal of work is being done within ICs and the broader research community to improve the reliability and validity of various SOCMINT sources. In particular, research into understanding how terrorists use social media for communication, intelligence, and operational planning is of central importance to ICs. Are there, for example, as Omand *et al.* speculate, 'thresholds, indicators and permissive conditions of violence; pathways into radicalization; an analysis of how ideas form and change' that can improve early warning and response to terrorist attacks (2012: 805–806). An increasing volume of research is now looking at tracking pathways to violence by radicalised individuals. In particular, there is a growing body of research into understanding grievance analysis using machine learning to identify clusters or anomalies in large data sets for behaviour that correlates statistically with emotions suggesting radicalisation (Al-Saggaf 2016: 13–27; Al Saggaf *et al.* 2016: 45–56).

However, as Omand *et al.* correctly point out, a 'crucial consequence of the rise of machine learning approaches within social media analytics is that we are currently much better at counting examples of online human behaviour than critically explaining why they are and what it might mean' (Ibid: 811). Importantly too, Omand reminds us that 'language is textured: the intent, motivation, social signification, denotation and connotation of any utterance is mutable and dependent on the context of situation and culture.'

> The accuracy of any interpretation depends on a very detailed understanding of the group or context that is being studied. For example, most groups of people use vernacular and group-specific language that a generic or standardized sentiment lexicon or thesaurus would often misinterpret.
>
> (Ibid)

As in the interpretation of SIGINT, therefore, analytical judgements about relationships and cultural nuances will remain key into the future.

The true meaning arising from social media analytics is fraught with other ongoing methodological difficulties. As noted in our earlier discussion of big data, ICs are in danger of misunderstanding the knowledge derived from machine learning if social media analytics solutions are developed solely by computer scientists and statisticians away from other disciplines that are better equipped to understand human behaviour such as psychology, political science, sociology, and anthropology.

The realisation by ICs and some law enforcement agencies is that if SOCMINT is 'to be methodologically robust enough to base decisions on and change policy,' a cross-disciplinary approach is required (both computer and social sciences). Such cross-disciplinary research efforts are underway particularly in 'Five Eyes' defence, science, and technology portfolios and in agencies such as IARPA (Omand *et al.* 2012: 816). However, future IC leaders and governments will need to continue making wise strategic investment decisions about what kinds of cross-disciplinary industry/research partnerships will best ensure ICs adapt and improve their social media collection methodologies.

Dark web

The dark web is the last example of methodological challenges we will discuss before turning our attention to the governance issues IC leaders will face in building sustainable and effective intelligence collection platforms and processes. There remains an ongoing concern amongst ICs about threat actor's communications 'going dark' either through exploited encrypted devices or using the dark web, which is a smaller part of the internet that is hard to access without the use of special browsers like Onion Router–Tor and passwords (Walsh 2018: 95). ICs and law enforcement agencies in recent years have had increasing success in penetrating, disrupting, and taking down several dark web Tor 'onion' domains, which have been used for a variety of criminal activity including terrorist communication and planning, drug trafficking, cyber-attacks, and child sexual exploitation. The FBI's 2014 takedown of Silk Road 2.0 used by multiple illicit drug networks, the 2016 disruption of the Avalanche syndicate (a global trafficker in botnet malware which infected over 180 countries), and the 2017 disruption of Alphabay (a dark web criminal market place) are recent examples of greater IC understanding and operational success against criminal dark web sites (Weiser 2014; European Union 2016; Broadhead 2018: 1180–1196).

It is difficult to gain outside the IC a full understanding of how 'Five Eyes' agencies are exploiting the dark web. However, there is now an increasing volume of openly available research that provides insights into the types of techniques and technologies ICs are using to collect information about dark web threats. Jardine lists a number of techniques currently in use by IC and law enforcement aimed at 'developing attacks on dark web hosting service to compromise the anonymity and privacy of the Tor network (including traffic correlation, protocol-level attacks, and website fingerprinting)' (Jardine 2018: 3). A number of machine learning techniques and web crawlers can also be used to categorise content on dark web forums (Dilip and Sharma 2018: 114–137; Chen 2012). Several other approaches such as passive surveillance of chatroom conversations are useful in providing details of criminal involvement and familiarity with cryptocurrencies and dark web markets (Jardine 2018: 3). Passive observation of dark web markets can provide opportunities to develop detailed case studies on both the intentions and capabilities of threat actors operating on illegal forums. Additionally, Jardine notes 'ethnographic investigations can reveal the catalytic effect of illegal markets on drug users and survey methods can be used to pinpoint perceptions of drug use among dark web market patrons' (2018: 3).

While the methods and approaches discussed above provide greater understanding of a diverse multitude of illicit markets, as Broadhead points out, the dynamic nature of the dark web, or one defined by a 'continuing transformation of the cyber-crime eco-system remains the only constant' (Broadhead 2018: 1180). The ability to get a really granular collection and analysis of both illicit vendors and users across various threat types is an ongoing challenge. The high churn rate for Tor hidden sites in real time conspires against research and IC efforts to improve analytical generalisability about 'market size,' threat assessment, and operational disruption.

An enduring challenge for IC leaders therefore is to know how best to support research and operational capabilities that will allow both a faster collection of dark web information—despite ongoing efforts by threat actors to use this part of the internet for increasing obfuscation and anonymity. Deep web information extraction has relied on several web crawling techniques to varying levels of success and research investment into other extraction protocols such as open framework protocol for collection could be considered in their place (Dilip and Sharma 2018: 133). Efforts also need to be made to improve knowledge about both the supply and demand side of illicit dark web markets and comparing these sources with surface web information and other more traditional collection sources. As noted in Chapter 8 (The Future IC Leader and Governance Challenges), IC leaders will need to work with external experts and researchers to improve collection capabilities against threat actors operating in the dark web.

Intelligence collection and governance challenges

In addition to some of the technical collection challenges leaders will face, a second set of issues relate to what kinds of organisational design within and across ICs best optimise collection capabilities. Related to this question also is how organisational cultural issues will inhibit and/or facilitate collection efforts in the future. As we saw in Chapter 3 (Tasking and Coordination), organisational structure and cultural identity have been powerful influencers historically in how intelligence is tasked, coordinated, and integrated. Both have also influenced significantly approaches to collection and analysis across 'Five Eyes' ICs. The role of organisational structure and culture are related to intelligence governance, which was defined in Chapter 2 as the strategies, habits, attributes, normative behaviour, and technical knowledge that leaders use to coordinate effective intelligence functions, processes, and outputs. In the following section, we will discuss both organisational structural and cultural factors that influence how IC leaders manage collection processes and capabilities.

Collection and organisational structure

Future IC leaders will need a keen understanding of not only how to build efficient, cost-effective and mission-focused collection capabilities, but also identify what organisational structural and cultural issues need addressing to achieve future collection requirements. As noted in Chapter 2, the Cold War saw the build-up of large SIGINT collection capabilities. Similarly, the post-Cold War and post-9/11 environment also required the development of additional digital collection capability responses. However, throughout all these stages advances in IC collection capability have not just been the result solely of technological transformation. It is true decisions made by IC leaders about investing in new collection technologies are usually made in order to adapt to changes in the security environment. But the adoption and integration of new collection capabilities have also been about how technologies have been integrated and adapted into the organisational structures and cultures of ICs.

For example, in the case of post-9/11, the security environment has become increasingly defined not just by state-based threats, but non-state-based global outlaws such as terrorists, drug and weapons traffickers as well as people smugglers. The question remains, though, has this changing security environment resulted in different organisational structures—ones better adapted to developing more effective collection capabilities to meet this complex post-9/11 environment?

Looking back to the early post-9/11 period, a common view by some observers, such as former senior intelligence officer Charles Cogan, was that the US IC 'a year after 9/11, America remains dangerously unprepared to prevent and respond to a catastrophic terrorist attack on US soil' (Cogan 2004: 305). In this context, Cogan added, 'we have to ask ourselves some urgent questions as to how we are organised and conditioned to conduct intelligence in the twenty-first century' (Ibid: 305). We have seen in previous chapters that in all 'Five Eyes' ICs a combination of policy, bureaucratic, and legislative reforms continue to raise questions about how ICs are structured and whether they are organised in ways that will result in effective intelligence collection on an increasingly mutable security environment. Cogan's question, therefore, is not just relevant to assessing whether the IC's organisational architecture was right immediately after 9/11, but it remains germane for future IC leaders as we advance further into the twenty-first century.

In terms of how leaders need to re-organise collection capabilities within their organisations, this will always be defined by *context* (national security, law enforcement, military), *legislation,* and *function* (SIGINT, HUMINT, GEOINT amongst others). But older definitions about what different types of collection mean has become increasingly blurred—such as the difference between foreign and domestic intelligence. Collection against threats that have both domestic and foreign dimensions such as terrorism continue to challenge older Cold War siloing of collection capabilities and organisational structures making IC structural redesign difficult in some cases (Walsh 2011). As too does collection against human security issues (e.g. pandemics, disasters, and human rights). Issues such as 'health security' while on the collection agenda of most 'Five Eyes' ICs have generally been peripheral issues. However, the significant health and national security threat posed by the 2020 COVID-19 pandemic again illustrates that IC leaders will need to at least in some contexts re-calibrate collection capabilities and organisational/structural responses to better deal with such health security threats in the future (Walsh 2020).

But is Cogan correct in his analysis that collection, particularly covert action, 'in the twenty-first century likely will be characterised by what could be termed an offensive hunt strategy' (2004: 305)? Or in his words: 'intelligence operatives in the twenty-first century will become hunters, not gatherers' (Ibid). His point implies that perhaps pre-9/11, IC's organisational structures including collection platforms waited passively for the information to come in rather than actively going out to get it. Of course this is not entirely true. Even during the Cold War, which relied heavily on vacuuming up large volumes of SIGINT, this period was also very much an aggressive HUMINT war, where each side actively hunted for information about the other. Nonetheless, Cogan's point is compelling in the sense that after 9/11 global outlaws like terrorists are frequently 'off the grid.' They also did not have large standing armies operating in locations that would be easily visible by IC geospatial assets.

Organisational structures, therefore, need to accommodate more flexible approaches to collection—ones as Cogan suggests 'hunts for intelligence' rather than just passively gathering it. Hunting for terrorists as we have has included a greater focus on special forces—often operating in countries that 'Five Eyes' countries were not officially at war with. Starting with the Bush administration, but continuing on in subsequent administrations, this hunter-focused collection approach has also seen the proliferation of paramilitary operations by some 'Five Eyes' IC agencies such as the CIA. The 'hunter collection' approach included the use of drones for enhanced surveillance and targeted killings of high-value targets (Walsh 2017: 429–433; Johnson *et al.* 2017: 411–440). As noted in Chapter 3 (Tasking and Coordination), in addition to a move towards a more hunter approach to *foreign intelligence collection*, legislative, policy, and greater integration of collection capabilities has also produced a hunter approach to *domestic intelligence collection*. The latter in particular as we shall see shortly, of course, has not been without its ethical, privacy, and community trust consequences.

While there is no doubt all 'Five Eyes' IC structures have changed to some extent in order to prosecute a hunter or proactive approach to intelligence collection, it remains difficult to know precisely how significantly each IC has changed. In short, it is difficult to know from the outside looking in whether current structural arrangements are optimal for the kind of proactive collection approaches now required against the evolving security environment. As discussed in Chapter 2 (Intelligence and Leadership), the history of all 'Five Eyes' ICs and the agencies therein are deeply imbued with institutional legacy constraints, including political cultural influences and organisational cultural issues. For example, one point of difference between the 'Five Eyes' ICs is that the US political culture is distrustful of government and institutions responsible for domestic security. This impacts on both the organisational structure of the US IC and to what extent security agencies can be active hunters of intelligence.

Chapters 2 (Intelligence and Leadership) and 3 (Tasking and Coordination) have already covered extensively many of the organisational cultural issues that have impacted on the structural development of our ICs. Similar cultural constraints also come into play when it comes to intelligence collection—particularly in areas of designing collection technology platforms, intelligence sharing, and identifying areas where collection sources can be more effectively fused to support a common mission (Tromblay 2017: 817–832). Future leaders will need to find ways to move through the negative or constraining aspects of their agency's cultural histories to improve collection outputs. As noted in earlier chapters, recent history shows inadequacies within intelligence collection methods and the way they have been organised structurally leading up to 9/11 and in the pre-war assessment of WMD in Iraq. This underscores the need for IC leaders to continually improve and test traditional approaches to collection, their validity, and relevance to a particular threat problem. The challenge is cultural and technological, but it is also how leaders manage the creation and distribution of knowledge across their agencies and the broader IC (Dearstyne 2005). For example, one of the aspects of collection failure leading up to the invasion of Iraq was whether other 'outside' sources such as the United Nations Special Commission (UNSCOM) weapons inspectors could have been taken more seriously by ICs over the traditional sources they have always been comfortable with, such as SIGINT and HUMINT (Morrison 2011: 513–514). Will organisational cultural bias and preferences over traditional collection sources blinker how future leaders arrange collection efforts against an increasingly complex security environment? This is not to suggest that traditional collection platforms like HUMINT are no longer required, in fact, the latter arguably is lacking against several threats—including terrorism and state-based ones such as an emboldening of Russia and China. But future leaders will need to continually review collection capabilities and structures against all threats to ensure that they remain fit for purpose, and collection strategies are based on the most effective way to retrieve the intelligence required. This will require a leaders' ability to implement organisational structures and responses that are more informed by evidence about how best to collect effectively against increasingly hardened targets and threats that mutate or are resilient over time. Part of their response will need to be a more agnostic perspective to long-cherished organisational and culture-bounded views about the merits of one kind of 'INT' over another. In the context of being constrained by history and culture, one IC leader surveyed summarised well what response was needed by future leaders when it comes to intelligence collection:

Don't be arrogant. Do not assume that anyone/company/group that does not have a TS SCI clearance has less information, expertise, insights, ideas about how to use innovative methods to collect information. Embrace OSINT and social media—but know its pitfalls. Understand what big data can do and cannot do. Reach out to the private sector OSINT community that is doing amazing "forensic" work (i.e. Bellingcat). Innovate, understand how technology can help collection, but also poses risks. Don't rely on old techniques, don't be hemmed in by CI concerns (people who are locals, but do not have a high level clearance can be valuable sources of information (survey respondent 78).[1]

Indeed, given the impact of the digital revolution globally, advances in cyber and biotechnology and now arguably a revolution in AI, IC leaders will need to as suggested in the above quote engage even more with the private sector and research community to gain knowledge and 'hard ware' in an attempt to stay ahead of emerging threat trajectories. In some cases, leaders will need to work closely with 'IC outsiders' in order to prolong 'old traditional INT' platforms, while in others they will seek advice on how they can be supplemented or replaced with a better fit for purpose-collection systems (Walsh 2018; Makridakis 2017: 46–60). Additionally, private-public partnerships between technology and knowledge providers, which can result in better collection capabilities, are already a major part of the post-9/11 'Five Eyes' IC landscape. In a global competitive market, as governments divest their interest in sensitive areas of critical infrastructure (telecommunications, energy, water, roads, airports, and ports), IC leaders will need to also demonstrate a broader understanding of 'security' at the same time as they look for opportunities to burden share-collection efforts with the private sector. This will require adept leadership that can reconcile the interest of governments and the private sector—yet still produce collection strategies that are ethical and aligned with liberal democratic principles (Petersen and Tjalve 2018: 21–35). Above all, managing the complexity of collection into the future will require, as noted by one IC leader surveyed for the project: 'being future focused, not thinking about current collection, but what will we need in 5 years' time' (survey respondent 60).

Intelligence collection ethics and efficacy

The third ongoing collection challenge for IC leaders will be as threat actors become more difficult to intercept, the 'Five Eyes' IC's proactive collection approaches will increasingly raise complex ethical and privacy issues. As we move further into the twenty-first century, several related issues will become more pressing. For example, the community discussion around what is considered legitimate surveillance and secrecy in liberal democratic states will gain further momentum. IC leaders in the decades to come therefore will likely be even more engaged in public discussions about the ethical and efficacy issues relating to the collection of intelligence than their post-9/11 colleagues. Limited space does not allow for a detailed discussion of the various ethics and efficacy collection issues that leaders will need to become more adept at understanding and handling.

For readers interested in detailed analyses of ethical challenges associated with intelligence collection, particularly since 9/11, there is now a growing body of work examining these issues in different collection applications, including electronic collection, covert action, and interrogation amongst others (Bellaby 2012; Omand and Phythian 2013; Omand and Phythian 2018; Walsh 2011; Walsh and Miller 2016). Many of these works have framed ethical challenges related to intelligence collection by using amended versions of 'Just War Theory,' often referred to as 'Just Intelligence Theory' (Bellaby 2012; Omand and Phythian 2012; Omand and Phythian 2013: 38–63). Although intelligence collection naturally occurs during a military conflict, wars morally should be a last resort, whereas other collection of course is enduring–occurring day to day in the absence of war conditions. Hence, at this stage it is less clear whether ethical principles governing military conflict are neatly transferrable to all the complex collection issues we have been discussing in this chapter.

While, as noted in Chapter 2, ICs have always had to contend with ethical dilemmas in the collection of intelligence; the advent of a more proactive and permissive collection culture; the digital revolution and now increasingly AI combined has taken historical ethical challenges to new levels. Added to this as mentioned earlier, both WikiLeaks and more significantly the 2013 Snowden leaks have also had a catalytic effect on ethics and efficacy debates within ICs and in the community about the legitimacy of various collection activities in liberal democratic states.

We will come back to the issue of ethics and intelligence collection in Chapter 8 (The Future IC Leader and Governance Challenges) and discuss how future IC leaders might engage further in managing them. But its clear researchers and political and IC leaders need clearer theoretical and practitioner frameworks in which to understand the ethical risks posed by increasingly complex technologically enabled collection platforms. This means all interested parties need to move away from historical and simplistic continuums for thinking about ethics in the intelligence collection context—such as privacy vs security—to frameworks that are both more nuanced and empirically informed.

At the heart of such a framework should be a careful analysis of three key aspects of intelligence collection (methods, context, and target) (Walsh and Miller 2016). In each case the *methods* (e.g. wiretaps, metadata, social media), the *context* (e.g. wartime, counter-terrorism) and the *target* of collection activity (e.g. the Chinese military vs economic espionage) throw up unique and distinct ethical and efficacy dilemmas that IC leaders will need to nimbly address in the future than hitherto has been the case up to now. In short, different methods, contexts, and targets of collection activity will raise their own unique ethical dilemmas and the IC leader will require a greater understanding of them and how principles such as necessity and proportionality apply or not in each case.

Conclusion

Chapter 4 introduced three themes (technological and methodological, governance, ethics, and efficacy) to frame our discussion on challenges IC leaders must navigate through if collection platforms and processes are to remain 'fit for purpose' against an increasingly complex security environment. The promise and potential of emerging technological innovation opens up for ICs other sources for collection as others may become more difficult to access due to encryption and counter-intelligence campaigns by threat actors. Yet governance issues such as organisational structure and culture will also impact on the kind of institutional progress ICs will be able to make on integrating new collection strategies and technologies. In Chapter 8 (The Future IC Leader and Governance Challenges) we will return to the collection governance themes raised here (technology, organisational structure, and ethics) to see how IC leaders will need to reconcile them in ways that can continue to facilitate adaptive collection platforms.

In the next chapter (Chapter 5 Analysis), we explore a sample of analytical methodological issues and how their application by analysts and others impacts on IC capabilities. The focus is not on how to improve the professional capabilities of analysts (i.e. training and education) as this will be a subject discussed in Chapter 7 (HR). Rather, Chapter 5 will investigate what methodologies, practices, and domain knowledge could improve analysis in the workplace and what developments in these areas might be most beneficial for IC leaders to embrace and why. It also explores what key governance challenges may arise as IC leaders seek to improve both human and technological analytical capabilities.

Note

1 Bellingcat is an independent international collective of researchers, investigators, and citizen journalists using open source media investigations to probe a variety of subjects: crime conflicts, corruption, secret operations, mis and disinformation, and extremist groups.

References

Al-Saggaf, Y. (2016). Understanding online radicalisation using data science. *International Journal of Cyber Warfare and Terrorism*, *6*(4), 13–27.

Al-Saggaf, Y., Utz, S., & Lin, R. (2016). Venting negative emotions on twitter and the number of followers and followees. *International Journal of Sociotechnology and Knowledge Discovery*, *8*(1), 44–55.

Bellaby, R. (2012). *The ethics of intelligence: A new framework*. Abingdon: Routledge.

Brantly, A. F. (2018). When everything becomes intelligence: Machine learning and the connected world. *Intelligence and National Security*, *33*(4), 562–573. doi: 10.1080/02684527.2018.1452555

Broadhead, S. (2018). The contemporary cybercrime ecosystem: A multi-disciplinary overview of the state of affairs and developments. *Computer Law & Security Review: The International Journal of Technology Law and Practice*, *34*(6), pp. 1180–1196. doi: 10.1016/j.clsr.2018.08.005

Chen, H. (2012). *Dark web: Exploring and data mining the dark side of the web*. New York, NY: Springer.

Clark, R. (2014). *Intelligence collection*. Thousand Oaks, CA: CQ Press.

Cogan, C. (2004). Hunters not gatherers: Intelligence in the twenty-first Century. *Intelligence and National Security*, *19*(2), 304–321. doi: 10.1080/0268452042000302010

Dearstyne, B. W. (2005). Fighting terrorism, making war: Critical insights in the management of information and intelligence. *Government Information Quarterly*, *22*(2), 170–186.

Dilip Kumar, S., & Sharma, A. K. (2018). Deep web information retrieval process: A technical survey. *The dark web: Breakthroughs in research and practice* (pp. 114–137). Hershey, PA: IGI Global.

Ding, F., Ge, Q., Jiang, D., Fu, J., & Hao, M. (2017). Understanding the dynamics of terrorism events with multiple-discipline datasets and machine learning approach. *PLoS One, 12*(6), e0179057. doi: 10.1371/journal.pone.0179057

European Union (2016). *Europol brings down global cybercrime syndicate*. Bangkok: Thai News Service Group.

Gill, P., & Phythian, M. (2018). *Intelligence in an insecure world* (3rd ed.). Cambridge: Polity Press.

Hayes, R. M., & Luther, K. (2018). *Crime: Social media, crime, and the criminal legal system*. Cham, Switzerland: Palgrave Macmillan US.

Higgins, O. (2009). The theory and practice of intelligence collection. In J. Ratcliffe (Ed.), *Strategic Thinking in Criminal Intelligence* (pp. 85–107). Sydney: Federation Press.

Jani, K. P., & Soni, A. (2018). Promise and perils of big data science for intelligence Community. In M. E. Kosal (Ed.), *Technology and the intelligence community: Challenges and advances for the 21st century* (pp. 183–203). Cham: Springer International Publishing.

Jardine, E. (2018). The trouble with (supply-side) counts: the potential and limitations of counting sites, vendors or products as a metric for threat trends on the Dark Web. *Intelligence and National Security*, 1–17. doi:10.1080/02684527.2018.1528752

Johnson, L. K., Dorn, A. W., Webb, S., Kreps, S., Krieger, W., & Schwarz, E. (2017). An INS Special Forum: Intelligence and drones/Eyes in the sky for peacekeeping: The emergence of UAVs in un operations/the democratic deficit on drones/the German Approach to Drone Warfare/Pursuing peace: The strategic limits of drone warfare/ Seeing but unseen: Intelligence drones in Israel/Drone paramilitary operations against suspected global terrorists: US and Australian perspectives/the 'Terminator Conundrum' and the future of drone warfare. *Intelligence and National Security, 32*(4), 411–440. doi: 10.1080/02684527.2017.1303127

Johnson, L., & Wirtz, J. (Eds.) (2015). *Intelligence: The secret world of spies*. New York: Oxford University Press.

Kaul, K., Tucker, M., McNamara, G. S., Hicks, J., Bliss, C., Tosi, S., & Loethen, L. (2018). *Going darker 2.0. Policy recommendations for law enforcement and the intelligence Community and private sector*. Washington, DC.

Lamarre, L. (1998). The digital revolution. *EPRI Journal, 23*(1), 26.

Lim, K. (2016). Big data and strategic intelligence. *Intelligence and National Security, 31*(4), 619–635. doi: 10.1080/02684527.2015.1062321

Lowenthal, M. (2012). *Intelligence from secrets to policy*. Thousand Oaks, CA: Sage Publications.

Makridakis, S. (2017). The [in press] Artificial Intelligence (AI) revolution: Its impact on society and firms. *Futures, 90*(C), 46–60. doi: 10.1016/j.futures.2017.03.006

Masys, A. (Ed.) (2014). *Networks and network analysis for defence and security*. Cham: Springer International Publishing.

Morrison, J. N. (2011). British intelligence failures in Iraq. *Intelligence and National Security, 26*(4), 509–520.

National Research Council (2013). *Frontiers in massive data analysis*. Washington, DC: The National Academies Press.

Newnham, J., & Bell, P. (2012). Social network media and political activism: A growing challenge for law enforcement. *Journal of Policing, Intelligence and Counter Terrorism, 7*(1), 36–50. doi: 10.1080/18335330.2012.653194

Olson, D. L., & Delen, D. (2008). *Advanced data mining techniques*. Berlin-Heidelberg: Springer Science & Business Media.

Omand, D., Bartlett, J., & Miller, C. (2012). Introducing social media (SOCMINT) intelligence. *Intelligence and National Security, 27*(6), 801–823.

Omand, S. D., & Phythian, M. (2013). Ethics and intelligence: A debate. *International Journal of Intelligence and Counterintelligence, 26*(1), 38–63. doi: 10.1080/08850607.2012.705186

Omand, D., & Phythian, M. (2018). *Principled spying: The ethics of secret intelligence*. Oxford: Oxford University Press.

Pannerselvam, John, Liu, Lu, & Hill, Richard (2015). An introduction to big data. In B. Akhgar, Saathoff, G. B., Arabnia, H. R., Hill, R., Staniforth, A., & Bayerl, P. S. (Eds.), *Application of big data for national security* (pp. 1–13). Oxford: Butterworth-Heinemann.

Pavlin, G., Quillinan, T., Mignet, F., & de Oude, P. (2013). Exploiting intelligence for national security. In B. Akhagar & S. Yates (Eds.). (pp. 181–198). Watham, MA; Boston: Butterworth-Heinemann.

Petersen, K. L., & Tjalve, V. S. (2018). Intelligence expertise in the age of information sharing: Public–private 'collection' and its challenges to democratic control and accountability. *Intelligence and National Security, 33*(1), 21–35. doi: 10.1080/02684527.2017.1316956

Pramanik, M. I., Lau, R. Y. K., Yue, W. T., Ye, Y., & Li, C. (2017). Big data analytics for security and criminal investigations. *Wiley Interdisciplinary Reviews: Data Mining and Knowledge Discovery, 7*(4), e1208-n/a. doi: 10.1002/widm.1208

Purda, L., & Skillicorn, D. (2015). Accounting variables, deception, and a bag of words: Assessing the tools of fraud detection. *Contemporary Accounting Research, 32*(3), 1193–1223.

Richey, M. K., & Binz, M. (2015). Open source collection methods for identifying radical extremists using social media. *International Journal of Intelligence and Counterintelligence, 28*(2), 347–364. doi: 10.1080/08850607.2014.962374

Rovner, J. (2013). Intelligence in the twitter age. *International Journal of Intelligence and Counterintelligence, 26*(2), 260–271. doi: 10.1080/08850607.2013.757996

Seel, P. B. (2012). *Digital universe the global telecommunication revolution*. Hoboken: John Wiley & Sons.

Shulsky, A., & Gary Schmitt, G. (2002). *Silent warfare understanding the world of intelligence*. Virginia: Potomac Books.

Skillicorn, D. (2009). *Knowledge discovery for counterterrorism and law enforcement*. Boca Raton, FL: CRC Press.

Skillicorn, D., & Reid, E. (2014). Language use in the jihadist magazines inspire and Azan. *Security Informatics, 3*(1), 1–16. doi: 10.1186/s13388-014-0009-1

Stottlemyre, S. A. (2015). HUMINT, OSINT, or something new? Defining crowdsourced intelligence. *International Journal of Intelligence and Counterintelligence, 28*(3), 578–589. doi: 10.1080/08850607.2015.992760

Tromblay, D. E. (2017). Information Technology (IT) woes and intelligence agency failures: The Federal Bureau of Investigation's troubled IT evolution as a microcosm of a dysfunctional corporate culture. *Intelligence and National Security, 32*(6), 817–832. doi: 10.1080/02684527.2017.1296947

Van der Hurst, R. (2009). Introduction to social network analysis (SNA) as an investigative tool. *Trends Organ. Crime, 12*(2), 101–121.

Walsh, P. F. (2011). *Intelligence and intelligence analysis*. Abingdon: UK: Routledge.

Walsh, P. F. (2017). Drone paramilitary operations against suspected global terrorists: US and Australian perspectives. *Intelligence and National Security, 32*(4), 429–433.

Walsh, P. F. (2018). *Intelligence, biosecurity and bioterrorism.* London: Palgrave Macmillan.

Walsh, P. F. (2020). Improving 'Five Eyes' health security intelligence capabilities: Leadership and governance challenges. *Intelligence and National Security, 35*(4), 586–602. doi: 10.1080/02684527.2020.1750156

Walsh, P. F., & Miller, S. (2016). Rethinking 'five eyes' security intelligence collection policies adn practice post snowden. *Intelligence and National Security, 31*(3), 345–368.

Warner, M. (2012). Reflections on technology and intelligence systems. *Intelligence and National Security, 27*(1), 133–153. doi: 10.1080/02684527.2012.621604

Weiser, B. (2014). *Man is charged with operating a black market website.* (Metropolitan Desk) (Blake Benthall and the Silk Road 2.0 website) (pp. A26), New York: The New York Times Company.

Zijuan, L., & Shuai, D. (2017, 25–27 December). Research on prediction method of terrorist attack based on random subspace. Paper presented at the 2017 International Conference on Computer Systems, Electronics and Control (ICCSEC), pp. 320–322. IEEE.

5 Analysis

Introduction

Analysis—both its cognitive and its technical dimensions—are at the heart of all core intelligence processes regardless of the context in which intelligence is practiced (e.g. national security, military, law enforcement, or the private sector). This chapter investigates common analytical techniques currently utilised in 'Five Eyes' countries and what the IC leadership (rather than analysts) need to know about them from a broader organisational perspective. Hence, the focus is not an in-depth discussion from an analyst's practice point of view of all analytical tools currently being deployed in our ICs. There is now an ever growing number of sources the reader can turn to for detailed background knowledge on both analytical techniques and general progress being made in the intelligence analysis area since 9/11 (see for e.g. Dahl 2017; Frank 2017: 579–599; Chang and Tetlock 2017: 903–920; Marrin 2007: 821–846, 2017, 2020: 350–366; Phythian 2017: 600–612; Lahneman and Arcos 2017: 972–985; Shelton 2014: 262–281; Walsh 2011, 2017; Pherson and Heuer 2020). Instead of attempting to provide a detailed evaluation of all available analytical techniques (which would be next to impossible), Chapter 5 provides a thematic exploration of a few well-known analytical techniques along with their strengths and weaknesses. Following this discussion, the chapter concludes with an assessment on how both the validity and utility of various analytical techniques impacts on broader leadership (governance) challenges within ICs.

For the sake of simplicity, I have decided to deliberately use the word 'technique' as a catch-all for what really is an increasingly diverse range of analytical methods, tools, approaches, and technologies in use or being developed for deployment in ICs. Methods, tools, and technologies are not the same thing as 'techniques,' nonetheless the latter does share commonality with all the former in that techniques are *ways of doing something*. 'Tools,' 'methods,' and 'approaches' also convey a similar meaning. Using the one word 'technique' to discuss a range of analytical methods, tools, approaches, and techniques *together* allows for a conceptually neater discussion—one less focused on the semantics between analytical techniques vs analytical methods and more on how in each case they enable or inhibit intelligence analysis of an increasingly complex threat environment.

As highlighted above, an assessment of the validity and reliability of analytical techniques discussed in this chapter reveals several governance issues for IC leaders. The most critical analytical governance issues will be highlighted here. However, in Chapter 8 (The Future IC Leader and Governance Challenges), we will revisit what governance challenges are likely to be the most pressing for future leaders to solve and how they might do so.

Analytical techniques

Before starting a thematic exploration of analytical techniques, it is necessary first to frame the discussion by defining how I will define 'intelligence analysis'—given that analytical techniques are primarily applied in support of it. Again, there is a healthy growing volume of research—some historical and others contemporary—that have sought to define what 'intelligence analysis' *is* and what analysts *do* (Walsh 2011; Marrin 2011, 2017; George 2010; George and Bruce 2008). A key strand in the intelligence studies literature over several decades has been to demonstrate that understanding 'intelligence analysis' requires a fuller exploration of its multi-disciplinary heritage. In other words, understanding fully the role of intelligence analysis is dependent on practitioners and researchers mapping how it is informed by different disciplines, and which of these may assist in improving analytical outcomes for decision-makers. Another strand in the 'intelligence analysis' literature asks whether intelligence analysis is an art or science (Richards 2010). While this second strand may be intellectually engaging, I argue that its actual application to improving analysis within ICs is limited. It may be still interesting to debate for some *how much* an art or science intelligence analysis is. But I think it is largely self-evident with even a cursory understanding of how intelligence analysis is practiced in different intelligence contexts that it is informed by *both* social scientific and natural science perspectives. In short, intelligence analysis is an amalgamation of the two broad branches of knowledge, and the practice context determines how aspects of social or natural sciences are deployed. Leaving this debate aside, it's clear that 'intelligence analysis' can be conceptualised from a variety of different perspectives depending on one's own disciplinary or practitioner background. For the sake of simplicity, I define 'intelligence analysis' as 'both a cognitive and methodological approach to processing and evaluating information—some of which is privileged—in order to produce an assessment for a decision-maker about the security environment' (Walsh 2011: 236). This definition is sufficiently vague that it can be applied in different intelligence contexts.

The analytical techniques we focus on in the following section are explored using three themes: *social network analysis, structured analytical techniques, and data mining/machine learning and behavioural sciences.* A brief discussion will introduce how each theme has been used in different intelligence contexts. We will not spend much time on data mining/machine learning techniques as these were discussed in detail in Chapter 4 (Collection). Data mining/machine learning will also be raised again in Chapter 6 (ICT). In the final section, the advantages and disadvantages of each analytical technique will be explored along with the critical governance challenges IC leaders will have to navigate as they relate to improving analytical practice.

Social network analysis

Social network analysis (SNA) is a broader theme category for a range of related analytical techniques seeking to assess the associations between threat actors (and other people), activity, and places. The principles underlying SNA are not new with 'the advent of modern social network analysis generally attributed to Jacob L. Moreno, a sociologist, who became interested in social psychology in the 1930s (NAS 2019: 89).' 'Moreno attempted to explain and understand social behaviour using "socio-grams"—graphical representations of the links between an individual and others' (Ibid: 89).

While SNA has been used in national security and law enforcement contexts across the 'Five Eyes' for several decades (e.g. Sparrow 1991; Koschade 2006; Ressler 2006; Leuprecht *et al.* 2017: 902–921), its intellectual heritage can be sourced back to a broader range of disciplines such as social psychology, sociology, mathematics and anthropology (Scott and Carrington 2011; Wasserman and Faust 1994: 10). As Van Der Hulst (2009) highlights, SNA has for many intelligence agencies become a critical analytical investigative tool for studying adversary networks—regardless of whether these are terrorist or criminal in nature. There may be:

> motivational and group dynamic differences between organized crime and terrorist groups, they (nonetheless) share the same loosely connected and fluid ad hoc organizational principles. Hence, social ties and connections are to a large extent crucial determinants for the performance, sustainability and success of both criminal and terrorist organizations.
>
> (Van Der Hulst 2009: 102)

In terms of SNA practice in law enforcement, Strang makes the distinction that law enforcement since the 1970s has actually been deploying 'network analysis' and only more recently SNA (Strang 2014: 2). He defines link analysis as 'exploring the connections between individuals involved in criminal activity through their links to each other and through their links to organisations, objects, places and events related to the crimes' (Ibid: 2). In contrast, Strang's definition of SNA as 'the study of patterns of social connections, communications, exchange, friendship, trust, cooperation, kinship also secrecy, competition, mistrust and enmity' (Ibid: 5) suggests a tighter focus concentrating on the relationships *between people*. The social interaction between criminal actors is clearly useful for targeting recommendations, intelligence collection, and operational disruption.

The large volumes of criminal intelligence accumulating in law enforcement agencies and the complexity of organised crime has seen the automation of SNA in many agencies using analytical software such as I2, Palantir, and others.

Researchers are also increasingly focused on computer-driven SNA that can more rapidly detect, for example, gang networks and counter their associated violence. For example, Paulo and colleagues (2013) documented their development of new software called the Organizational, Relationship, and Contact Analyzer (ORCA) 'that is designed from the ground-up to apply new techniques in social network analysis and mining to support law enforcement.' The software combines techniques from logic programming, viral marketing, and community detection in a usable application custom-tailored for law enforcement intelligence support. The authors note their 'work is inspired by recent work in law enforcement that recognizes similarities between gang members and insurgents and identifies adaptations that can be made from current counter-insurgency (COIN) strategy to counter gang violence' (Paulo *et al.* 2013: 1). The research team evaluated ORCA on a police data set of 5418 arrests from a single police district over three periods of time, finding 11,421 relationships among the arrests (Ibid: 3). From this data, Paulo *et al.* 2013 used ORCA to assemble a social network consisting of 1468 individuals (who were members in one of 18 gangs) (Ibid: 3–4).

> ORCA was able to complete this assembly in addition to all analysis (determining degree of membership, finding seed sets, and developing ecosystems) taking 34.3 seconds to do so on a commodity laptop (Windows 8, B960 2.2 GHz processor with 4 GB RAM).
>
> (Ibid: 4–5)

This kind of research shows the potential of automated SNA techniques, but further work is required to improve their speed and accuracy.

SNA techniques have also been deployed for several decades in assessing the interaction within and between terrorist groups (Arquilla and Ronfeldt 2002). In the 1960s, the CIA deployed network analysis to understand the relationships between families and communities in communist strong areas of Thailand (Ressler 2006: 6). After the 9/11 attacks, there has been an increased interest in SNA from some IC agencies such as the CIA and NSA along with a greater number of scholars attempting to do SNA research on terrorist groups using open source information (Ibid: 3). Shortly after 9/11, Valdis Krebs mapped Al Qaeda's network using publicly available data on the AQ hijackers and running basic network principles through computer software (Ressler 2006: 3). Marc Sageman's 2004 book *Understanding Terrorism Networks* also provided a detailed understanding of clusters of regional AQ groups using open sources (Sageman 2004). Large databases now exist such as the Global Terrorism Database and the Profiles of Incidents involving CBRN and Non-State Actors (POICN) database (Binder and Ackerman 2019: 4–5), which provide scholars with additional opportunities to conduct SNA research on various terrorists and criminal groups. Researchers within and outside the IC continue to experiment with how best to use SNA techniques to destabilise and disrupt terrorist groups, and for understanding recruitment and resilience (Choudary and Singh 2015; Bright *et al.* 2020: 638-656). Increasingly, this research involves attempts to improve algorithms that can both automate and assess the significance of social interactions between threat actors closer to real time using YouTube, Twitter, Facebook, and other social media (Klausen *et al.* 2012; Ball 2013: 147–168; Zeng *et al.* 2015: 13–16; Chen 2008). Other research is looking at how computational networks can reflect changes in terrorist activity based on the implementation of counter-terrorism policies (Horne and Bestvater 2016: 87–110). In summary, it's clear that attempts are being made to improve the accuracy and automation (using big data and machine learning) of various SNA techniques. Equally though, as we shall see in the second section (intelligence governance issues), not only analysts but intelligence leaders will increasingly be challenged in their understanding on which machine learning-driven SNA techniques will be most useful and how they can be effectively deployed in ways that optimise collection and analytical processes.

Structured analytical techniques

The second cluster of analytical techniques explored here is structured analytical techniques (SATs). Structured analytical techniques include a diverse number of analytical tools (e.g. analysis of competing hypotheses (ACH), key assumptions check, red teaming, foresight analysis, and scenario generation) that developed originally and mainly in the US IC (particularly the CIA), but have also been picked up by other 'Five Eyes' countries over the last few decades (Walsh 2011, 2017; Heuer 1999, 2009: 529–545; Heur and Pherson 2010; Beebe and Pherson 2014; Pherson and Pherson 2017; Pherson and Heur 2020). SATs are informed by an amalgamation of a number of quantitative and qualitative social science methodologies: from cognitive psychology to political science as well as other disciplines such as business and engineering. SATs remain an evolving knowledge area in the intelligence studies field and within ICs. Their propagation across 'Five Eyes' ICs have waxed and waned in the last four decades for a range of reasons. There are lots of complex factors involved in both their utilisation and under-utilisation—one of which relates of course to whether IC leaders have been willing to fund training in SATs and their integration into work practice. Additionally, the extent to which SATs are used in some IC agencies has also varied due to differing organisational cultural attitudes about their utility to improving analysis. The key objectives of SATs is that they provide a structure for analysts to both enhance their critical thinking and contest cognitive biases, which may lead to faulty judgements. They also promote greater collaboration among analysts whose thinking and expertise can become siloed when writing products. For several decades now and particularly since 9/11, SATs have been promoted and analysts trained in them as a response to significant intelligence failure (e.g. Cuban Missile Crisis, 9/11, Assessment of WMD in Iraq). Anecdotally, from SATs analytical training sessions I have run in Australia and in other 'Five Eyes' countries, some analysts have reported to me that their use in the workplace have helped them think more critically and improve analytical judgements. Though, from an evidence-based perspective, there is less empirical evidence of whether SATs can improve both the reliability and validity of judgements made.

For example, in what ways do they add value to the analytical process beyond giving analysts systems and structures to think critically about complex issues? Some SATs such as ACH have been used for several decades now, but do they significantly improve validity and reliability of analytical judgements? In simple terms, what expectations should IC leaders, practitioners, and researchers have about their strengths and limitations in various analytical contexts?

We may now be starting to get some answers to these questions. More recently, empirical studies have investigated the value of SATs to improving the accuracy of analytical assessments and/or reducing cognitive biases. To date these studies have suggested they may be of limited value (Coulthart 2017; Whitesmith 2020). Both of these studies were mentioned briefly in Chapter 3 (Tasking and Coordination) in the context of how IC leaders need to address capability issues within strategic intelligence. However, we did not go into any detail about either. It's worth here in the context of our discussion of various analytical techniques that IC leaders need to evaluate for impact to briefly discuss each. In the US-based study, Coulthart systematically reviewed several sources in the literature as well as surveying 80 analysts at the US State Department's Bureau of Intelligence and Research (INR) for evidence that particular SATs improve analysis. Looking at six SATs in particular (e.g. devils advocacy, futures analysis, brainstorming, ACH, red teaming, team A/B), he concluded that 'in the aggregate there is low to moderate credible evidence that 6 techniques improve analysis most of the time' (2017: 384). Whitesmith's study in the UK is a little more detailed. Whitesmith conducted an experimental study to test whether one structured analytical method Analysis of Competing Hypotheses (ACH)—taught by the Cabinet Office to the United Kingdom's intelligence community—provides effective mitigation of the cognitive biases of *serial position effect*s and *confirmation bias* during intelligence analysis. She found that ACH had no statistically significant mitigative impact on the proportion of participants that exhibited serial position effects or confirmation bias, or the impact of confirmation bias on the analytical process. The most significant factor that influenced participants' judgements of the credibility of information was the possibility of deception or dishonesty (2020: 380-405).

Data mining/machine learning techniques

A third cluster of analytical techniques which IC leaders will continue to grapple with yet benefit from are data mining/machine learning techniques. In Chapters 3 (Tasking and Coordination) and 4 (Collection)—but particularly the latter—we discussed in detail how data mining, machine learning/AI is now continually driving both the tasking/coordination and collection of intelligence for analysis. Hence, there is no need to repeat that discussion here. But in brief, and based on discussions in earlier chapters, it's clear that data mining, machine learning/AI techniques are also changing the ways many of the analytical techniques covered above are now being applied. Data mining, machine learning/AI is helping to automate in some ways traditional analytical techniques as well as providing new capabilities in areas such as social network analysis, artificial neural networks, text mining, computational intelligence, swarm intelligence, and link analysis (see Chapter 3 Tasking and Coordination; Skillicorn 2009; Pedrycz and Chen 2014; Agarwal and Sureka 2015; Leuprecht *et al.* 2017: 902–921).

However, as highlighted in previous chapters, while big data analytical techniques are in many contexts improving the speed in which some data and intelligence can be collected and assessed, the signal to noise ratio within data can be low in many complex threat types such as terrorism and organised crime (Pedrycz and Chen 2014; Agarwal and Sureka 2015; Pramanik *et al.* 2017). Additionally, the predictive power of algorithms in complex multi-actor threat types such as terrorism and organised crime is not yet able to correlate confidently either what could be just data noise from signals or able to estimate future activities of threat actors. So regardless of the data mining techniques being used, there are significant governance issues remaining in how these techniques are deployed within ICs. These are briefly summarised in the final section of this chapter, but is also discussed again in Chapter 8 (The Future IC Leader and Governance Challenges), along with key governance issues identified in other chapters.

Social and behavioural sciences

Several psychological and other social sciences perspectives have also become relevant to intelligence analysis. In the earlier two sections, the focus was on SATs and how technical analytical tools (big data/machine learning) can improve analysis. In the next chapter (Chapter 6 ICT), we will come back to how social-behavioural sciences (SBS) can help improve the technical support for analysis. SBS can also help inform analytical workforce issues and these will be discussed in detail in Chapter 7 (Human Resources). In this third and final sub-section, (before the focus is shifted to a summary of key governance issues), we explore how SBS can improve analytical processes and outcomes. There are several SBS disciplines (e.g. psychology, economics, criminology, demography, political science, philosophy, and sociology) which can inform how intelligence analysts understand complex threat and risk issues (Fischoff 2011). As now underscored several times in previous chapters, the list of threat and risk issues since 9/11 have expanded both in volume and complexity. Nation states such as China and Russia are challenging the post-World War II order, which is bringing increased uncertainty and the possibility of mis-calculation in relations with others such as the United States. Jihadist terrorism, transnational criminal networks, border security, cyber security, and exploitation of dual-use technology for WMD/CBRN are also becoming more complex to understand. All of these threat/risk issues have at their core the need for ICs to understand the human behaviour that is behind them. The SBS discipline in a sense has long helped ICs to understand various aspects of human behaviour, but the links between both communities has been ad hoc and often at arm's length. The SBS academic community and analysts working in ICs while having much in common in terms of trying to understand human behaviour are different in other key ways. One point of difference is culture. Analysts, for example, generally have less time to research extensively topics given the often short deadlines in providing assessments for senior policy leaders. Intelligence analysts will often have to go with what information they can assemble in the available time without the luxury SBS researchers have in extensive collection of data to test hypotheses or generate theories. Additionally, intelligence analysts do not have the time to consider different methodological approaches to improve reproducibility, reliability, and validity of results as SBS researchers generally do.

Despite these workplace cultural differences, the growing complexity of threat/risk issues, particularly how threat actors are interacting with technology, is demanding that analysts embrace more formally SBS researchers in their assessment of evolving security threats. Since 9/11, there has been a greater awareness in ICs about how various SBS, particularly psychology, political science, and sociology, can help them understand threat actors. Nowhere has this been more obvious in SBS research than in studies of social media behaviour, which has helped shape IC understanding of terrorist's communications, propaganda, radicalisation, and operational planning. But also SBS studies of political (sentiment) behaviour is helping ICs understand emotions/behaviour in regime change and state failure. As noted earlier, social network analysis has also been informed by a range of SBS fields (anthropology, communication, sociology, and political science). It is increasingly the combination of different disciplines rather than one approach that is providing ICs with increasingly sophisticated network analysis for 'identifying key actors, their group identifications, and other network features' such as network adaptation (NAS 2019: 89).

The 2019 *National Academy of Sciences Decadal Survey of the Social and Behavioural Sciences* provides a detailed survey of SBS disciplines that may help intelligence analysts improve assessments across a range of threat/risk issues (NAS 2019). A similar, smaller report on the same topic as the NAS report (*Social Science Research and Intelligence in Australia*) was commissioned by Australia's ONI in 2019 (Withers *et al.* 2019).[1] In addition to understanding social network analysis of different state and non-state actors, the NAS report provides insights into other cross-disciplinary SBS areas such as the emerging field of social cybersecurity, which seeks to understand the human behaviours and motivations behind various types of cyber-attacks (e.g. malware, denial of service attacks, data breaches, disinformation campaigns, deception, and manipulation). SBS researchers can work with computer scientists to understand 'cyber-mediated changes in individual, group, societal, and political behaviours and outcomes, as well as to support the building of the cyber infrastructure needed to guard against cyber-mediated threats' (Ibid: 141–142). The objective of SBS researchers working in social cybersecurity is not just to understand behaviour or inform more robust protective cyber infrastructure, but to develop technology (e.g. cyber-forensics, social-media analytics, text mining, spatiotemporal data mining) and knowledge that will help 'assess, predict and mitigate instances of individual influence and community manipulation in which either humans or bots attempt to alter or control the cyber-mediated information environment' (Ibid: 142). In summary, social cybersecurity researchers are increasingly useful for intelligence analysts trying to understand the socio-political context of cyber activity that seeks to influence, persuade, and manipulate behaviour in the cyber realm—such as hostile state actors involved in foreign interference seeking to manipulate elections or non-state actors seeking to recruit or communicate with other like-minded individuals or groups. In the next section, the focus will shift from a summary of key analytical techniques to the governance challenges associated with their application in ICs. Space does not allow a full discussion of all the challenges, though there are several common governance problems to all 'Five Eyes' ICs which are raised briefly in the next section. The challenges raised here will also be revisited in the context of what IC leaders might do about them in Chapter 8 (The Future IC Leader and Governance Challenges).

Intelligence governance issues

In the discussion of analytical techniques above, one clear and common governance challenge is how IC leaders can promote innovation in these techniques (and others not discussed here) in an integrated, strategic, and sustainable way. There are several strands to this innovation challenge. One relates to addressing workforce and capability issues, including the education and training of analysts in various analytical techniques and/or facilitating the creation of operational environments that allow analysts easier access to external expertise. Analytic workforce issues will be discussed in detail in Chapter 7 (Human Resources). Another challenge in implementing analytical innovations is the ability of ICs to assess the performance of various analytical techniques such as those discussed above (e.g. SATs, machine learning and social-behavioural applied knowledge to intelligence analysis). Resources are limited and IC leaders will come under greater pressure to not only defend analytical capability investments, but demonstrate they are effective. George refers to 'a taxonomy of errors in intelligence analysis that impact on improving tradecraft (2010: 297).' These are cognitive, organisational, cultural, and political errors (Ibid). A key governance challenge, therefore, is how IC leaders can influence in a positive way the reduction of these errors in order to maximise the organisational integration of various innovative analytical techniques. All four of George's errors have played roles in poor implementation of various analytical techniques in ICs and law enforcement agencies in the past. Even potentially really useful techniques such as SNA have been either poorly implemented or as Van der Hulst (2009) argued 'neglected by law enforcement, intelligence and policy research, which has hampered the ability to counteract organized crime and terrorism' (Bruinsma and Bernasco 2004; Coles 2001; Chattoe and Hamill 2005; McIllwain 1999). Part of this neglect can be explained by the lack of experienced staff within ICs and law enforcement agencies of SNA and poor understanding of the most appropriate methodology to analyse networks.

Additionally, the introduction of various analytical techniques, particularly ones which require significant investment, are not solely decided by analysts because as George (2010) reminds us analytical performance is determined by a broad range of variables beyond the analyst's cognitive abilities such as organisational, political, and cultural factors. IC leaders also need to consider how from an agency or community perspective analytical innovation is evaluated to investigate whether they can make demonstrable improvements in the analytical processes and products. These questions will be returned to in the context of a range of other governance challenges future IC leaders will need to deal with in Chapter 8 (The Future IC Leader and Governance Challenges).

A second key governance issue related to the uptake of innovations in analytical techniques is how IC leaders ensure these tools can not only result in more skilled analysts, but also promote improved collaborative environments between analysts within agencies and across ICs. An increasingly complex security environment will require not only greater use of innovative analytical techniques, but a cross agency and community team-based approach to using them to maximise their utility in assessing emerging threats/risks. Since 9/11, there has been an increase in the number of collaborative tools and communities of practice established that can help analysts come together to make better use of analytical techniques and processes. For example, in the US IC, collaborative tools such as Intellipedia and A-Space have enabled the creation of living documents that can be updated and peer-reviewed periodically (Fingar 2011: 16–17). There are a myriad of other technical solutions being investigated to enhance analytical collaboration at tactical, operational, and strategic levels (e.g. Bier *et al.* 2010; Svenson *et al.* 2010; Wollocko *et al.* 2013). Given many collaboration tools are software or web based, a key challenge for IC leaders will be determining which systems can genuinely promote new and more efficient ways for analysts to work together that improves analytical reliability and validity, while at the same time does not add extended periods of time, particularly in circumstances when assessments are time sensitive.

A third governance challenge related to intelligence analysis and use of analytical techniques concerns whether analytical innovations can result in better evidence that underpins assessments. It should not just be up to analysts alone to determine at an agency or community-wide level how to improve the systems and processes for assessing analytical information quality, including how this is communicated, particularly strategic assessments which involve probability and forecasting (Dhami *et al.* 2015, 2018; Barnes 2016: 327–344; Mandel and Barnes 2018: 127–137; Tetlock & Mellers 2011). As noted earlier, improving the quality of information, including a stronger integration of more evidence-based information from SBS and the scientific community, should increase the reliability and validity of intelligence assessments. In terms of increasing the reliability and validity of assessments in the future, the governance challenge is two-fold. First, IC leaders will need to identify strategies which can better integrate quality evidence-based knowledge from within and outside ICs. Second, IC leaders will also need to implement initiatives that monitor and evaluate how the uptake of new analytical knowledge and techniques is improving assessment outcomes. There were a number of suggestions by IC leaders who completed the survey for the study on how to improve assessment outcomes. For example, one said:

> intelligence analysis tradecraft can be improved by integrating evidence-based assessment methodologies, exercising, war gaming, red teaming,

and case studies to assess accuracy and relevancy of intelligence products. Formal review workshops including decision makers and analysts should be considered. (survey respondent 4)

Another survey respondent suggested IC leaders needed to promote evidence-based approaches to determine how analytical innovations impact on performance and ultimately improve assessments (survey respondent 22). It is pleasing to see in the survey data IC leaders expressing the importance of validating analytical innovations, though there are few comments from participants on areas in particular that such an approach should be applied. Another important aspect of evaluating analytical performance and outcomes should include building on studies within decision-science. As Dhami *et al.* argue, this is 'because of its quantitative methods for measurement and testing cognition and behaviour, its theoretical models of human judgement and decision making, and its history of dealing with applied problems' (2015: 756). The growing complexity of the security environment and creeping volume of deceptive or 'fake' open source material creates additional risks to the rigor of the analytical process. Accordingly, it is likely IC leaders will be increasingly focused on how to improve agency/community systems for monitoring analytical performance over time to reduce significant episodes of cognitive bias or poor decision-making based on fake, deceptive, or low evidence information sources.

Related to better IC wide monitoring systems for evaluating analytical judgements is another metric—time. A key focus for IC leaders in the future will not just be how to increase the reliability and validity of analytical judgements, but also the speed in which analytical outcomes can reach decision-makers. Policy makers are saturated with information from various sources including ICs. A key governance challenge in an increasingly competitive information environment is how IC leaders can not only increase the value of assessments, but the speed in which they can be consumed by policy makers. Increasing the speed of analysis is both a cognitive and technological consideration. Improving the cognitive aspects will be addressed in the broader context of workforce planning issues discussed in Chapter 7 (HR). The technological aspects of 'speeding up analysis' will be considered in Chapter 6 (ICT).

Conclusion

This chapter explored thematically key analytical techniques used by ICs to support analytical processes and judgements. In each case, their strengths and weaknesses were identified. Second, the chapter discussed how innovation in analytical techniques and processes is the responsibility of both analysts and IC leaders. The increasing complexity of the security environment, limited resources, and a competitive information environment places more pressure on IC leaders now to adopt whole of agency and enterprise wide initiatives. In the case of analytical innovations, this means ones that are cost effective and can demonstrate empirically (to the extent that this is possible) how they increase the validity and reliability of assessments. This is not to suggest that all analytical techniques and innovations can or should be amenable to 'empirical testing.' Intelligence analysis will remain an art and science. However, the complexity of the security environment will demand additional analytical innovations that can augment traditional tradecraft. Innovations are likely to come from SBS and the scientific community whose traditions of deploying empirical methods for testing the validity and reliabilty of data sources will improve IC assessments. And indeed a number of IC leaders surveyed echoed the greater need for them to engage with SBS academics and the broader academic community (survey respondents 7 and 36). It will be up to IC leaders, however, to assess what constraints in their organisational structures, processes, and cultural environments might be limiting progress on analytical innovations—both endogenous and exogenous to IC—including their evaluation and implementation. How will IC leaders address the institutional obstacles to analytical innovation and create sustainable communities of analytic practice that result in more reliable and valid assessments for decision-makers? In the following chapters (Chapters 6 ICT; 7 HR; and 8 The Future IC Leader and Governance Challenges), we will address aspects of these questions further.

In the next chapter (Chapter 6 ICT), the focus shifts away from the leadership aspects of core intelligence processes (e.g. tasking and coordination, collection, and analysis) to two chapters which are centred on two key enabling activities (ICT, HR).[2] Chapter 6 will discuss the leadership challenges associated with information communications and technology (ICT) which support core intelligence processes. It will primarily focus on the role of artificial intelligence (AI) given this topic remains an enduring priority for ICs to manage and because its implementation is linked as noted earlier to our discussions on analytical innovation, but also other topics in the rest of the book.

Notes

1 I peer reviewed the Social Science Research and Intelligence in Australia report.
2 You will recall from Chapter 2 we mentioned there were five key enabling activities: ICT, HR, Legislation, Research, and Governance. While the book's next two chapters focus exclusively on ICT and HR, the other activities (research, legislation, and governance) cross over all chapters and are also explored more deeply in Chapter 8 (The Future IC Leader and Governance Challenges) and Chapter 9 (Leadership Development).

References

Agarwal, S., & Sureka, A. (2015). Applying social media intelligence for predicting and identifying online radicalisation and civil unrest oriented threats. *Computers and Society*, 1–18.

Arquilla, J., & Ronfeldt, D. (Eds.). (2002). *Networks and netwars: The future of terror, crime and military*. Washington, DC: RAND.

Ball, L. (2016). Automating social network analysis: A power tool for counter-terrorism. *Security Journal*, *29*(2), 147–168. doi: 10.1057/sj.2013.3

Barnes, A. (2016). Making intelligence analysis more intelligent: Using numeric probabilities. *Intelligence and National Security*, *31*(3), 327–344. doi:10.1080/02684 527.2014.994955

Beebe, S.M., & Pherson, R.H. (2014). *Cases in intelligence analysis: Structured analytic techniques in action*. Thousand Oaks, CA: CQ Press.

Bier, E.A., Card, S.K., & Bodnar, J.W. (2010). Principles and tools for collaborative entity-based intelligence analysis. *IEEE Transactions on Visualization and Computer Graphics*, *16*(2), 178–191.

Binder, M.K., & Ackerman, G.A. (2019). Pick your POICN: Introducing the profiles of incidents involving CBRN and non-state actors (POICN) database. *Studies in Conflict and Terrorism*, 1–25. doi: 10.1080/1057610X.2019.1577541

Bright, D., Whelan, C., & Harris-Hogan, S. (2018). On the durability of terrorist networks: Revealing the hidden connections between jihadist cells. *Studies in Conflict and Terrorism*, *43*(7), 638–656. doi: 10.1080/1057610X.2018.1494411

Bruinsma, G., & Bernasco, W. (2004). Criminal groups and transnational illegal markets. *Crime, Law and Social Change*, *41*(1), 79–94.

Carrington, P.J. (2011). Crime and social network analysis. In J. Scott and P. Carrington (Eds.), *SAGE handbook of social network analysis* (pp. 236–255). London: Sage Publications.

Chang, W., & Tetlock, P.E. (2016). Rethinking the training of intelligence analysts. *Intelligence and National Security*, *31*(6), 903–920.

Chattoe E., & Hamill H. (2005). It's not who you know - it's what you know about people you don't know that counts. *British Journal of Criminol*, *45*, 860–876.

Chen, H. (2008). *Sentiment and affect analysis of dark web forums: Measuring radicalization on the internet*. Paper presented at the 2008 IEEE international conference on intelligence and security informatics. 17–20 June 2008, Taipei, Taiwan.

Choudhary, P., & Singh, U. (2015). A survey on social network analysis for counter-terrorism. *International Journal of Computer and Applications*, *112*(9), 24–29.

Coles, N. (2001). It's not what you know - it's who you know that counts: Analysing serious crime groups as social networks. *British Journal of Criminol*, *41*, 580–594.

Coulthart, S.J. (2017). An evidence-based evaluation of 12 core structured analytic techniques. *International Journal of Intelligence and CounterIntelligence*, *30*(2), 368–391.

Dahl, E.J. (2017). Getting beyond analysis by anecdote: Improving intelligence analysis through the use of case studies. *Intelligence and National Security*, *32*(5), 563–578. doi: 10.1080/02684527.2017.1310967

Dhami, M.K. (2018). Towards an evidence-based approach to communicating uncertainty in intelligence analysis. *Intelligence and National Security*, *33*(2), 257–272. doi:10.10 80/02684527.2017.1394252

Dhami, M.K., Mandel, D.R., Mellers, B.A., & Tetlock, P.E. (2015). Improving intelligence analysis with decision science. *Perspectives on Psychological Science*, *10*(6), 753–757. doi:10.1177/1745691615598511

Fingar, T. (2011). *Reducing uncertainty*. Stanford, CA: Stanford University Press.

Fischoff, B. (2011). *Intelligence analysis: Behavioural and social scientific foundations*. Retrieved from Washington, DC.

Frank, A. (2017). Computational social science and intelligence analysis. *Intelligence and National Security*, *32*(5), 579–599. doi: 10.1080/02684527.2017.1310968

George, R.Z. (2010). Beyond analytic tradecraft. *International Journal of Intelligence and Counterintelligence*, *23*(2), 296–306. doi: 10.1080/08850600903566124

George, R.Z., & Bruce, J.B. (2008). *Analyzing intelligence: Origins, obstacles, and innovations*. Washington, DC: Georgetown University Press.

Heuer, R. (1999). *Psychology of intelligence analysis*. Washington, DC: Center for the Study of Intelligence.

Heuer Jr., R.J. (2009). The evolution of structured analytic techniques. *Presentation to the National Academy of Science, National Research Council Committee on Behavioural and Social Science Research to Improve Intelligence Analysis for National Security*, 529–545.

Heuer, R., & Pherson, R. (2010). *Structured analytical techniques for intelligence analysis*. Washington, DC: CQ Press.

Horne, C., & Bestvater, S. (2016). Assessing the effects of changes in British counterterrorism policy on radical Islamist networks in the UK, 1999–2008. *Behavioral Sciences of Terrorism and Political Aggression*, 8(2), 87–110.

Klausen, J., Barbieri, E.T., Reichlin-Melnick, A., & Zelin, A.Y. (2012). The YouTube jihadists: A social network analysis of Al-Muhajiroun's propaganda campaign. *Perspectives on Terrorism*, 6(1), 36–53.

Koschade, S. (2006). A social network analysis of Jemaah Islamiyah: The applications to counterterrorism and intelligence. *Studies in Conflict and Terrorism*, 29(6), 559–575.

Lahneman, W.J., & Arcos, R. (2017). Experiencing the art of intelligence: Using simulations/gaming for teaching intelligence and developing analysis and production skills. *Intelligence and National Security*, 32(7), 972–985. doi: 10.1080/02684527.2017.1328851

Leuprecht, C., Walther, O., Skillicorn, D.B., & Ryde-Collins, H. (2017). Hezbollah's global tentacles: A relational approach to convergence with transnational organized crime. *Terrorism and Political Violence*, 29(5), 902–921.

Mandel, D.R., & Barnes, A. (2018). Geopolitical forecasting skill in strategic intelligence. *Journal of Behavioral Decision Making*, 31(1), 127–137.

Marrin, S. (2007). Intelligence analysis theory: Explaining and predicting analytic responsibilities. *Intelligence and National Security*, 22(6), 821–846. doi: 10.1080/02684520701770634

Marrin, S. (2011). *Improving intelligence analysis: Bridging the gap between scholarship and practice*. Abingdon, UK: Routledge.

Marrin, S. (2017). Understanding and improving intelligence analysis by learning from other disciplines. *Intelligence and National Security*, 32(5), 539–547. doi: 10.1080/02684527.2017.1310913

Marrin, S. (2020). Analytic objectivity and science: Evaluating the US Intelligence Community's approach to applied epistemology. *Intelligence and National Security*, 35(3), 350–366. doi: 10.1080/02684527.2019.1710806

McIllwain, J.S. (1999) Organized crime: A social network approach. *Crime Law & Soc Chang 32*, 301–323.

NAS. (2019). *A decadal survey of the social and behavioural science: A research agenda for advancing intelligence analysis*. Retrieved from Washington, DC.

Paulo, D., Fischl, B., Markow, T., Martin, M., & Shakarian, P. (2013). *Social network intelligence analysis to combat street gang violence*. Paper presented at the 2013 IEEE/ACM international conference on advances in social networks analysis and mining (ASONAM), 25–28 August, Niagara Falls, ON.

Pedrycz, W., & Chen, S.-M. (2014). *Information granularity, big data, and computational intelligence* (Vol. 8). Berlin: Springer.

Pherson, K., & Pherson, R. (2017). *Critical thinking for strategic intelligence*. Washington, DC: CQ Press.

Pherson, R.H., & Heuer Jr., R.J. (2020). *Structured analytic techniques for intelligence analysis*. Thousand Oaks, CA: CQ Press.

Phythian, M. (2017). Intelligence analysis and social science methods: Exploring the potential for and possible limits of mutual learning. *Intelligence and National Security, 32*(5), 600–612. doi: 10.1080/02684527.2017.1310972

Pramanik, M.I., Lau, R.Y.K., Yue, W.T., Ye, Y., & Li, C. (2017). Big data analytics for security and criminal investigations. *Wiley Interdisciplinary Reviews: Data Mining and Knowledge Discovery, 7*(4), e1208. doi: 10.1002/widm.1208

Ressler, S. (2006). Social network analysis as an approach to combat terrorism: Past, present, and future research. *Homeland Security Affairs, 2*(2).

Richards, J. (2010). *The art and science of intelligence analysis*. Oxford: Oxford University Press.

Sageman, M. (2004). *Understanding terror networks*. Philadelphia, PA: University of Pennsylvania Press.

Shelton, A.M. (2014). Teaching analysis: Simulation strategies in the intelligence studies classroom. *Intelligence and National Security, 29*(2), 262–281. doi: 10.1080/02684527.2013.834219

Skillicorn, D. (2009). *Knowledge discovery for counterterrorism and law enforcement*. Boca Raton, FL: CRC Press.

Sparrow, M. (1991). Network vulnerabilities and strategic intelligence in law enforcement. *International Journal of Intelligence and Counterintelligence, 5*(3), 255–274.

Strang, S.J. (2014). Network analysis in criminal intelligence. In A. Masys (Ed.), *Networks and network analysis for defence and security* (pp. 1–26). Berlin: Springer.

Svenson, P., Forsgren, R., Kylesten, B., Berggren, P., Fah, W.R., Choo, M.S., & Hann, J.K.Y. (2010). *Swedish-Singapore studies of Bayesian Modelling techniques for tactical Intelligence analysis*. Paper presented at the 2010 13th International conference on information fusion (FUSION), 26–29 July, Edinburgh, UK.

Tetlock, P. E., & Mellers, B. A. (2011). Structuring accountability systems in organizations: Key trade-offs and critical unknowns. In Committee on Behavioral and Social Science Research to Improve Intelligence Analysis for National Security (Eds.), *Intelligence analysis: Behavioral and social scientific foundations* (pp. 249–270).

Van der Hulst, R.C. (2009). Introduction to Social Network Analysis (SNA) as an investigative tool. *Trends in Organized Crime, 12*(2), 101–121.

Walsh, P.F. (2011). *Intelligence and intelligence analysis*. Abingdon: UK: Routledge.

Walsh, P.F. (2017). Teaching intelligence in the twenty-first century: Towards an evidence-based approach for curriculum design. *Intelligence and National Security, 32*(7), 1005–1021. doi: 10.1080/02684527.2017.1328852

Waniek, M., Michalak, T.P., Wooldridge, M.J., & Rahwan, T. (2018). Hiding individuals and communities in a social network. *Nature Human Behaviour, 2*(2), 139–147. doi: 10.1038/s41562-017-0290-3

Wasserman, S.W., & Faust, K. (1994). *Social network analysis: Methods and applications*. Cambridge: Cambridge University Press.

Whitesmith, M. (2020). Experimental research in reducing the risk of cognitive bias in intelligence analysis. *International Journal of Intelligence and CounterIntelligence, 33*(2), 380–405. doi:10.1080/08850607.2019.1690329

Withers, G., Buchanan, E., West, L., Clements, D., & Austin, G. (2019). *Social science research and intelligence in Australia*. Canberra, ACT: Australian Academy of Social Sciences.

Wollocko, A.B., Farry, M.P., & Stark, R.F. (2013). *Supporting tactical intelligence using collaborative environments and social networking.* Paper presented at the SPIE defense, security, and sensing, 28 May, Baltimore, MD.

Zeng, D., Chen, H., Lusch, R., & Li, S.-H. (2010). Social media analytics and intelligence. *IEEE Intelligent Systems, 25*(6), 13–16.

6 Information and communication technologies (ICT)

Introduction

In Chapters 2–5, the discussion focused on the challenges leaders face in directing and optimising various *core intelligence processes* (tasking and coordination, collection, and analysis). You will recall from Chapter 2 that the core intelligence processes combined are like the machinery on the 'factory floor.' Without each of the component parts there is no process or product which can ultimately produce the intelligence decision-makers rely on. Chapters 2 to 5 highlighted several governance challenges and it should be clear by now that these do not have simple solutions particularly as the ever changing and increasingly complex security environment conspires further against 'hard and fast' remedies. In the next two chapters, I discuss several additional governance challenges, but these relate to *key enabling activities* (ICT and Human Resources). Again, you may recall that key enabling activities are those activities that provide the structure and support upon which core intelligence processes take place—whether that is within just one intelligence agency or across an entire community.

Having effective ICT systems, architecture, and processes has always been vital to the intelligence mission. Data, information, and knowledge may represent the lifeblood of the intelligence enterprise, but even the most valuable information in the world becomes redundant if it cannot be stored, accessed, shared, and integrated through reliable and adaptable ICT systems and processes.

Chapter 2 (Intelligence and Leadership) presented a number of themes that spoke to the kinds of ICT issues intelligence leaders have had to manage historically. In many respects, the ICT challenges remain persistently similar to the ones that emerged following the establishment of modern ICs from 1945 onwards. You will recall in Chapter 2 several themes were discussed, and the critical roles each played in the evolution of IC institutions from 1945 to the present. The fourth theme mentioned was 'knowledge management and information sharing.' Under this theme several issues were presented. As technological innovation facilitated a greater collection of open and covert information sources (particularly SIGINT)—the challenge for intelligence leaders quickly turned to finding technical and institutional solutions for extracting meaning from abundant sources. The other main difficulty became managing information overload and having organisational cultural and knowledge systems available to promote information sharing across ICs.

Similarly, Chapter 4 (Collection) presented a detailed discussion about technological and methodological approaches to information collection and processing. In particular, a significant amount of time was spent on how rapid changes in ICT facilitated the uptake of new collection platforms including using big data and machine learning, social media, and the exploitation of the dark web. In summary, discussion of ICT-related issues in Chapters 2 and 4 have provided much of the historical context for understanding what challenges IC leaders have faced in collecting, managing, and sharing information. This chapter builds on that foundation by focusing exclusively on the role of artificial intelligence (AI) in our ICs. It explores the likely challenges intelligence leaders will confront with the integration of AI into other ICT processes.

While the incorporation of AI technologies and processes into ICs are not new, I argue that understanding the opportunities and downsides for the further integration of AI remain complex, uncertain in many cases—and will continue to occupy current and future leaders into the next decade. Given the integration of AI into existing IC systems, processes, and cultures is likely to be consequential, it is fitting that we focus on it in this chapter, and the role intelligence leaders have in integrating it into various core intelligence processes. Simply put, as far as being the major ICT challenge IC leaders will face well into the next decade and longer, AI is the stand out.

Intelligence and AI

For many, AI is not just another trajectory in global technological change that all sectors of our societies need to both understand and harness. But is AI that consequential a change? Klaus Schwab, the former executive chairman of the World Economic Forum, argued that a series of technical, economic, and scientific changes begun to usher in AI at the turn of this century. But these changes were not just an 'add-on' to the digital revolution that brought rapid and significant innovation in computers from the 1960s and the internet in the 1990s. For Schwab, the rise of AI embodies what he refers to as the Fourth Industrial Revolution. Why a fourth revolution beyond the first (Industrial Revolution 1760–1840), second (mass-production late nineteenth century to early twentieth), and third (computer/digital 1960s to 1990s)?

Schwab argues that current and future developments in AI are ushering in a distinct and fourth revolution because of the velocity, breadth, depth, and transformative systems impact of change being facilitated by AI (Schwab 2017: 3). He suggests that it is not just the critical role of AI in bringing about this fourth revolution, but breakthroughs in closely related fields such as robotics IoT, autonomous vehicles, 3D printing, nano-technology, biotechnology, materials science, energy storage, and quantum computing are also contributing to ongoing, major disruptions to economies and societies in ways never seen before (Ibid).

Whether Schwab is correct and the cumulative impact of all AI innovations from the turn of the century to the present and beyond represents a fourth revolution globally is not entirely clear. It is likely that the significance of change can only be fully assessed in the rear vision of history. Regardless, as will be seen shortly, there is no question AI has and continues to be transformative across most economic and social sectors nationally and internationally. While the true extent of any transformative impact of AI globally cannot be known at least in the short to medium term, expectations are high across many economic and social sectors that AI will bring a profound change in nation-states and globally. For example, just in the commercial sector alone, business researchers Davenport and Ronanki (2019: 1) surveyed 250 executives familiar with their companies' use of cognitive technology and it showed three-quarters of them believed that AI will substantially transform their companies within three years.

Suggesting that AI is and will continue to bring substantial change to companies, industries, and society as a whole seems clear enough, but given the rapid development in multiple AI technologies it is less clear what we mean by AI. Lu suggest that AI is 'any theory, method, and technique that helps machines (especially computers) analyse, simulate, exploit, and explore human thinking process and behaviour' (2019: 1–2). It involves 'the computation and computing of data in intelligent ways in order to construct intelligent systems that allow computers to complete tasks that only humans were able to do in the past' (Ibid). Lu also describes AI as involving the application of 'computer hardware and software to simulate the underlying theories, approaches and techniques of human behaviour' (Ibid).

Nilsson in his historical study of AI defines it as 'that activity devoted to making machines intelligent, and intelligence is that quality that enables an entity to function appropriately and with foresight in its environment' (2010: preface). His account details the AI's contributions to achievements in multiple fields, including but not limited to biology, linguistics, psychology and cognitive sciences, neuroscience, mathematics, philosophy and logic, engineering and computer science. Lu's definition above is not dissimilar to Nilsson's, particularly on AI being multidisciplinary and interdisciplinary of natural sciences and social sciences consisting of many diversified disciplines (Lu 2019: 1–2).

Other definitions of AI emphasise the human and rational dimensions of what this kind of technology is meant to achieve. Russel and Norvig lay out eight definitions of AI against two dimensions that typify its objectives. The first (*human dimension*) is how machines might think humanly (i.e. problem solving, learning) or act humanly (i.e. creating machines that perform functions that require intelligence). The second dimension (*rationality*) refers to whether an AI system's performance can be 'rational.' This means it does the 'right thing' given what it knows (2016: 1–2).

What AI *is* and *does* can also be understood by surveying its historical development, which stretches back now for more than 60 years. It is not germane to our discussion of AI in the intelligence context to provide an exhaustive historical survey of AI. There are now an increasing number of good sources that do just that (see for example: Lu 2019; Flasinki 2016: 3–13; Russel and Norvig 2016). However, a quick historical overview is useful in providing a foundation and context for how AI has developed so that discussion in the next section (AI: National Security and Military Applications) is more meaningful for the reader.

Lu (2019) describes the evolution as being in three phases. The three developmental steps are the *initial phase (1956–1980)*, *the industrialisation phase (1980–2000)*, and *the explosion phase* (2000–) (2019: 7). In the initial phase (1956 to 1980), AI was only used to solve algebraic problems and prove geometric theorems. Nonetheless, progress was made during this earlier period. In 1956, at Dartmouth University in the United States, scientists participated in a conference to study and explore the use of machine simulation intelligence. The Dartmouth conference became a watershed moment and is also known as the origin of AI (Ibid: 7). In the second major development of AI (1980–2000), "knowledge processing" became the focus of AI research (Ibid: 8). Several European countries, Japan, and the United States started to allocate larger sums of money to support AI. A key goal was to 'create machines that support human-machine dialogue, translation and image recognition' (Ibid).

The third major developmental phase in AI (2000 to the present) was fuelled on the back of an increasing volume of data since the development of the internet. Sensors too were collecting a lot of different data, and in the first ten years of the twenty-first century the AI field built the foundations of machine learning tools to process the explosion in the volume and variety of data. Lu argues that at this time algorithms that have gone through generations of trials and errors started to produce impressive results. In the public arena at least, AI and machine learning began to grab extensive attention with IBM's "Deep Blue" defeating Kasparov in chess games and Google's AlphaGo defeating world champion Li Sedol. In essence, this third phase of the AI evolution has encapsulated a growth in deep learning and deep learning algorithms.

Deep learning can be thought of as a branch of machine learning which has pushed the boundaries of AI to higher levels. Deep learning techniques simulate large-scale structures of the cerebral cortex through large-scale data training and design complex multi-layer artificial neural networks (Lu 2019: 9–11). Artificial Neural Networks (ANNs) enable robots to learn and think like humans and to handle more complex tasks. In essence, progress in deep learning techniques is now allowing the development of even more complex machine learning models that can work on (train) ever increasing volumes of data to improve the accuracy of classification or prediction possible from such models. After now several decades of development, deep learning has produced many algorithms and models. Lu categorises deep learning into two types: *supervised* and *unsupervised* learning.

Supervised learning makes full use of AI prior knowledge to build robust data analysis models. Supervising training and learning models can improve the universality of model applications and improve the accuracy of data analysis. Unsupervised learning does not require any prior knowledge. Data analysis models can automate information mining and automatically build learning models. Unsupervised learning has been widely used in speech recognition and text retrieval.

(Lu 2019: 12–14)

The advancements in deep learning and big data now means AI applications are expanding across several commercial sectors including in monitoring water, energy, the stock market, logistics, health care, transport, retail, agriculture, and education. And naturally several deep learning and big data models continue to be developed across the national security and intelligence sectors. In the next section, we focus on a brief survey of how AI technology and knowledge is being applied across national security intelligence and the military sectors. In addition to exploring what kinds of AI innovations are being used by the broader national security intelligence and military enterprise, the section shows how these potentially strengthen intelligence capabilities by creating enhanced opportunities for more effective collection and analysis of information.

AI: national security intelligence and military applications

The discussion here is not exhaustive; rather the objective is to provide sufficient context to allow a more detailed exploration of the challenges AI poses for IC leaders. The discussion is organised around three broad sub-headings: *national security*, *cyber*, and *military* applications. I recognise using these headings is fairly arbitrary given how the issues discussed under each frequently intersect across all three. Nonetheless, using sub-headings provides some organisation— particularly in how AI has improved intelligence capabilities across different areas of both the national security and military enterprises. After a discussion of how AI/machine learning has been applied by ICs, the final section will explore the challenges leaders confront with integrating such technology, methodologies, and processes into their agencies. On this last point, Chapter 8 (The Future IC Leader and Governance Challenges) also reflects further on the implications of challenges raised here and how IC leaders might begin to address them.

National security

For decades now, but particularly since the digital revolution of the 1990s, 'Five Eyes' ICs have not been able to analyse the burgeoning volumes of information available to them despite increased capabilities to collect it. The volume, velocity, and variety of information now available, particularly unstructured sources (documents, social media, digital pictures, videos), and an increasing volume of information from sensors (i.e. IoT) means more information is collected than can be analysed by any IC (Brantly 2018: 566). This point was also made earlier in Chapter 4 (Collection).

Most of this new data is unstructured sensor or text data and stored across unintegrated databases. For intelligence agencies, this creates both an opportunity and a challenge; there is more data to analyse and draw useful conclusions from, but finding the needle in so much hay is getting tougher. All 'Five Eyes' ICs each day collect more raw intelligence data than their entire workforce could effectively analyse in their combined lifetimes. So analysts must prioritise and triage which collected information to analyse, and increasingly this has meant relying on computer searches and databases to more quickly access, manage, and assess the information. The ability to quickly interrogate databases has clearly been advantageous for the analysis of SIGINT, but the other trend has been the partial automation in the analysis of some kinds of GEOINT such as satellite reconnaissance using machine learning techniques. Machine learning techniques will likely continue to be useful in processing SIGINT and ELINT, but also allow even more sophisticated pattern recognition across data sets (Allen and Chan 2017: 27; Horowitz *et al.* 2018). Further, as discussed in the next section, it's increasingly clear that AI will continue to play a significant role in cyber security and defence issues (Payne 2018: 7–32).

Additionally, over the last decade several AI and machine learning projects have been developed to improve predictive analytics and sense-making capabilities of ICs. In the United States, the Intelligence Advanced Research Projects Activity (IARPA) has sponsored several programs to improve the forecasting of complex and emerging events. Many programs have used forecasting tournaments involving people from around the world to generate forecasts about 'thousands of real-world events.' 'All of our programs on predictive analytics do use this tournament style of funding and evaluating research,' according to Jason Matheny, IARPA's former director (Seffers 2015: 19–22). Matheny cites several programs that have demonstrated 'predictive success' including the Open Source Indicators program, where he suggested they were able to predict disease outbreak earlier than traditional reporting (Ibid). This program used a crowdsourcing technique in which people across the globe offered their predictions on several events (e.g. political uprisings, disease outbreaks, and elections). The data analysis relied on social media trends and web queries indicating potential behaviour suggestive of a disease outbreak or political uprising. The collection methods were automated and used machine learning to filter through several billions of data points looking for a signal that an event may be about to happen (Ibid).

Other IARPA sponsored AI/machine learning analytical programs have been developed to improve IC's capability to detect earlier cyber-attacks. One program looked not just at suspicious activity on a computer, but data outside of a network that might indicate an impending cyber-attack. Such external indicators sources could include patterns of web search queries and black market activity relating to malware (Ibid). Still other programs such as the Scientific advances to Continuous Insider Threat Evaluation (SCITE) program examines a broad array of insider threats, including mass shootings, cyber-attacks, and industrial espionage. The objective again is to use AI/machine learning methodologies to look for indicators for insider threat detection that could include kinetic attacks in IC (including military facilities) as well as cyber-attacks resulting in the loss of intellectual property (Seffers 2015: 19–22).

The next section expands on how AI/machine learning applications have been used to improve cyber capabilities of ICs. For the remaining space here, the discussion focuses on AI/machine learning and counter-terrorism. The increase in the scale and reach of global terrorism since 9/11 has shown that 'Five Eyes' ICs needed to develop faster ways to collect and analyse vast amounts of data and information in real time in order to prevent and disrupt as much as possible attacks in their homelands or abroad. IC's traditional reliance on SIGINT and even HUMINT to some extent has made getting a close to real-time picture of terrorist activities, plans, and movements increasingly difficult. Counter-intelligence awareness by AL-Qaeda and the Islamic State of IC's interception capabilities and the growth in sophistication and their use of encrypted communications is making traditional physical and technical surveillance challenging. Against this backdrop, advancements in data mining, AI/machine learning have provided ICs new platforms to collect and synthesise information useful in identifying terrorist activity in real time. As Ganor suggests, 'everyone has a digital footprint (e.g. cell phones, email, biometrics, social network, smart phone applications) that can be tracked and processed' (2019: 3). In particular, certain kinds of social media such as Twitter can be studied to better understand terrorist communications, particularly operational planning—but also individuals that may be in the process of becoming radicalised (Ibid). For 'Five Eyes' ICs, collecting or accessing bulk digital data as will be discussed later is not without its ongoing concerns about what is appropriate, proportionate, and what might become an excessive invasion in the privacy of other law-abiding citizens. These privacy issues were flagged previously in Chapter 4 (Collection). But the increasing advances in the collection and analytical synthesis of big data/AI/machine learning systems clearly will continue to have benefits for ICs in identifying more quickly and accurately those suspected of terrorist activities. It is not just tracing the digital footprint of individuals working in larger terrorist groups such as the Islamic State that this type of technology will continue to be useful, but also in harder counter-terrorism cases involving lone actor attacks, which in some cases can be more spontaneous. AI/machine learning applications may not have the capability to predict 'the next lone actor' attack, but they can be used to develop a pattern of life on suspects, which can increase the chances that ICs can detect and disrupt their plans. Another application of AI/machine learning technology in the counter-terrorism context—autonomous drones—has been in place now for several decades. The CIA and US Department of Defense has used them in para-military missions in Afghanistan, Iraq, and West Africa and more broadly globally for surveillance and targeted killing of high-value terrorist targets from the Bush administration onwards (Johnson *et al.* 2017). Other 'Five Eyes' countries such as Australia are now more actively deploying drones too for counter-terrorism operations overseas (Walsh 2017: 429–433).

AI and cyber applications

The effectiveness of various AI/machine learning techniques to 'predict' indicators for an impending cyber-attack—whether state or non-state-based—in origin remains an open question. However, what is clearer is how the development of various cyber tools has significantly increased ICs, defence and law enforcement agencies' surveillance and espionage capabilities (Leenen and Meyer 2019: 42–63). Physical surveillance, i.e. people following persons of interest in physical spaces, is not extinct, yet advances in digital surveillance reduces the number of intelligence officers now required to collect intelligence on people.

To put this in perspective, Schneier shows the significance in the lift in AI capabilities by comparing how:

> the exceptionally paranoid East German government had 102,000 Stasi surveilling a population of 17 million: that's one spy for every 166 citizens. By comparison, using digital surveillance, governments and corporations can surveil the digital activities of billions of individuals with only a few thousand staff.
>
> (cited in Allen and Chan 2017: 18)

Increased adoption of AI in the cyber domain will further augment the power of those individuals operating and supervising these surveillance tools and systems, which brings with it not only efficacy issues, but also ethical ones, particularly related to reasonable expectations of privacy and free speech in liberal democratic countries. The challenges and downsides to enhanced AI/machine learning applications to cyber and other threats are discussed in greater detail below. We also come back to the broader ethical dilemmas IC leaders will confront in Chapter 8 (The Future IC Leader and Governance Challenges).

But what about other AI/machine learning applications to improve IC cyber capabilities? For some time now, cyber security/defence has been relying on the capabilities of AI and big data processing (Leenen and Meyer 2019: 42–63; Seker 2019; Alazab and Tang 2019). Big data provides the huge sets of data AI algorithms require to train data and to learn, i.e. to determine what normal behaviour is and thus to be able to detect abnormal events. These technologies are used for intrusion detection, malware classification and attribution, attack prediction, and other applications. There are several military applications of AI, but that discussion will occur under the next section. One area, however, that is critical to the ongoing effective functioning of all ICs is the protection of information security. AI/machine learning innovations have improved security protection capabilities for ICs by searching in real time through large volumes of data for cyber-attacks, system vulnerabilities and failures, IoT security, and other network anomalies (Lu 2019: 20). Along with advances in information security, however, adversaries will also be able to use similar AI machine learning technology for offensive cyber-attacks by deploying email phishing and botnet attacks (Johnson 2019: 151).

Military applications of AI

In a broader sense, several militaries are now employing at an increasing rate aspects of AI into their capabilities and broader doctrines. In particular, three countries—the United States, China, and Russia—are reported to be developing serious *military* AI technologies, which likely in the future will provide significant military advantage to these nation's militaries. Strategic military plans and increased investment for the development of and investment in AI/machine learning of course is not just about advantage, but larger powers seeking to grow military superiority over other similar powers. Vladimir Putin has publicly announced Russia's intent to pursue AI technologies, stating, 'whoever becomes the leader in this field will rule the world' (cited in Hoadley and Lucas 2018: 1). Russia has targeted reportedly 30 per cent of its entire military force structure to be robotic by 2025 (Johnson 2019: 148).

Further, in July 2017, China's State Council issued the new generation Artificial Intelligence Development Plan (AIDP), which is meant to enhance national (economic) competitiveness and protect national security (Allen 2019: 5). The AIDP also clearly articulates a role for AI technology becoming even more embedded in the field of national defence innovation (Ibid). In February 2019, the United States Department of Defense also launched a defence strategy, which included amongst other things an increased focus on speed and agility, improving situational awareness, and creating a leading AI workforce (DOD 2018: 7). This strategy has built on earlier work done in the Pentagon such as the 2016 release of a National Artificial Intelligence Research and Development Plan (Johnson 2019: 149).

Such military AI strategies attempt to provide a more coordinated approach to research and development and application of AI/machine learning than hitherto has been the case in the last two decades in the United States and other 'Five Eyes' countries. In the last two decades, AI/machine learning has been applied to a range of military objectives at the strategic level (e.g. managing cognitive heuristics and group think) and operational tactical levels (e.g. reducing command decision-making time, improving situational awareness, and autonomous weapon systems).

Several sources provide detailed summaries and analysis of various applications (Wasilow and Thorpe 2019; Johnson 2019: 147–169; Lele 2019: 29–42; Payne 2018: 7–32). In this section, however, I will summarise thematically some of the ways AI/machine learning have been applied in military contexts as both force enablers and multipliers (Johnson 2019: 148) rather than providing detailed analysis of specific technology. Readers looking for more in-depth analysis of AI/machine learning technology can explore the references listed in the preceding paragraph. The first thematic area (surveillance) is not dissimilar to some of the AI developments discussed above (see national security and cyber sections). AI/machine learning applications have automated some of the surveillance functions soldiers and military intelligence personnel may traditionally have carried out. For instance, neural networks can scrutinise surveillance video and alert soldiers to specific frames that contain objects of interest such as vehicles, weapons, or persons (Wasilow and Thorpe 2019: 37). Additionally, as noted in the context of counter-terrorism, facial recognition software is also useful in alerting military forces when a person of interest emerges in video surveillance. Just as in the national security and cyber contexts, the application of AI/machine learning also holds the promise potentially of fusing more effectively large amounts of disparate structured, unstructured as well as data from sensors in the battlefield. The key advantages are less manual processing and the possibility of more informed and quicker decisions in the battle space.

A third discernible AI/machine learning theme in the defence context is the development of AI enhanced autonomous weapons and robotic systems that 'can be given dull, dirty, and dangerous jobs, reducing physical risk to soldiers and enabling them to concentrate their efforts elsewhere' (Wasilow and Thorpe 2019: 37; Payne 2018: 7–32). For example, it is likely soon that leaving aside the ethical and legal issues, several larger states may deploy fully autonomous armed aerial and marine vehicles. Israel is already operating a variant of this kind of AI enabled technology, the Loitering Attack Munitions (LAM), which can loiter over targets (enemy radar or ships) and is pre-programmed with targeting criteria (Johnson 2019: 151).

Developments in swarm technology will also be able to deploy weaponised drone swarms in the battle space—making it difficult even for larger militaries to counter them. It is increasingly possible that development in lethal autonomous weapons systems (operated by robots instead of humans) may result in the obsolescence in some military platforms over the next five to ten years. As Wasilow and Thorpe note:

> as of 2013, the United States possessed 14,776 military aircraft, some of which cost more than $100 million per unit. A high-quality quadcopter UAV currently costs roughly $1,000, meaning that for the price of a single high-end aircraft, a military could acquire one million drones.
>
> (2019: 21–22)

Given the growth in the robotics market, prices for autonomous vehicles with military applications such as drones are expected to decrease further this decade. Leaving aside the investments larger countries such as the United States, China, and Russia can spend on this technology, advances in the precision of drones with larger payload present military advantages to smaller states with weaker militaries as well. Such AI/machine learning-enabled technology is likely to present force posture and protection challenges for all militaries as they seek to train and re-train personnel and develop counter-measures to lethal autonomous weapons.

IC leadership challenges

It should be clear from the summary above there are plenty of advantages in the application and integration of AI/machine learning across 'Five Eyes' ICs. Nonetheless, with advantages comes challenges that both the current and future IC leadership cadre will need to address. Left unaddressed they will result in the reduction of the capability dividend many AI/machine learning applications can offer ICs. A failure by IC leaders to engage with the many AI/machine learning challenges will also increase the friction of non-technical factors associated with AI in ICs, and potentially degrade the legitimacy of the work intelligence agencies do in liberal democratic states. In this last section, I summarise key challenges for leaders using three broad sub-headings: *technology, counter-intelligence*, and *social and ethical challenges*. Limited space does not allow a 'deep dive' into all the issues associated with each sub-heading. The key objective instead is to contextualise and summarise the key leadership challenges going forward, particularly those that create intelligence governance issues into the foreseeable future. Chapter 8 (The Future IC Leader and Governance Challenges) will pick up on what leaders will need to do to address the governance issues raised here.

Technology challenges

As noted, AI advancements in the form of deep learning and machine learning have shown significant breakthroughs for supervised learning applications including, for example, in computer vision, speech recognition, chatbots, and autonomous driving (Zhao and Flenner 2019: 35). While many supervised learning applications are improving, there remain technological constraints on using them when precision, rigor, and deeper clarity is required in many security applications ICs are confronted with. As Payne (2018: 10) suggests, at least in the military context:

> there is considerable wariness that the hype and publicity surrounding deep learning will not pan out as dramatic breakthroughs in cognition that might approach human-level capacity—for example in satisficing between conflicting goals, or in using imagination and memory flexibly to cope with novel scenarios. The AI of today is rather narrow and brittle—adept in its area of expertise, but not at shifting to new tasks. Nevertheless, the rapid progress in AI research, especially of hybrid approaches that utilise multiple AI techniques, along with increasingly powerful hardware on which to run algorithms, suggests the potential for AI to significantly affect existing military activities in the short to medium term, even if it falls short of simulating human-level cognition any time soon.

It may be that in more high-volume crimes such as break and enters or credit card fraud, there is growing confidence in the ability of algorithms by end users that their performance can demonstrate irregularities in large volumes of crime which are indicative a crime is committed or about to be committed. However, in other complex security threats (e.g. organised crime and terrorism) which require more sophisticated use of deep learning algorithms, IC end users cannot yet trust in all circumstances their performance or ability for them to classify relevant examples. For example, to 'find a terrorist pattern' or 'predict' the likelihood of such an offence requires the algorithmic classification of a range of data, but in many cases there is insufficient data for data scientists to build high confidence level deep learning networks for such an offence.

As noted earlier, in the United States, IARPA has funded several AI/machine learning analytical programs to improve IC's capability to detect earlier more complex threat and events such as cyber-attacks and political instability. While progress is being made in improving the confidence levels of deep learning networks, there is still a lot more understanding required about how deep learning algorithms perform and how to get them to perform better. As Zhao and Flenner note:

> it is easy to find examples that are easily classified by humans but misclassified by deep learning algorithms. Furthermore, it has been demonstrated that a small but visually imperceptible change to a correctly classified image will result in the misclassification of the image. Therefore, there exists a fundamental instability in the learned functions.
>
> (2019: 36)

In summary, Zhao and Flenner highlight four of the main challenges in applying the AI revolution to security applications: 'the lack of adequate samples for classification tasks, short timescales for learning, fewer computational resources, and adversarial behaviour' (Ibid). At a high level, national and international security needs AI in a wide range of forms but the results and the limitations of deep learning continue to raise many questions with respect to applications in security contexts (Ibid). Other key questions that IC leaders and military commanders will need to address from future developments in machine learning techniques relate to critical operational areas where lives may be at stake. For example, how well are autonomous systems going to be at not only processing data but perceiving, learning, deciding, and acting on their own? Will future AI/machine learning technology deployed in the IC and broader security context also be unable to 'explain their decisions and actions' to human users? Both questions are important because they go to the 'intelligent reliability,' safety, and explainability power of autonomous capabilities in critical life and death situations. DARPA defines explainable AI as 'AI systems that can explain their rationale to a human user, characterize their strengths and weaknesses, and convey an understanding of how they will behave in the future' (Gunning and Aha 2019: 44–58). DARPA launched its explainable artificial intelligence (XAI) program in May 2017 to address such issues.

Another challenge with AI/machine learning technology in general, but particularly applied to IC and security issues, is how to integrate a variety of big data sets with other existing intelligence information systems. A related problem to the integration of AI/machine learning is how to improve semantic technology so that there exists common vocabularies for information and shared understanding of domains in how information is described before it is automated for processing and decision-making. Current improvements in some semantic technologies will likely improve the management and integration of different data sets by extracting commonly understood meaning and insights—thereby reducing large numbers of false positives in areas such as cyber security and terrorism. But IC leaders will need to keep abreast of these developments to ensure a coordinated approach to technical solutions across their agencies and their broader intelligence communities.

Counter-intelligence challenges

In addition to IC leaders being able to navigate the inevitable technological challenges arising from applying AI/machine learning systems in their agencies, they will also need to address several counter-intelligence issues that will likely rise with the use of such technology and by others—particularly adversaries. The development of AI has relied on access to cloud computing, the internet, and big data, but as Lu suggests on the other hand, internet-based hackers and viruses can pose a huge threat to AI (2019: 22–23). Many applications of AI in the military, national security, and intelligence context are also dual-use technology—making them open to malignant exploitation by state and non-state actors of concern for 'Five Eyes' countries. Machine learning advancements to protect from cyberattacks could make intelligence and national security information systems vulnerable to newer kinds of attacks— given bad actors could have access to similar knowledge and skills than ICs. The automation of systems, particularly in cyber to detect threats, could be targeted for disruption or distributing fake information. Allen and Chan list several examples of how developing AI/machine learning applications could pose counter-intelligence issues for IC leaders, who will be responsible for preventing, disrupting, and reducing them. For example, the training data used in machine learning systems for facial data, voice, videos, audios, and documents could be manipulated, enhanced, or forged (2017: 25).

We have also seen in recent years an increasing volume in and sophistication of state actors such as Russia prepared to manipulate social media sources with fake information in order to influence the 2016 US presidential election. It is likely that Russia and other state actors (China, North Korea) will continue to exploit new AI/machine learning developments in 'Five Eyes' countries, including as Allen and Cohen suggest:

> using hackers to take control of an official news organisation website; or social media account being used to spread not only false text, but also false video and audio. A network of social media bots could then be used to spread the fake messaging rapidly and influence a broad number of individuals.
>
> (Ibid)

In summary, as the growth in AI/machine learning generated data and other information available to ICs grows, so too does its vulnerability to non-state and adversarial state actor exploitation. This complicates an already difficult environment ICs face about how to assess the provenance of intelligence collected and the impacts it has on analytical assessments. IC leaders along with their military counterparts will need to design counter-intelligence strategies that can more effectively detect, disrupt, and manage malevolent exploitation of AI/machine learning automated collection and analytical systems. However, as seen in other dual use technology areas that could be weaponised, such as biotechnology (Walsh 2018), there remain critical uncertainties around how 'Five Eyes' adversaries will exploit dual use AI technology in ways that weaken capabilities or present new threats to their ICs.

Social and ethical challenges

The rapid development of AI is bringing significant change, much of it positive across a range of economic sectors—but on the other hand, there are now equally profound concerns about many of its potential downside effects—many of which present social and ethical challenges. From a social and ethical perspective, several open questions have now been raised by the public, commentators, policy makers, and researchers. The objective in this final section is not to provide a detailed analysis of all the social and ethical challenges associated with AI applications in either 'Five Eyes' ICs or society more generally. Instead, given limited space, it is more germane to raise in a general sense some of the key questions that IC leaders will need to think about when applying AI/machine learning to support and/or lead intelligence capabilities and activities.

One key question is whose responsibility is it to ensure increasingly automated and robotic systems remain both secure and controllable by humans? Who for instance is responsible for accidents and deaths that occur when a robot is operating, for example, a vehicle or as noted earlier a surveillance drone? Secondly, although different intelligence contexts may raise specific ethical dilemmas, in a broader sense what kinds of ethical risk management of AI is needed in 'Five Eyes' ICs? Thirdly, while AI systems have demonstrated their ability to increase productivity in several sectors by releasing humans from monotonous work such as collating or monitoring information sources, the automation of aspects of some roles in the workplace including in ICs will continue to impact on labour markets and potentially on the structure of society itself (Lu 2019: 22–23).

It's not yet possible to provide a complete answer to the first question on who is responsible legally or ethically for the security and control of AI systems. It's clear that the international community, nation-states, and the public and private sector likely all have a role. The increasing incorporation of AI/machine learning applications into ICs means that their leadership needs to consider the ethical and legal dimension of using them, particularly those that act autonomously in defence and intelligence contexts, which can have privacy or lethal consequences. We have seen in other chapters how ICs' improved data mining capabilities have sped up and expanded intelligence collection—yet has also raised concerns about how even anonymised data can disclose personal privacy of citizens (Walsh and Miller 2016). Continued advances in AI systems that can be used for surveillance beyond data such as biometrics will only compound further the ethical dilemmas IC leaders currently face in using a range of collection platforms.

The second question posed above: what kind of ethical risk management of AI is needed in 'Five Eyes' ICs? Again, a definitive answer to such a question is difficult.

It is likely that ethical dilemmas will be contextually driven for different agencies depending on their mission and legislative framework. AI technological development is rapid and it's also likely that IC leaders will need to adopt ethical risk management frameworks that can be revisited in some cases in real time as opposed to necessarily via set and forget guidelines. It's clear that in some countries such as China many of the ethical risks associated with AI applications in national security and broader societal contexts have been put aside as Beijing seeks to build further its social credit scoring system—a system which results in a greater 'digital repression' of citizens via intrusive AI enabled surveillance systems (Feldstein 2019; Allen 2019). In liberal democracies such as the 'Five Eyes' countries, IC leaders of course should not be expected, nor is it advisable that they develop risk management frameworks on their own. AI/machine learning scientists, policy makers, and ethicists should collaborate with leaders to ensure that frameworks will identify risks to privacy and human rights—yet still promote the use of new AI technologies in ways that improve collection and analytical functions. Encouragingly, in recent years some research is emerging which seeks to inform the kinds of frameworks IC leaders and those also in the broader military and national security context might need to consider in order to navigate ethics and efficacy issues related to AI applications (Babuta *et al.* 2020; Yu *et al.*: 1–7; Akerkar 2019: 1–18; Tuffley 2019: 170–189; Wasilow and Thorpe 2019; Iphofen and Kritikos 2019: 1–15).

For example, research by Wasilow and Thorpe developed an ethics assessment framework for the Canadian Armed Forces (CAF) 'to help technology developers, policymakers, decision makers, and other stakeholders identify and broadly consider potential ethical issues that might arise with the military use and integration of emerging AI and robotics technologies of interest' (2019: 37–38). The assessment framework includes 12 principles, which are compliant with Canada's Department of National Defense and Defense Force code of values and ethics. The 12 principles are based on Jus Ad Bellum criteria. In other words, just as in the conventional warfare sense, the use of AI in conflict should still be justifiable (in self-defence) and proportional (Ibid).

Similarly, it is encouraging that AI ethics assessment research is not just being generated by social scientists, but also technical experts such as computer scientists and engineers in the private sector, who are also raising the importance of designing in ethical principles into algorithms/AI systems (Yu *et al.* 2018; Whittlestone *et al.* 2019). Whittlestone *et al.* (2019) provide a road map for working on the ethical and societal implications of algorithms, data, and AI. Whittlestone *et al.*, like others, offer a set of high-level guidelines such as personal data access, embedding values into autonomous intelligence systems, ethical research, and design, safety and benefit, addressing economics and legal issues (Ibid). But how any of the principles articulated in recent studies can be implemented across 'Five Eyes' ICs or agreed to by nations more universally remains unclear. It's clear though that IC leaders now and into the future have the opportunity to encourage and learn from a cross-fertilisation of ideas across academia, the public, and private sector to more proactively address potential ethical issues that will arise with the application of AI into their intelligence enterprises.

The third key question that will need consideration by IC leaders is while automating some collection and analytical functions will likely improve efficiencies and in some case even accuracy it is less clear what the impact of adopting AI technology will have for the workforce across 'Five Eyes' ICs. It is difficult to know precisely whether impacts on workforce will be mainly positive or negative in the short to medium term. It is likely intelligence agencies across each IC will be affected in different ways depending on their missions (e.g. military, national security, and law enforcement) and functions (analytical, collection, or mixed). Another important variable will be the level of decision-making that the intelligence agency is using its AI capability for. In other words, you might expect at least in the short to medium term, machine AI/machine learning technology will automate more tactical and operational rather than strategic intelligence activities. As discussed earlier, AI/machine learning applications are already either supplementing or replacing humans in a range of high volume data collation activities in SIGINT and IMINT.

But will robots take over more complicated tasks in ICs such as making analytical judgements, which go beyond merely assembling data or looking for patterns, but also require higher cognitive assessments about human thinking and understand human intentions? This question is currently the subject of extensive research. A key part of this research is can robots ever learn like humans. This question itself requires a deeper epistemological reflection, understanding, and agreement about what constitutes learning. Already, advances now in AI applications suggest machines like humans use rules to learn, but human learning is also highly contextual, intuitive, and socio-culturally bounded (Hasse 2019: 335–364).

Nonetheless, larger-scale AI applications in ICs will inevitably see the development of more intelligent machines that may replace certain analytical skills and knowledge of humans (Hare and Coghill 2016: 858–870). But this trend is neither linear nor can technological determinism be the only lens in which IC workforce changes are determined. IC leaders and policy makers will have a significant role in engineering how enhanced intelligent machines replace parts of the workforce, rather than it being a case of humans being removed completely in for example two decades. It is likely that as some traditional IC analytical workforce roles will be replaced by AI applications (e.g. filtering, categorising, and searching) yet other human knowledge and skill sets will grow in demand, particularly in assessing complex emerging threats and in assessing counter-intelligence vulnerabilities 'Five Eyes' IC will face as state and non-state actors attempt to use AI against them. But workforce changes will bring anxieties and require adept management by IC leaders—a key theme to be explored in our next chapter (Chapter 7 Human Resources).

Finally, AI work force changes will not just impact on individuals in 'Five Eyes' who may lose their jobs or retrain for new roles, AI/machine learning will result in organisational cultural change. In particular, how ICs collaborate in using AI applications will likely require IC leaders to steer cultural change as their organisations move away from more rigid, closed, conventional intelligence and military doctrines that have underscored 'Five Eyes' intelligence operations from the start of the Cold War to the present. To grasp the opportunities and minimise the downsides of AI innovations, IC leaders will be challenged to foster more open, flexible, and agile organisational cultures that allow even greater collaboration and information within 'Five Eyes' communities and externally where the bulk of AI innovation is taking place.

Conclusion

Chapter 6 focused on both the advantages and challenges AI/machine learning applications will pose for IC leaders. Integrating, managing, and coordinating new AI capabilities will not of course be the only ICT challenge for leaders in the foreseeable future, but I argue it will remain the primary challenge as it will impact profoundly on existing and traditional ways ICs have managed, collected, and assessed information. At this stage, it's impossible to assess what the full impact of AI will be on IC's core intelligence processes, or indeed other key enabling activities (e.g. human resources, research, and legislation). It's wise I think, to avoid much of the hyperbole that AI will be so revolutionary that it will do away with the humans in 'Five Eyes' ICs. Regardless of whether ongoing AI technological development is revolutionary or evolutionary, the key point is that IC leaders will need to become even more adept in their understanding of AI/machine learning technological development and be able to along with their ICT staff identify what investments to make. However, the even bigger challenge for most IC leaders will not be understanding necessarily or selecting the required AI technology, but how to integrate this strategically operationally and tactically into their organisations so AI research and technology has the intended and meaningful difference on the ground. Achieving integration of AI operational capability will require both doctrinal and organisational change. This will be the biggest leadership challenge and history demonstrates that when it comes to ICT transformation in ICs, these don't always reach the intended potential due to various reasons but including leadership coordination and change management failures, resourcing issues, and institutional cultural factors. ICT transformation tends to be built on existing legacy systems rather than a complete rethink of systems and processes. The cultural barriers to ICT innovation and change in ICs is another key intelligence governance issue that we come back to in Chapter 8 (The Future IC Leader and Governance Challenges). In Chapter 7 (Human Resources), we explore the second key enabling activity and the governance challenges associated with it.

References

Akerkar, R. (2019). Introduction to artificial intelligence. In R. Akerkar (Ed.), *Artificial Intelligence for Business* (pp. 1–18). Cham: Springer International Publishing.

Alazab, M., & Tang, M. (2019). *Deep learning applications for cyber security*. Berlin: Springer.

Allen, G., & Chan, T. (2017). *Artificial intelligence and national security*. Cambridge, MA: Belfer Center for Science and International Affairs.

Allen, G.C. (2019). *Understanding China's AI strategy: Clues to Chinese strategic thinking on artificial intelligence and national security*. Washington, DC: Center for a New American Security.

Babuta, A., Oswald, M., & Janeva, A. (2020). *AI and UK national security policy considerations*. London: Royal United Services Institute for Defence and Security Studies.

Brantly, A. F. (2018). When everything becomes intelligence: Machine learning and the connected world. *Intelligence and National Security, 33*(4), 562–573. doi:10.1080/026 84527.2018.1452555

Davenport, T., & Ronanki, R. (2019). Artificial intelligence for the real world. In HBR's 10 Must Reads (Ed.), *On AI, Analytics, and the new machine age* (pp. 1–19). Boston, MA: Harvard Business Review.

DOD. (2018). *Summary of the 2018 Department of Defense AI strategy. Harnessing AI to advance our security and prosperity*. Washington, DC: DOD.

Feldstein, S. (2019). Artificial intelligence and digital repression: Global challenges to governance. Available at SSRN: https://ssrn.com/abstract=3374575.

Flasiński, M. (2016). History of artificial intelligence. In M. Flasinski (Ed.), *Introduction to artificial intelligence* (pp. 3–13). Cham: Springer International Publishing.

Ganor, B. (2019). Artificial or human: A new era of counterterrorism intelligence? *Studies in Conflict and Terrorism*, 1–20. doi: 10.1080/1057610X.2019.1568815

Gunning, D., & Aha, D.W. (2019). DARPA's explainable artificial intelligence program. *AI Magazine, 40*(2), 44–58.

Hare, N., & Coghill, P. (2016). The future of the intelligence analysis task. *Intelligence and National Security, 31*(6), 858–870. doi: 10.1080/02684527.2015.1115238

Hasse, C. (2019). Posthuman learning: AI from novice to expert? *AI and SOCIETY, 34*(2), 355–364. doi: 10.1007/s00146-018-0854-4

Hoadley, D.S., & Lucas, N.J. (2018). *Artificial intelligence and national security*. Washington, DC: Congressional Research Service.

Horowitz, M. C., Scharre, P., Allen, G. C., Frederick, K., Cho, A., & Saravalle, E. (2018). *Artificial intelligence and international security*. Washington, DC: Center for a New American Security (CNAS).

Iphofen, R., & Kritikos, M. (2019). Regulating artificial intelligence and robotics: Ethics by design in a digital society. *Contemporary Social Science*, 1–15.

Johnson, J. (2019). Artificial intelligence & future warfare: Implications for international security. *Defense and Security Analysis, 35*(2), 147–169. doi: 10.1080/14751798.2019.1600800

Johnson, L.K., Dorn, A.W., Webb, S., Kreps, S., Krieger, W., Schwarz, E., & Wirtz, J.J. (2017). An INS Special Forum: Intelligence and drones/Eyes in the sky for peacekeeping: The emergence of UAVs in UN operations/the democratic deficit on drones/The German Approach to Drone Warfare/Pursuing peace: The strategic limits of drone warfare/Seeing but unseen: Intelligence drones in Israel/Drone paramilitary operations against suspected global terrorists: US and Australian perspectives/the 'Terminator Conundrum' and the future of drone warfare. *Intelligence and National Security, 32*(4), 411–440. doi: 10.1080/02684527.2017.1303127

Leenen, L., & Meyer, T. (2019). Artificial intelligence and big data analytics in support of cyber defense. In *Developments in information security and cybernetic wars* (pp. 42–63). Hershey, PA: IGI Global.

Lele, A. (Ed.) (2019). Defence and disruptive technologies. In *Disruptive technologies for the militaries and security* (pp. 29–42). Singapore: Springer Singapore.

Lu, Y. (2019). Artificial intelligence: A survey on evolution, models, applications and future trends. *Journal of Management Analytics*, *6*(1), 1–29. doi: 10.1080/23270012.2019.1570365

Nilsson, N. (2010). *The quest for artificial intelligence: A history of ideas and achievements*. Cambridge: Cambridge University Press.

Payne, K. (2018). Artificial intelligence: A revolution in strategic affairs? *Survival*, *60*(5), 7–32. doi: 10.1080/00396338.2018.1518374

Russell, S.J., & Norvig, P. (2016). *Artificial intelligence: A modern approach*. Malaysia: Pearson Education Limited.

Schwab, K. (2017). *The fourth industrial revolution*. New York: Crown Business.

Seffers, G. (2015). Decoding the future for national security. *SIGNAL*. https://www.afcea .org/content/Article-decoding-future-national-security

Şeker, E. (2019). Use of artificial intelligence. Techniques/Applications in Cyber Defense. *arXiv preprint arXiv:1905.12556*.

Tuffley, D. (2019). Human intelligence+ artificial intelligence= human potential. *Griffith Journal of Law & Human Dignity*, *6*(3), 170–189.

Walsh, P.F. (2017). Drone paramilitary operations against suspected global terrorists: US and Australian perspectives. *Intelligence and National Security*, *32*(4), 429–433.

Walsh, P.F. (2018). *Intelligence, biosecurity and bioterrorism*. London: Palgrave Macmillan

Walsh, P.F., & Miller, S. (2016). Rethinking 'five eyes' security intelligence collection policies and practice post snowden. *Intelligence and National Security*, *31*(3), 345–368. doi: 10.1080/02684527.2014.998436

Wasilow, S., & Thorpe, J.B. (2019). Artificial intelligence, robotics, ethics, and the military: A Canadian perspective. *AI Magazine*, *40*(1), 37–48. Retrieved from https://se arch-proquest-com.ezproxy.csu.edu.au/docview/2213786823?accountid=10344

Whittlestone, J., Nyrup, R., Alexandrova, A., Dihal, K., & Cave, S. (2019). *Ethical and societal implications of algorithms, data, and artificial intelligence: A roadmap for research*. London: Nuffield Foundation.

Yu, H., Shen, Z., Miao, C., Leung, C., Lesser, V.R., & Yang, Q. (2018). *Building ethics into artificial intelligence*. Ithaca, NY: Cornell University.

Zhao, Y., & Flenner, A. (2019). Deep models, machine learning, and artificial intelligence applications in national and international security. *AI Magazine*, *40*(1), 35–36.

7 Human resources

Introduction

This chapter explores another key enabling activity (human resources), which like information communications technology (ICT) (Chapter 6) is also critical to supporting core intelligence processes (tasking and coordination, collection, analysis, production, and evaluation). Any public or private sector organisation will eventually fail if leaders cannot attract, develop, and keep human talent that can progress its mission. ICs and the agencies that make them up are no different. Chapter 6 (ICT) focused on the technological impact AI/machine learning will likely have for ICs in the future. The chapter also discussed the impact of technology on the workforce and underscored how both technological changes in ICs and the workforce are linked. The introduction of any significant technological change will always impact the workforce—sometimes positively and on other occasions negatively. In this chapter, we explore the critical role IC leaders will need to play in addressing evolving workforce planning issues against the backdrop of an ever increasingly complex technological and security environment.

At this point you may be asking, but haven't IC leaders always had to turn their minds to workforce planning as their operating environment changed? Yes, but I argue now and even more in the future the pace, variety, volatility, and complexity of the security environment will require IC leaders to demonstrate an even greater ability to respond and adapt quickly to workforce planning requirements. IC leaders will need to implement both strategic and operational workforce planning responses that are flexible to the velocity and complexity now seen in the security environment. Naturally, workforce planning strategies, plans, and the necessary resourcing are required for all aspects of IC operations. This includes but is not limited to those that support analysts, intelligence operations, technical services, science and technology, and administration areas. Given space limitations, however, and also because of the centrality of the analyst's role to the IC mission, this chapter focuses on workforce planning issues as they relate to the recruitment, training, and retention/attrition of analysts. It's clear also that workforce planning issues are both influenced and impacted by other broader IC leadership governance challenges discussed in earlier chapters as well as organisational cultural factors. The chapter highlights some of the governance issues as they relate to human resource planning. However, Chapter 8 (The Future IC Leader and Governance Challenges) discusses in greater detail the significance of these governance issues and how IC leaders may begin to address them. In particular, it explores three inter-related workforce areas (recruitment, training and education, and retention and attrition) and provides a thematic discussion of the key governance challenges in each workforce area.

Workforce planning issues

Chapter 5 (Analysis) discussed several analytical techniques and methodologies such as social network analysis, structured analytical techniques, data mining/machine learning, and behavioural sciences, amongst others. One key point arising from that discussion was that IC leaders will be called upon to bear greater responsibility for the earlier integration of new analytical techniques in ways that can optimise mission priorities—but also in a manner that is sustainable from a human resource perspective. However, also noted in Chapter 5, what is best practice or even good practice is unclear in the application of many analytical techniques and technologies. Being able to define 'good practice' is also dependent on a clear articulation of strategic planning that identifies ways to improve capabilities. The role of IC leaders in sponsoring and evaluating innovation is a defining leadership attribute for future IC leaders—a point we come back to in the next chapter (Chapter 8 The Future IC Leader and Governance Challenges). Harnessing innovation more proactively and effectively will be determined in no small measure by how IC leaders can promote a skilled and adaptive workforce. Workforce planning is as we see in this chapter complex, but in simple terms it is about how IC leaders build human capacity to meet organisational missions by making good decisions around recruitment, training, and retention. In other words, what knowledge and processes can IC leaders invest in that hires, nurtures, and holds onto the 'right kind' of human capability? In the space available and noting that much of the detail of specific HR initiatives for 'Five Eyes' ICs is close-held or classified—this chapter examines the workforce issues and challenges IC leaders will continue to be confronted from an open sources perspective.

The objective is to present a normative discussion of what IC leaders need to consider in promoting effective workforce planning of analysts into the future. Every IC will continue to develop its own approaches to workforce planning that works best for them. However, for reasons we will discuss shortly, specific 'home-grown' workforce planning strategies should be underpinned as much as possible by both normative and better practice evidence-based processes to improve IC HR outcomes.

Recruitment

The first workforce planning issue—recruitment—is arguably the most critical to get right. Training and retention strategies that keep good talent is important, but if you do not have a clear picture of the role you expect people to do now or in the future then recruited staff will not be fit for purpose. At best this might be a waste of resources for that recruitment round—at worst poor selection processes have a cumulative effect that degrades IC agencies' ability to adapt to the fast-changing security environment. If we glance across all 'Five Eyes' countries, a lot of synergies in practice and collaboration have been forged over several decades between agencies across all five nations. But it is also true that the size, missions, and political institutional structures upon which each 'Five Eyes' IC operate shows a great deal of diversity. For example, just going by one metric—'size'—at both ends of the extremes there is the US IC with 17 and at the other the NZ IC with three agencies. While it is difficult to get an accurate number on the total headcount of the US IC, ODNI reporting on the number of secret and top secret security clearances being actively used in the United States in the FY 2017 was 2.8 million (ODNI 2017a: 3). This was for the entire US federal government including intelligence staff and contractors—though a large portion of them would be working for civilian or military intelligence agencies. In comparison, the NZ IC with its three core intelligence agencies has perhaps no more than 1,000 personnel—the later not including NZ Police or the NZ Defence Force (Whibley 2014). Somewhere in the middle is the ICs of Australia, Canada, and the United Kingdom. Given key differences in size, number of personnel, missions, and funding of agencies within and between 'Five Eyes' countries, there can be no 'one size fits all' approach to recruitment. But are there broader normative attributes across 'Five Eyes' ICs about the role analysts play, which can inform workforce planning issues such as recruitment?

In a 2019 US National Academies of Science, Engineering and Medicine report (commissioned by the ODNI), the authors provide an overview of a number of broad factors defining the role of analysts (NAS: 65–79). The authors argue that the role of the analyst hasn't changed significantly in the last two decades. I am not sure I would agree with this observation entirely. It may have been true to some extent, but as discussed in Chapter 6, over the last two decades, I argue that AI/machine learning and data mining technology has impacted on the way analysts have traditionally done their jobs in ways not completely understood. Nonetheless, the NAS report authors provide a good list of the skills and activities most ICs would expect from their analysts. Unsurprisingly, these include things like the ability to 'recognise patterns in behaviours, trends and relationships among actors' (Ibid: 67), critical thinking, sense-making, communication skills, and the ability to coordinate and collaborate with peers and decision-makers (Ibid: 65–79).

Demonstrated research skills are of course also critical when recruiting personnel to analyst's positions. But like the general skills and activities analysts are expected to learn that are mentioned by the NAS report and others (Johnson 2017: 881; Walsh 2017b: 1005–1021; Caddell and Caddell 2017: 889–904; Dylan *et al.* 2017: 944–960; Kreuzer 2016: 579–597; Shelton 2014: 262–281; Dahl 2017; Lowenthal 2017: 986–994), IC leaders will need even clearer articulation of what we want an analyst to do in the future as the security environment rapidly changes. For example, no one would argue that IC recruitment strategies for analysts would no longer be looking for essential skills, knowledge, and behaviours such as 'critical thinkers.' But there needs to be a lot more granularity and clarification amongst IC leaders and their recruiters on what is meant by such terminology both organisationally and externally as job descriptors get rolled out the door in position wanted advertisements (Clarke 2010).

Being able to pass a psychometric test might be one indicator of critical thinking, but on its own may not be sufficiently diagnostic to determine recruitment decisions in the future. Does the IC, for example, want critical thinkers who can flexibly move from one (analyst) account to another quickly? And/or do ICs need other types of critical thinkers—the so called 'slow thinking' variety that decision-making psychologists Kahneman (2011) and Tversky have raised that might be better at assessing complex strategic analytical problems? Similarly, IC recruiters and leaders need to develop greater clarity by what they mean behind statements such as 'must have advanced research skills.' What research skills are required for an analysts role are contextual. For example, if recruitment is for a tactical analyst working in a national law enforcement agency that has an intelligence function such as the FBI or Australian Federal Police (AFP), the research skill set required may look very different from one where the role is for a strategic analyst in a national security intelligence agency that has an assessment function like Australia's Office of National Intelligence (ONI) or the US State Department's Bureau of Intelligence and Research (INR). Leaving such contextual issues to one side and on the question of research skills and activities, more broadly IC leaders and recruiters will also need to reflect deeply on the complexity of the security environment and whether the research skills current analysts have will continue to be fit for purpose (Walsh 2017b: 548–562). While some research skills such as collation activities that were once core duties of analysts might become automated—others may become more important, such as recruits having stronger backgrounds in qualitative social research and quantitative analysis (Ibid).

In addition to assessing the kinds of attributes, skills, and knowledge ICs might need from analysts in the future, there are other important recruitment criteria that require further consideration by leaders and HR officials. Recruitment is not just about what the 'day job' is. It is also about where ICs find the analytic staff needed. Given the increasing complex range of current and emerging threats in the security environment, ICs must develop the ability to adapt to it by hiring analysts whose skills are applicable—but also have personal and cultural backgrounds that assist in understanding a diverse spectrum of threats. Some ICs have struggled historically to recruit a sufficiently broad spectrum of personnel not just for analyst's roles—but others such as undercover roles and linguists. George (2011: 79) and Lieberthal (2009) have both argued that the US context, particularly in the CIA recruiting and vetting processes, have 'ruled out hiring many ethnic-Americans—who have exactly the kinds of cultural experiences that would make them better analysts of foreign cultures and decision-making styles' (George 2011: 79). George's quote raises two inter-related recruiting issues. IC leaders may have in some instances legitimate concerns about proceeding with security vetting of individuals from certain ethnic backgrounds. However, an overly prescriptive or cautious approach increases the possibility of not employing suitable candidates whose rich ethnic and cultural backgrounds would only enhance the validity and reliability of analytical outputs in a range of areas. All 'Five Eyes' ICs need to continually assess how they risk manage relevant security vetting procedures to ensure candidates, who have much needed ethnic and cultural backgrounds, are not overly disadvantaged on applying and gaining positions. In 2014, the US DNI under Jim Clapper launched a *US IC Human Capital Vision 2020*—a strategic plan to restructure workforce planning and policies across the IC (ODNI 2014)[1]. It was built around three central themes: *shaping an effective workforce, embracing continuous learning,* and *embedding agility, innovation and inclusion* (Ibid: 3). The 2014 strategic plan looked like the first significant attempt by the US IC to draft and address a comprehensive set of standards for a range of workforce planning issues, including in areas of ensuring compliance with EEO requirements and building cultural competencies in agencies (Ibid: 7–8). For example, the plan referred to a workforce strategy that 'would give careful consideration of each individual's unique situation using the 'whole of person' concept' (Ibid: 5). Assuming the latter quote referred to the recruitment of individuals from ethnically and culturally diverse backgrounds, such rhetoric is important to see from IC leaders. But with all strategic plans, of course the real test is how strategic objectives are actioned in the workforce planning activities of individual ICs over time. Roughly at the same time that the 2014 US IC Human Capital Vision 2020 was released, the ODNI implemented in 2016 the *IC Equal Employment Opportunity Enterprise Strategy (2015–2020)*. The Strategy provided in contrast to the broader 2014 (Human Capital Vision) plan more specifics on how ICs could operationalise plans to increase the employment of minorities and diversity groups—including but not limited to African-Americans, Hispanics, women, persons with targeted disabilities, lesbians, gays, bisexuals, and transgenders (ODNI 2016). Again there is less detail in the 2016 ODNI publication on how strategic measures are being implemented when it comes to recruiting minority groups. A further 2017 ODNI report (Annual Demographic Report—Hiring and Retention of Minorities, Women and Persons of Disabilities in the US IC) suggests improvements are being made. The report cites for FY 2017 there was a 2 per cent increase up from FY 2016 in the recruitment of minority groups by the IC, though the overall percentage of minorities working in the US IC is 22.5 per cent compared to 35.4 per cent for other federal agencies and the broader population of 38.7 per cent (2017b: 1–3). So clearly there is more progress to be made and at the time of writing it remains unclear how all 17 US IC agencies are performing against ONDI strategies and their own workforce planning objectives.

In the United States, ODNI has also established other programs aimed at broadening the ethnic and cultural diversity of recruits coming into the IC. One example is the IC Centers for Academic Excellence program (IC CAE) that commenced in 2005. IC CAE's objective was to create an increased pool of culturally and ethnically diverse job applicants for intelligence community agencies. It also sought through grants to help universities establish intelligence training programs aligned to the mission skill sets and competencies of the IC. It was originally operated by the DNI, moved to the DIA in 2011, and recently the DNI has taken back its management. Recent research, which received survey returns from 19 out of 40 college grant recipients of the IC CAE program, suggests the IC CAE program has had impact. Of all college program managers surveyed, 36 per cent said their graduates were able to get intelligence jobs (federal and state) and 58 per cent of their program managers believed that they were supporting the ODNI's mission of diversifying the workforce (Landon-Murray and Coulthart 2020: 270–275). However, the US Congress independent auditing agency—the Government Accountability Office (GAO)—also reviewed this program in 2019 and determined it was still unclear to what extent all US ICs engaged in its objectives and whether it really has created the increased pool of culturally and ethnically diverse job applicants its architects hoped for (GAO 2019). Deficiencies in ethnic inclusion and diversity recruitment issues are also seen across other 'Five Eyes' ICs though public discussion of them has lagged somewhat compared to those that have taken place in the US IC. Space does not allow a comprehensive coverage of these issues as they are playing out in the other four countries (e.g. UK, Canada, Australia, and New Zealand). But in brief, the UK's intelligence oversight committee—the Intelligence and Security Committee (ISC)—released a detailed report on diversity and inclusion issues in that country's IC (Grieve 2018). It stated that though 'significant progress has been made in recent years with IC agencies adopting more innovative recruitment campaigns that seek to attract a more diverse range of applicants from under-represented groups and other measures, much more needs to be done' (Ibid: 1, 5). Just looking at one group, the report stated that 35 per cent of MI5's senior positions were women, but for other IC agencies it dropped down to only 25 per cent (Ibid: 1). The UK Government responded later in the same year with how the IC was going to enact further improvements in addressing these issues (UK Government 2018). In Australia's IC, it's clear that individual agencies have been focusing on improving ethnic, cultural, and inclusion recruitment barriers—but a community-wide approach is needed. With the creation in 2018 of the Office of National Intelligence (ONI), which has a legislative mandate to provide enterprise management oversight for all agencies in the IC—hopefully such a community-wide strategy to all recruitment and broader workforce planning issues can be implemented.

In addition to IC leaders working on recruitment strategies that increase both the ethnic and cultural diversity across 'Five Eyes,' ICs also need to give further consideration to inter-generational factors (Constanza *et al.* 2012). As at the time of writing, the last cohort of the baby boomers (born 1964) will likely retire by 2030. Their earlier-born generational compatriots would have mostly worked in ICs where the Cold War dominated analyst's attention and upon retiring will take with them valuable corporate memory. I recall my own experience working as an analyst just prior to 9/11 in the late 1990s 'peace dividend period.' During this time, older Afghanistan and Soviet analysts seemed to have disappeared overnight along with their much-needed experience that was required only a few years later. In contrast, Generation X (1965–1976), depending when they were born, have now accrued between 20 to 30 years professional experience working as analysts—or have moved onto other senior analytical or non-analyst roles. Those Generation X cadre born earlier would have gained extensive analytical experience just prior to 9/11. Many Generation X analysts have probably lived and breathed post-9/11 counter-terrorism for most of their careers. Again, many are close to retirement, while others in their forties are now in middle-ranking manager positions as analysts or moved onto non-analyst jobs. Like their predecessors, Generation X on retirement will take a lot of corporate knowledge with them. Their seniority and experience once gone also reduces the number of highly skilled senior analysts who can mentor and manage younger junior staff—most of whom are now millennials/Gen Y.

In contrast, Generation Y (or millennials) analysts have no direct working knowledge of the Cold War and some will not have lived through 9/11. Depending on when they were born some careers would overlap those of Generation X and have been shaped by the post-9/11 'war on terror.' However, those born after 1982 may likely need to pivot their careers to respond to new demands in the ever increasingly complex security environment—beyond counter-terrorism wars in the Middle East. The growing uncertainty of a multipolar rather than the Cold War bi-polar security world order will require re-skilling by late Generation X and Ys as other threats equal to terrorism demand analytical attention (e.g. resurgence of bad state actors and foreign interference).

Again, Generation Y analysts, depending on when they were born, would now be in the 10–20 year range of professional experience in ICs. There is a growing body of human resource research on the differences between generations and how this impacts on recruitment strategies in the private sector, though there is next to no research on why millennials/Gen Y might be interested in applying for a job in the IC (Weinbaum 2016). Many studies on Gen Y attributes in other non-IC industries emphasise them as being technologically savvy than earlier generations, which is advantageous to ICs as they confront a range of challenges including rapid changes in AI/machine learning in the workplace. However, the research is not settled on all the attributes Gen Y embody (both good and bad). It's clear that knowing the general personality attributes of a generation demographic may be helpful to a point. But there are variations between individuals which IC leaders need to take into further consideration when trying to attract and recruit young people to the changing workforce (Sharma 2020; Hobart and Sandek 2014; Walker *et al.* 2010).

Finally, there is Generation Z (born 1996 to 2012)—the oldest of which are now just leaving university—some of whom may be contemplating working in the IC as an analyst. They are likely to be better educated and skilled in AI/machine learning than even their Gen Y predecessors, but by the time the youngest in this cohort enter the IC workforce in around 2050 the challenges they will face and the skills required will be different again. While IC leaders need to develop an end to end (recruitment to retirement) continuing professional development program for analysts born in earlier generations, recruitment strategies now need to plan for Generation Z and beyond to ensure personalities, beliefs, values, skills, and experience can be best matched up to how the job of an analyst is likely to change in the next one to two decades.

Several researchers suggest that Generation Z are even more focused on 'corporate responsibility' and want to believe the organisation has an ethical mission. Like Generation Y they want to quickly obtain autonomy and expect inclusion based on race, ethnicity, sexual orientation, and religion to be fully normalised and integrated into the fabric of society and their potential employer. Generation Z are also carrying large college debt and expect a potential employee to be generous with remuneration. This expectation might be more difficult to meet in the foreseeable future, particularly after the global impact of the COVID-19 pandemic. But nonetheless, expectations need to be managed in proactive and transparent ways.

Interesting too, they are less likely to be influenced by recruitment advertisement and will look to friends to provide advice on whether an employee is likely to deliver on their key personal and professional goals (Robinson 2018; Adamy 2018; Williams *et al* 2010: 21–36). Many Generation Y/millennials, according to Weinbaum *et al.*'s study (2016: X), 'have a lack of trust in government, yet believe it has a responsibility to respond to war, terrorism, social unrest and political instability.' So for both Generations Y/millennials and Z to come, how do IC leaders attract suitably qualified personnel, who may have an interest in national security issues, yet have concerns about notions of secrecy, intelligence collection, operations, or even the legitimacy of IC activities in liberal democracies?

No one has a crystal ball about how exactly the security environment will evolve in the next two decades. But as seen with the development of machine learning/AI over the last two decades, a number of macro trends will begin to emerge in the security environment. In response, the focus of IC leaders should be on the implementation of reliable risk and foresight analytical frameworks in order to inform recruitment planning and strategies for analysts. Inter-generational attributes and skills variations between workforce generations are also important considerations for recruiting other positions, including IC leaders and managers. But we will come back to what skills and attributes IC leaders will need in Chapters 8 (The Future IC Leader and Governance Challenges) and 9 (Leadership Development).

There is one final important question on recruitment which IC leaders need to consider in the future. This is how the mechanics of workforce selection is done across 'Five Eyes' ICs, and if these processes are the most optimal approaches to matching the right person to analyst's position (Nemfakos *et al.* 2013). IC workforce selection, like other non-IC recruitment, has been informed for several decades by extensive psychological and cognitive testing tools to try to predict how an individual may perform in an analyst's role. In addition to assessing cognitive functioning, psychological testing also provides recruiters with insights into personality, values, and interest—all of which are critical things to know about when determining if a candidate is a good fit for working in the closed IC working environment. Psychological testing is also relevant to security vetting requirements, such as determining good character, probity, and life history. In addition to psychological testing, other selection tools rely on interviews, assessment centres, and working candidates through scenarios with problem solving.

IC selection testing is underscored by over a century of research in broader industrial organisational psychology and human resource management. Though the recruitment selection practice has grown organically in a lot of agencies across 'Five Eyes' ICs, there is less evidence-based knowledge available about what practices are most effective and why this is so. As Ployhart *et al.* suggest, the efficacy of recruiting practices have been well researched by applied psychologists. But even in a field that has improved empirically the recruitment practice in a range of industries, methodological challenges still preclude consensus by researchers on how best to assemble evidence of validity in studies and putting theory into practice (2017: 299; Farr *et al.* 2017; Ryan and Derrous 2016). Ployhart *et al.* also correctly point out that improving evidence-based research on recruitment strategies needs a two-pronged approach. The first is further refinement of traditional recruitment research, which seeks to assess which people have the best skills against the position. The second and likely increasingly important approach is given personality traits of Gen Y, Z, and beyond—research is needed that can help IC leaders understand how candidates respond to different recruiting and selection strategies (Ibid).

Again, IC leaders can look to the research in applied psychology disciplines that over several decades have been assessing behavioural changes and their relationship to job performance in different industries. Although research progress has been made in non-IC industries, evaluating how someone is likely to perform pre-recruitment and after is difficult given the complex inter-play of a range of organisational and individual variables (Ones *et al.* 2018; Sackett *et al.* 2017). Leaving aside differences in knowledge, skills, and abilities, there are also individual behavioural differences impacting on job performance including ability, personality, interests, emotional intelligence, and motivational traits (Sackett *et al.* 2017). Researchers also point out a number of other behavioural traits that may impact on an individual's performance. One key distinction being made is between what some psychologists refer to as the difference between a typical performance (the choices about *what people will do* in the workplace) compared to maximum performance (or *what people can do* when they are highly motivated to do so) (Ones *et al.* 2018: 156). In the recruitment of analysts and indeed any other position across the IC, as argued earlier, context will greatly inform recruitment strategies; understanding such variations in an individual's performance is about recruiting the 'right candidate' with the right mixture of behavioural traits.

Accordingly, it's clear that IC leaders can do more to engage in research that assesses behavioural characteristics of both potential and actual job performance. It's also clear that IC leaders and their HR departments need to articulate both a normative approach to what knowledge/skills and personality attributes they are looking for. Additionally, in the future consideration must be given to how both inter-generational change and individual behavioural traits impact recruitment. Given the changing security environment, assessing likely performance and matching to organisational culture will need to look more deeply at key differences in a person's typical and maximum performance pre and post recruitment. It will also be important to match assessing individual typical job performance against how they may potentially perform in a range of crisis situations. Again, IC leaders need to either fund or access relevant/translatable evaluation research that can assess how to improve selection systems and psychological evaluation of personal attributes in other work contexts to see how they can be better integrated into IC recruitment strategies.

Training, education, and competency

As discussed earlier, the chapter's objective is to identify broad normative principles that IC leaders and their HR staff can use to anchor their strategic and operational workforce planning in the future. Since 9/11, an ever increasing body of work addressing various aspects of training and education has emerged. Though I would argue there is still less focus on competencies required in analytical training/education as well as evaluating the various pedagogical approaches to the training and education of analysts (Walsh 2017a: 1005–1021; Harrison *et al.* 2020). In other words, how do we tie curriculum development ultimately to what skills analysts need to demonstrate on the job? And how can we be sure that teaching strategies deployed whether inside or external to ICs are developing the professional performance required (Walsh 2017a: 1005–1021)? Making the right calls about how to map an entire continuing professional development program for analysts at varying stages (i.e. during training, education, and demonstrating competency) will remain a difficult challenge and responsibility for IC agency heads and their HR teams. Across and within the 'Five Eyes,' diverse roles, functions, and agency mandates will always require different approaches to analyst's training, education, and building of competencies. There will never be a 'one size fits all.' However, just as IC leaders can identify normative approaches to recruitment there are likely also discernible common principles to guide training, education, and competencies for analysts regardless of where they are working across the 'Five Eyes' ICs. The literature provides some ideas on what principles might help frame training, education, and competencies relating to the professional development of analysts. Space limitations precludes a detailed discussion, though the intelligence training and education literature seems to have coalesced around a few key themes: curriculum, accreditation, continuing professional development, teaching and learning, and content and assessment (Walsh 2017a: 1006).

In the United States, it's clear that efforts have been made over the last two decades to operationalise policies and processes underpinning many of the themes raised in the intelligence training and education literature. For example, after 9/11, with the establishment of the ODNI a series of common IC-wide analytical standards and directives (e.g. ICD 203 and ICS 610–3) were progressively released to provide guidance on analytical standards and competencies.[2] The eventual establishment of the National Intelligence University (NIU) and developments in other universities saw a proliferation of intelligence analysis majors or whole degree programs (Spracher 2017: 231–243). The 9/11 Commission seemed to be a major catalyst by some within the IC and externally (contract trainers and places of higher learning) that analyst's training, education, and competencies needed overhauling. Such clarion calls for improvements in training and education are not unique just to the events of 9/11, however, they go back decades. For example, previous US-independent reviews such as the Jeremiah Review commissioned by then CIA Director George Tenet into the intelligence failures contributing to the United States' surprise at the Indian nuclear tests suggested improvements to better coordinate analytical expertise and training.[3]

Other 'Five Eyes' countries have also implemented efforts to improve training, education, and competency levels of analysts after major independent reviews. After the Butler review, for example, the position of Professional Head of Intelligence Analysis (PHIA) was established to promote a greater sense of intelligence professionalism in the UK IC, including helping coordinate and lead improvements in analytical standards and training (Devanny *et al.* 2018: 86). Similarly, the 2004 Flood Report, which examined intelligence assessments provided to the Australian government prior to the coalition invasion of Iraq in 2003, also made comments on the need for further development of analysts, particularly strategic analysis (Flood 2004: 2–3). But on the whole, post-review reforms to training, education, and competency in non-US 'Five Eyes' ICs at least in the first decade after 9/11 have been more incremental and modest compared to their US counterparts. It is difficult to know how each 'Five Eyes' IC will approach future training, education, and competency reforms moving forward. The 2020 COVID-19 crisis has resulted in significant fiscal stress for their treasuries and this could impact substantially IC leaders' ability to implement training, education, and professionalisation initiatives for analysts and other staff. Equally though, and despite resource constraints, the enduring and unrelenting demands of the changing security environment could be a driver for 'Five Eyes' ICs to implement further root and branch reviews and renewals of analytical training and education.

As mentioned earlier, intelligence failures (e.g. 9/11 and Iraq) and the extensive legislative and independent reviews that inevitably follow them have a way of escalating the actual or perceived need for urgent IC reform. Reform measures of course can include a range of areas, better collection, coordination, and analysis, which were discussed in previous chapters. And as discussed briefly here, they can also include recommendations for improving analyst training and competencies. But often these reviews make only general suggestions such as 'more training' or 'better training' without necessarily providing the IC leadership with specific suggestions on how or where actual or perceived deficiencies can be addressed.

Independent and legislative branch IC reviews post an intelligence failure event can generate a sense of urgency in and pressure on ICs to quickly address sometimes vague recommendations on what training and education deficiencies need fixing. Such pressure situations, however, when there is political and/or public imperative to do something can often be the wrong environment for IC leaders to address actual/perceived weaknesses in training and education measures. This is because under political pressure IC leaders may make reform decisions that are about being seen to be doing something rather than implementing measures in slower time—when there has been more time to gather sufficient evidence for what will work longer term.

Now at the end of the second decade after 9/11, other independent and government reviews across some 'Five Eyes' ICs continue to highlight ongoing deficiencies about analytical training and broader workforce capability issues. I have already mentioned earlier the 2019 US NAS study commissioned by the ODNI that examined analytical workforce issues, including training and education. A similar report was released in 2019 by Australia's Office of National Intelligence (ONI). ONI commissioned the Australian Academy of Social Sciences a similar study which I was asked to peer review. The report summarised the views of a number of Australian social scientists about ways for the IC to gain more capability and expertise from social-behavioural sciences, but also raised analyst workforce issues (AASS 2019). In the UK, a recent annual report of the Intelligence and Security Committee of Parliament quoting the then acting chairman of the Joint Intelligence Committee conceded by the middle of this decade the Assessment Staff had become under-funded, under-staffed relative to priorities, and was 'no longer at the cutting edge of where we should be' (Devanny *et al.* 2018: 80).

As noted above, this chapter cannot go into the minutiae of what every 'Five Eyes' IC is (or is not) doing specifically to address deficiencies in training and education. The literature listed above provides a road map for readers wanting to drill down on different approaches to training, education pedagogy, and institutional reforms across 'Five Eyes' ICs. In summary though, two decades out from 9/11, some concerted efforts have been made across the intelligence training and education sector to build on training and education programs. Different sectors have played a role. For example, some improvements have been made around accreditation of training and education programs by professional organisations (IAFIE, IALEIA).[4] And as mentioned, ICs and individual agencies have promoted the establishment of universities or seeded grants to promote applied intelligence analysis programs in universities. Universities, ICs, and other external training providers too across the 'Five Eyes' are having better conversations about what is best taught within and outside ICs and who might be better placed to deliver content.

As a former intelligence analyst and now educator for the last 17 years, it's pleasing to see greater reflection in ICs and by external education providers on what factors may lead to better training and education outcomes for analysts. Nonetheless, I still assert both in the literature and in practice there needs to be a greater strategic focus on curriculum development than currently is the case. It's not just that training and education stakeholders should collaborate more in order to holistically assess how to improve curriculum development. It's even more fundamental than that. In short, IC leaders need a strategic focus to analytical workforce issues including training and education. Such a focus must be underpinned by an evidence-based approach that determines what educational/ training factors specifically improve workplace capabilities (Walsh 2017a: 1014). In a 2017 article, I outlined in greater detail core features for an evidence-based framework that could be used to evaluate training and education programs for analysts. I also argued that any framework should be informed by a multi-discipli-nary approach (education theorists, intelligence studies, and workplace learning experts). Additionally, any framework ideally would include evaluation research of a range of inter-connected training and education issues: curriculum, accredita-tion, continuing professional development, teaching and learning, and content and assessment (Walsh 2017a: 1014–1016). IC institutional change and how agencies can adapt to the changing security environment will demand a concerted and con-sistent strategic approach to curriculum development and continuing professional development. How IC leaders build training and education frameworks in the future will be crucial.

Retention and attrition

Managing retention and attrition is the third and final workforce planning issues we will discuss. Retention and attrition of course are linked but not the same thing. In short, effective retention strategies should result in maintaining the right amount of skilled people who are matched to the organisation's key values and remain motivated to meet its objectives. Attrition, in contrast, results in either natural loss of head count (when people retire) or when the organisation's leaders are unable to address staff turnover due to a range of personal, financial, or organi-sational cultural factors. Since the foundation of the 'Five Eyes' ICs in modern history (1945) to the present, all IC leaders have had to deal with not just who to recruit and how to train them but how to keep them.

Managing both retention and attrition in any organisation (large or small) pre-sent challenges and these are no different in our ICs. A loss of expertise, corporate and tacit knowledge, and potentially greater workloads and stress on remaining employees are all adverse and impactful by-products from poorly managed reten-tion and attrition strategies. The exact rate of attrition in agencies across all 'Five Eyes' at this point is difficult to know. Some IC agencies in their public annual reports to government will provide head count or articulate the broad details of their capability frameworks that include workforce issues. I have not yet seen any details on exact attrition numbers. This is understandable to some extent as it is a sensitive matter for any organisation, but this kind of information even if it was only provided publicly from a IC-wide perspective would provide greater transparency in annual reporting—and help researchers engage with ICs on how potential issues could be addressed. In summary, it seems that without perhaps a few exceptions (Treverton and Gabbard 2008), there is both a lack of research and absence of detailed studies commissioned by agencies within ICs that evaluates retention strategies in use and how best to reduce attrition of skilled useful staff.

I emphasised in the earlier two sections (in recruitment and training and educa-tion) that IC leaders and their HR departments should reach out to social research-ers to help benchmark their processes on these issues, including learning from them what factors are causing retention and attrition issues in other industries and what to do about it. There is an increasing body of research from the health sector, particularly doctors, nurses, and surgeons, on how students progress through their training and clinical practice. For example, Salles *et al.*'s (2017: 288–291) study assessed grit (a measure of perseverance) and wellbeing and found they were positively correlated with general wellbeing. Likewise, a lack of grit was inversely correlated with depression and attrition from a surgical residency program. There would also likely be lessons IC leaders could learn from researchers who are investigating factors that contribute to retention and attrition in other knowledge sectors of the economy such as education, IT, and the research community. Other workforce researchers are now focusing on whether it's possible to assess risk of attrition within an organisation using predictive analytics. Predictive analytics as discussed in Chapter 6 (ICT) employs a range of statistical analysis, data mining, and machine learning techniques to 'predict' potentially future events based on past or current trends (Srivastava and Nair 2017).

Such data-driven approaches may have their merits, but rely on designing algorithms based on reliable and valid data. At the time of writing, I would argue that such data (both quantitative and qualitative) is insufficient and incomplete in most agencies across the 'Five Eyes' ICs. So the first step for IC leaders and HR teams is to audit current data holdings on attrition and retention to diagnose where current data deficiencies reside and then assess the best strategies to collect missing data. This is the logical place to start before any evaluation can be made about whether current IC retention programs are reducing attrition to organisationally acceptable levels. While each IC agency should collect their own relevant data for their future operational planning purposes, it makes sense if a central coordinating body in each 'Five Eyes' (e.g. in the US ODNI and in Australia ONI) IC can ensure these efforts allow a whole of community picture, which identify where for the entire IC are the main attrition risks—and what strategic level capability measures can be put in place to mitigate emerging risks.

Assessing attrition risks means being able to understand employee retention, career mobility, and transition factors, which are equally not well understood in non-IC industries as well (Chudzikowski 2012). Organisations may have developed the right rhetoric around how they maintain talent retention, but this can be different from the reality or what is actually required (Tlaiss *et al.* 2017: 426–455). Technological and digital changes in the workplace continue to change the way people work with more people collaborating virtually or from home. Beyond technological factors, research in non-IC contexts does suggest that several other factors also influence staff retention and reduce attrition rates. Corporate culture, development and progression opportunities, role, incentives and rewards, and relationships with managers and colleagues are all key factors. This can make it difficult for an organisational leader to gauge what personal and organisational factors influence staff to stay or leave a job.

As with developing better recruitment, training, and education strategies, IC leaders can look to and collaborate with external researchers from organisational psychology fields, sociologists and intelligence studies that can bring cross-disciplinary perspectives on the retention and attrition issues. Again, workplace research that is investigating generational influences on retention and attrition suggest there are differences in values and behaviours between generations that frame how they view their interest and commitment to remaining with an organisation. Baby boomers and to a slightly lesser extent Generation X have tended to value staying in the one organisation—resulting in fewer organisation transitions than Generation Y (Millenials) (Culpin *et al.* 2015; Lyons *et al.* 2012: 333–357; Constanza *et al.* 2012). In starker contrast, the millennial rate of job turnover is much higher. Seibert *et al.*'s (2013: 177) study of 337 participants (with an average age of 25.5 years) showed that 34.4 per cent left employers after a 16-month period. Further, as discussed earlier, Generation Y and possibly Generation Z also care about the 'brand value' of where they work. ICs are no doubt starting to think about designing retention strategies for Generations Y and Z, but their success will be contingent on how adeptly leaders can provide a rewarding, supportive, flexible, and value-focused working environment.

While the bulk of this chapter has focused on how IC leaders might address workforce planning issues as they relate to analysts, there are other specialisations within ICs (e.g. collectors, technical, legal, and administrative) that the executive must also develop. The common denominator, however, for all workforce planning regardless of the position falls back on how well the IC leadership can navigate through difficult governance issues that may impact on the effective delivery of the recruitment, development, and retention of staff.

Conclusion

This chapter outlined the broad challenges IC leaders will confront as they relate to the recruitment, training, and retention of analysts. There is now growing evidence that IC leaders in most 'Five Eyes' countries are giving much more of their capability thinking time to workforce planning issues. While at this point a lot of this thinking is going on behind the closed doors of our ICs, this chapter has provided examples in broad terms of the kinds of issues, challenges, and remedies leaders are developing to address workforce planning. There are no quick fix or 'one size fits all' solutions to addressing the many workforce challenges to come as the security becomes even more uncertain and volatile. Indeed, resolving any HR challenge leaders face will be a function of how equipped they are personally to manage them and these are dealt with in the context of intelligence governance issues raised in the next chapter (Chapter 8 The Future IC Leader and Governance Challenges) where we shift the focus away from specific areas of leadership responsibility (e.g. tasking and coordination, collection, analysis, ICT, and Human Resources) towards a broader analysis of what key governance issues IC leaders will need to deal with. Chapter 8 also includes a discussion on how IC leaders may address the many governance challenges identified before concluding with an exploration of what kind of leadership attributes are likely to be more effective in tackling governance issues.

Notes

1 The 2014 Strategic Human Capital Plan was built on an earlier and first attempt at laying the groundwork for workforce planning and innovation—the Strategic Human Capital Plan (2006).

2 Intelligence Community Directive 203– Analytic Standards sets out broad standards (such as objectivity, independence from policy makers, and timeliness) meant
to embody the production and evaluation of analytic products, as well as provide
foundations for analytic training and education. ICD 610 provided a list of competencies for the entire IC workforce, not just analysts. ODNI Intel Community
Directive Number 610 Competency Directories for the Intelligence Community
Workforce.
3 While the full text of the Jeremiah Report remains classified, a summary of its recommendations has been declassified by the CIA. See Director of Central Intelligence,
'Recommendations of the Jeremiah Report,' June 1998, <https://nsarchive2. gwu.edu/
/NSAEBB/NSAEBB187/IN38.pdf>, accessed 19 November 2018.
4 IAFIE, or the International Association For Intelligence Education, was formed in
2004 with a mission to expand research, knowledge, and professional development in
intelligence education. It seeks to exchange ideas and advance the intelligence profession by focusing on intelligence studies. IALEIA, or the International Association for
Law Enforcement Intelligence Analysts, has a similar mission but focuses more on law
enforcement.

References

AASS. (2019). *Social science research and intelligence in Australia.* Canberra: AASS.
Adamy, J. (2018, September 07). Ready, set, strive -- Gen Z is coming --- Battle-scarred,
they are sober, driven by money and socially awkward; a 1930s throwback. *Wall Street
Journal.* Retrieved from https://search-proquest-com.ezproxy.csu.edu.au/docview/
2100179262?accountid=10344
Caddell Jr, J., & Caddell, Sr, J. (2017). Historical case studies in intelligence education:
Best practices, avoidable pitfalls. *Intelligence and National Security, 32*(7), 889–904.
doi: 10.1080/02684527.2017.1328854
Chang, W., & Tetlock, P.E. (2016). Rethinking the training of intelligence analysts.
Intelligence and National Security, 31(6), 903–920.
Chudzikowski, K. (2012). Career transitions and career success in the 'new' career era.
Journal of Vocational Behavior, 81(2), 298–306. doi: 10.1016/j.jvb.2011.10.005
Clarke, C.M. (2010). Gen next: Are we adequately training our next generation of China
intelligence analysts? *Asia Policy, 9*(1), 12–20. doi: 10.1353/asp.2010.0008
Costanza, D.P., Badger, J.M., Fraser, R.L., Severt, J.B., & Gade, P.A. (2012). Generational
differences in work-related attitudes: A meta-analysis. *Journal of Business and
Psychology, 27*(4), 375–394. doi: 10.1007/s10869-012-9259-4
Culpin, V., Millar, C., Peters, K., Lyons, S.T., Schweitzer, L., & Ng, E.S. (2015). How have
careers changed? An investigation of changing career patterns across four generations.
Journal of Managerial Psychology.
Dahl, E.J. (2017). Getting beyond analysis by anecdote: Improving intelligence analysis
through the use of case studies. *Intelligence and National Security, 32*(5), 563–578. doi:
10.1080/02684527.2017.1310967
Devanny, J., Dover, R., Goodman, M.S., & Omand, D. (2018). Why the British Government
must invest in the next generation of intelligence analysts. *The RUSI Journal, 163*(6),
78–89. doi: 10.1080/03071847.2018.1562027
Dylan, H., Goodman, M.S., Jackson, P., Jansen, P.T., Maiolo, J., & Pedersen, T. (2017).
The way of the Norse Ravens: Merging profession and academe in Norwegian national
intelligence higher education. *Intelligence and National Security, 32*(7), 944–960. doi:
10.1080/02684527.2017.1328833

Farr, J.L., Tippins, N.T., Borman, W.C., Chan, D., Coovert, M.D., Jacobs, R., & Schneider, B. (2017). *Handbook of employee selection* (2nd ed.). Abingdon, UK: Taylor and Francis.

Flood, P. (2004). *Report of the inquiry into Australian Intelligence Agencies*. Canberra, Australia: Department of Prime Minister and Cabinet.

GAO. (2019). *Intelligence community: Actions needed to improve oversight and oversight of the centers for academic excellence program*. Washington, DC: GAO.

George, R.Z. (2011). Reflections on CIA analysis: Is it finished? *Intelligence and National Security*, *26*(1), 72–81. doi: 10.1080/02684527.2011.556360

Grieve, D. (2018). *Diversity and inclusion in the UK intelligence community*. London: ISC/HMSO.

Harrison, M., Walsh, P.F., Lysons-Smith, S., Truong, D., Horan, C., & Jabbour, R. (2018). Tradecraft to standards—Moving criminal intelligence practice to a profession through the development of a criminal intelligence training and development continuum. *Policing: A Journal of Policy and Practice*, *14*(2), 312–324.

Hobart, J., & Sandek, H. (2014). *Gen Y now: Millenials and the evolution of leadership*. Hoboken, NJ: John Wiley & Sons.

Johnson, L.K. (2017). Special Issue on the teaching of intelligence. *Intelligence and National Security*, *32*(7), 881–881. doi: 10.1080/02684527.2017.1328826

Kahneman, D. (2011). *Thinking, fast and slow*. London: Macmillan.

Kreuzer, M.P. (2016). Professionalizing intelligence analysis: An expertise and responsibility centered approach. *Intelligence and National Security*, *31*(4), 579–597. doi: 10.1080/02684527.2015.1039228

Landon-Murray, M., & Coulthart, S. (2020). Intelligence studies programs as US public policy: A survey of IC CAE grant recipients. *Intelligence and National Security*, *35*(2), 269–282. doi: 10.1080/02684527.2019.1703487

Lieberthal, K. (2009). *The US Intelligence Community and foreign policy: Getting analysis right, John L. Thornton China Center Monograph series*, *2*(September). Washington, DC: Brookings.

Lowenthal, M.M. (2017). My take on teaching intelligence: Why, what, and how. *Intelligence and National Security*, *32*(7), 986–994. doi: 10.1080/02684527.2017.1328856

Lyons, S.T., Schweitzer, L., Eddy, S., Ng, & Kuron, Lisa K.J. (2012). Comparing apples to apples. *Career Development International*, *17*(4), 333–357.

NAS. (2019). *A decadal survey of the social and behavioural science: A research agenda for advancing intelligence analysis*. Washington, DC: NAS.

Nemfakos, C., Rostker, B.D., Conley, R.E., Young, S., Williams, W.A., Engstrom, J., & Temple, D. (2013). *Workforce planning in the intelligence community*. Santa Monica, CA: RAND Corporation.

ODNI. (2014). *US Intelligence Community's human Capital vision, 2020*. Washington, DC: ODNI.

ODNI. (2016). *The intelligence community's equal opportunity employment diversity enterprise strategy (2015–2020)*. Washington, DC: ODNI.

ODNI. (2017a). *National Counter Intelligence and Security Center. Fiscal year 2017 annual report on security clearance determinations*. Washington, DC: ODNI.

ODNI. (2017b). *Annual demographic report. Hiring and retention of minorities, women, and persons with disabilities in the United States Intelligence Community. FY 2017*. Washington, DC: ODNI.

Ones, D.S., Anderson, N., Viswesvaran, C., & Sinangil, H.K. (2015). *The SAGE handbook of industrial, work & organizational psychology: V1: Personnel psychology and employee performance*. London, UK: SAGE Publications.

Ployhart, R.E., Schmitt, N., & Tippins, N.T. (2017). Solving the supreme problem: 100 years of selection and recruitment at the journal of applied psychology. *Journal of Applied Psychology, 102*(3), 291–304. doi: 10.1037/apl0000081

Robinson, R. (2018). Gen Z enters the Workforce…Now what?: Top 3 things gen Z expect from companies they work for. *Recognition and Engagement Excellence Essentials.* Retrieved from https://search-proquest-com.ezproxy.csu.edu.au/docview/2043555406 ?accountid=10344

Ryan, A., & Derous, E. (2016). Highlighting tensions in recruitment and selection research and practice. *International Journal of Selection and Assessment, 24*(1), 54–62. doi: 10.1111/ijsa.12129

Sackett, P.R., Lievens, F., Van Iddekinge, C.H., & Kuncel, N.R. (2017). Individual differences and their measurement: A review of 100 years of research. *Journal of Applied Psychology, 102*(3), 254.

Salles, A., Lin, D., Liebert, C., Esquivel, M., Lau, J.N., Greco, R.S., & Mueller, C. (2017). Grit as a predictor of risk of attrition in surgical residency. *The American Journal of Surgery, 213*(2), 288–291. doi: 10.1016/j.amjsurg.2016.10.012

Seibert, S.E., Kraimer, M.L., Holtom, B.C., & Pierotti, A.J. (2013). Even the best laid plans sometimes go askew: Career self-management processes, career shocks, and the decision to pursue graduate education. *Journal of Applied Psychology, 98*(1), 169–182. doi: 10.1037/a0030882

Sharma, D. (2020). *How to recruit, incentivize and retain Millennials.* New Delhi: SAGE Publications.

Shelton, A.M. (2014). Teaching analysis: Simulation strategies in the intelligence studies classroom. *Intelligence and National Security, 29*(2), 262–281. doi: 10.1080/02684527.2013.834219

Spracher, W.C. (2017). National Intelligence University: A half century educating the next generation of U.S. Intelligence Community Leaders. *Intelligence and National Security, 32*(2), 231–243. doi: 10.1080/02684527.2016.1248316

Srivastava, D.K., & Nair, P. (2018). *Employee attrition analysis using predictive techniques.* Cham: Springer.

Tlaiss Hayfaa, A., Martin, P., & Hofaidhllaoui, M. (2017). Talent retention: Evidence from a multinational firm in France. *Employee Relations, 39*(4), 426–445. doi: 10.1108/ ER-07-2016-0130

Treverton, G.F., & Gabbard, C.B. (2008). *Assessing the tradecraft of intelligence analysis.* Santa Monica, CA: Rand Corporation.

U.K. Government. (2018). *Government response to the intelligence and Security Committee of Parliament Report on Diversity and Inclusion in the intelligence community.* London, UK, Cabinet Office: HMSO.

Walker, James W., & Lewis, Linda H. (2010). *Dealing with X, Y, Zs how to manage the new generations in the workplace.* London, UK: FTPress Delivers.

Walsh, P.F. (2017a). Teaching intelligence in the twenty-first century: Towards an evidence-based approach for curriculum design. *Intelligence and National Security, 32*(7), 1005–1021. doi: 10.1080/02684527.2017.1328852

Walsh, P.F. (2017b). Improving strategic intelligence analytical practice through qualitative social research. *Intelligence and National Security, 32*(5), 548–562. doi: 10.1080/02684527.2017.1310948

Weinbaum, C., Girven, R.S., & Oberholtzer, J. (2016). *The millennial generation: Implications for the intelligence and policy communities.* Santa Monica, CA: Rand Corporation.

Whibley, J. (2014). One community, many agencies: Administrative developments in New Zealand's intelligence services. *Intelligence and National Security*, *29*(1), 122–135. do i:10.1080/02684527.2012.746416

Williams, K.C., Page, R.A., Petrosky, A.R., & Hernandez, E.H. (2010). Multi-generational marketing: Descriptions, characteristics, lifestyles, and attitudes. *The Journal of Applied Business and Economics*, *11*(2), 21–36. Retrieved from https://search-proquest-com.ez proxy.csu.edu.au/docview/815978214?accountid=10344

8 The future IC leader and governance challenges

Introduction

As noted earlier, intelligence community (IC) leadership, particularly at the operational level, may play out differently in a range of diverse organisational contexts such as the national security, law enforcement/homeland security, military, and private sectors. Given the diverse roles of IC leaders across these sectors, it should come as no surprise that there is no single source of truth or 'leadership map' pointing to how to lead within and across the 'Five Eyes' ICs. Hence, all leaders regardless of the level of responsibility (team, branch, agency, or entire IC) will be shaped by the unique organisational contexts in which they work. However, while an IC leader working within a specific context might be called upon at times to demonstrate particular behavioural and technical competencies, leadership in any IC environment is nonetheless informed by common normative personal and technical attributes. As we will discuss shortly, what these personal leadership attributes are remains an open debate.

Based on a synthesis of key governance challenges identified from primary (survey results, semi-structured interviews) and secondary data sources (scholarly literature, government reports, documents), this chapter and the following one (Chapter 9 Leadership Development) circle back on the book's four objectives listed in Chapter 1 (Introduction). First, given the many governance challenges raised in earlier chapters, what will be the most critical for IC leaders to manage in the future? Second, in what ways can IC leaders seek to address key governance challenges?

Third, what personal attributes are more likely to result in leadership behaviours that impact positively on the key intelligence governance issues identified? And based on a synthesis of the data collected, what attributes, skills, knowledge, and practice can we develop in the next IC leadership cadre that can address governance challenges in ways that result in resilient and adaptive ICs? The answers to this fourth question are addressed in Chapter 9 (Leadership Development).

The chapter is organised into three main headings: key governance challenges, addressing governance challenges, and leadership attributes. While the chapter is a synthesis of both primary and secondary sources, the analysis here will draw heavily on insights gathered from the 208 former and current IC leaders who participated in the study's survey. Finally, just to remind the reader, I define intelligence governance as 'a set of attributes and rules pertaining to strong leadership, doctrine design, evaluation and effective coordination, cooperation and integration of intelligence processes' (Walsh 2011: 135). Attributes and rules of course need not only be prescriptive or directives set by the leader. In many or even most cases, strong leadership will be about making collective decisions on doctrine, integration, and coordination of intelligence processes.

Key governance challenges

There were a number of governance challenges identified in the preceding chapters. In this section, and given space limitations, we will explore thematically those that seem to be the most difficult or urgent for IC leaders to address. However, it's important to keep in mind that the actual number of governance challenges—particularly in larger IC agencies and across communities—are likely to be an even more extensive list than the summary provided here. Determining what governance challenges are discussed here was also informed by a qualitative thematic analysis of both primary and secondary data collected, particularly the insights gathered from survey participants. In short, the identification of the governance challenges below is meant to provide a foundation for further deeper theorising, research, and practitioner reflection on whether they represent sufficiently areas where future IC leaders should be concentrating their efforts. The challenges are discussed thematically and grouped under the names of previous chapters (tasking, coordination and integration, collection, analysis, information and communication technologies (ICT), and human resources).

Tasking, coordination, and integration

In Chapter 3 (Tasking and Coordination), several governance issues were raised which could impact on effective tasking, coordination, and integration. For example, the role politicisation can play in influencing intelligence processes such as tasking and coordination within the ICs will be an ongoing concern for IC leaders. As we saw, in some contexts the malignant effects of politicisation can be mitigated against by IC leaders building constructive engagement strategies with policy makers and having the presence of strong independent oversight and accountability mechanisms to help address actions by decision-makers that result in excessive interference in IC activities. But as many IC leaders surveyed indicated, 'tasking and requirements are driven by policy makers and customers, not intelligence chiefs' (survey respondent 55). Ultimately, tasking and priority setting is bounded in politics and as in the past so too in the future IC leaders will need to adeptly as possible navigate the political/policy world in ways that allow for effective tasking, coordination, and integration of intelligence activities within and between the agencies they lead. Unfortunately, there will never be straightforward solutions for IC leaders seeking to deflect completely the increasingly malignant influence of some political leaders on the intelligence enterprise.

Chapter 3 also raised several other governance issues related to organisational risk/threat assessment, structure, and cultural issues and how they impact on the tasking, coordination, and integration of intelligence. However, the key governance issues arising out of the research in tasking and coordination seem to be how do IC leaders create and adapt their organisational structural environments in ways that can use very broad national intelligence priorities set by policy makers 'to establish multi-dimensional (tactical and strategic) tasking, collection and assessment priorities' (survey respondent 56). Or put another way, the key governance challenge is determining how ICs organisationally can ensure that operationalising national intelligence priorities 'is happening in a way that is effective and efficient' (survey respondent 86).

Collection

Chapter 4 (Collection) highlighted three themes—*technological and methodological, collection strategies*, and *intelligence collection and ethics and efficacy challenges*. All of these raise governance challenges that will continue to occupy the attention of IC leaders into the future. For example, the intersection of issues within both the technological and collection strategy themes raises critical governance challenges. In particular, there will be ongoing challenges around how ICs can improve their knowledge and use of Open Source Intelligence (OSINT) and social media capabilities. In future this will be critical for not just enhancing collection, but for ICs being able to check rapidly and accurately the provenance of these sources for assessment verification and counter-intelligence reasons. Another key collection governance issue that will consume IC leaders' energy will be responding to what Lim refers to as 'data asphyxiation and the decision paralysis that can come from the collection of large volumes of data' (2016: 628). From a collection perspective too, it's clear that many ICs are taking big bets on big data, machine learning, and AI to more effectively manage collection and assessment processes and capabilities. We will come back to the key kinds of governance challenges posed by investing in AI shortly under the sub-heading ICT.

Finally, it's also clear from discussions in Chapter 4 (Collection) that IC leaders will continually be challenged by hardened threat actor/targets who are increasing their use of encrypted platforms and the dark web for communications and illicit markets. It is likely that ongoing advances in AI and other science and technological solutions will provide new collection platforms for ICs to help ameliorate some encryption barriers. However, IC leaders will continually need to balance investments in these capabilities against more informed ethical risk assessments that can evaluate effective surveillance/interception collection strategies against privacy, trust, and legitimacy in liberal democratic states.

Analysis

In Chapter 5 (Analysis), two broad governance challenges were identified. One related to promoting collaboration and the other can broadly be described as advancing innovation. On collaboration, the analysis of primary and secondary sources (including comments from surveyed IC leaders) suggests that improvements have been made since 9/11 in ICs to promote better collaboration between analysts. However, several survey comments highlighted further progress was required to promote more effective collaboration that would result in stronger cross agency virtual and physical communities of analytical practice. A key governance challenge for IC leaders, therefore, is how to build on what analytical collaborative tools currently exists that promotes efficiencies and are most likely to be utilised by multi-agency analysts. In the context of the need for further development of collaboration strategies to promote analytical collaboration, several IC leaders surveyed also commented that collaboration required the regular inclusion of outside experts (survey respondents 7, 20, 85). The inclusion of outside experts has been a recurring theme throughout this book concerning a range of capability issues, not just analytical innovation.

The second key governance challenge for analysis is innovation. Innovation includes improving knowledge, skills, and the acquisition of technology that can increase the validity and reliability of analysis. It also includes IC leaders being able to validate through evidence-based research or other means that innovations are making a demonstrable effective difference to analysis. Chapter 5 (Analysis) discussed examples of recent evidence-based studies such as Dhami's work on improving analytical probability and forecasting (2018: 205). But there are now several other issues impacting on the reliability and validity of analysis, such as 'fake news' and foreign interference, where it will be important to evaluate their impact on analysis as a result of analytical bias, poor evidence, and deception. Finally, resolving analytical collaboration or innovation challenges naturally will not just be dependent on technological solutions. Often improving existing analytical processes and innovation will rely on IC leaders reaching out to analysts and other staff at the 'coal-face,' who may have simple, elegant solutions to managing challenges. In the words of one IC leader surveyed:

> Intelligence and security agencies are notoriously slow to change and adapt to an ever changing tactical environment. A reliance on traditional practices have shown to be ineffective. Leaders must maintain relationships with front-line practitioners and be fully cognizant of emerging challenges and the ad hoc 'workarounds' that personnel in the field have self-developed. Often leaders surround themselves with other leaders and insulate themselves from the work of front-line practitioners, thereby creating a disconnect from perception and reality. (survey respondent 31)

ICT governance issues

In Chapter 6 (ICT) we discussed how IC leaders are increasingly investing in AI; and the chapter provided examples of how AI has been applied in cyber, military, and national security settings. As expected there were a number of insights from survey respondents on the advantages of a greater uptake of AI technologies by

ICs in order to drive collection and analysis (survey respondent 74). Aligned with discussion in Chapter 6 (ICT), several IC leaders surveyed mentioned the critical role AI will have in managing what one referred to as 'the tsunami of data available to intelligence organisations' (survey respondent 14). Additionally, others suggested that training, integrating, and working with AI-enabled bots in the intelligence workforce would be important in overcoming other ongoing ICT governance issues, including 'the cost of resolving technical debt from the maintenance of legacy systems, and the absence of an "enterprise" intelligence architecture' (survey respondent 88).

But as discussed in Chapter 6 (ICT), there are several intelligence governance challenges related to the adoption of AI technologies into existing ICT platforms within ICs. For example, there are technological issues. In short, AI algorithmic performance needs to be more reliable and has failed in simpler applications like facial recognition. So the question going forward for IC leaders is to decide on where machine learning/AI applications can most reliably perform for critical missions. The incorporation of AI into ICs raises other challenges that will demand the attention of IC leaders, such as counter-intelligence, legislative, and social-ethical issues. Several comments from IC leaders surveyed demonstrated a level of scepticism and caution about AI. A general concern was that some IC leaders do not fully understand AI and will take a 'techno-centric' view in its integration to existing ICT and other organisational processes. One respondent said AI 'will challenge a range of leadership demands and skills as senior executives place more dependence on technology at the expense of the human operator without a solid understanding of the pros and cons of establishing such reliance' (survey respondent 40).

Other respondents suggested leaders were being pressured by vendors and governments to invest further in AI. One said that the 'government and business seem to be obsessed with big data and AI in an attempt to make the best use of money expedited to acquire information, but responding to external pressures to adopt AI will be a balancing act' (survey respondent 15). Several respondents also made the point that it was up to IC leaders to make stronger cases for the integration of AI into existing ICT, collection, and analytical processes. One IC leader suggested that being able to articulate the real value of AI was an ongoing challenge. Further elaborating their point, the respondent admitted that 'with AI one may be able to collect more information and faster. However, when one is looking for a needle in a haystack, to quote Tom Fingar, one does not need more hay' (survey respondent 72).[1]

Others pointed to the many technological challenges related to identifying new AI capabilities 'and figuring out the interaction between hardware and software development and AI. There are so many complex possible outcomes that anticipating issues is very difficult' (survey respondent 66). Part of the many challenges, as identified several times in Chapter 6 (ICT) and by survey respondents, was how to understand both the advantages of new AI capabilities for ICs yet 'also mitigate risk created by adversaries acquiring new technology' (survey respondent 87).

In addition to specific concerns about AI, a number of survey respondents made general observations about the limited capability development of ICT systems in ICs—which in some agencies will likely compound the introduction and effective integration of next generation machine learning/AI technologies for ICs. One IC leader surveyed said:

> The intelligence community is years behind in capability development compared to industry. The future of building in house for intelligence operations is dead, and they have not seen this yet. To scale, co-develop and innovate and the pace of their adversaries, they need to work in a trusted eco-system to get things done. Joint R&D goes a long way to delivering on new technologies and capabilities. Government is often years behind in technology because they think they know how it works, but fail to understand its interrelated aspects globally with its broader ecosystem on both access to additional functionality and capabilities. (survey respondent 73)

On this issue of ICT capability being well behind industry standards, other survey respondents suggested this was compounded by a lack of flexibility in funding arrangements, particularly in the law enforcement context. As survey respondent 10 remarked:

> no criminal group ever had to write a business case to acquire new technology so if law enforcement in particular is to avoid losing pace, a more flexible approach has to be allowed to the flow of funding. This might require governments to cede more authority to intelligence leaders to have discretion over funding use, but new policy proposals simply delay the process and flag to the target what it is that the community might be capable of in 3–4 years hence.

Other survey respondents also commented on the level of skills, knowledge, and competence of IC leaders to implement and oversee existing ICT systems let alone a broader suite of deep learning AI systems now in the research and development pipeline. In the context of analytical technology, one IC leader suggested how:

> multiple cycles of intelligence leaders with very little background in intelligence practice have overseen a major decline in the capabilities of analytical software and related tradecraft of practitioners. Analysts have less ability now to interrogate and compare data holdings than they did ten years ago. (survey respondent 29)

On the same point of whether IC leaders are effectively managing ICT implementation, one former IC leader (in the Australian context) said:

> Intelligence agencies will still grapple with ICT as they fundamentally have old school thinking and it would be wise to have new blood from outside to

refresh their thinking. I would go back in as a senior executive, as would others, happy to take a pay cut, but really show them how to do Joint Technology Capability Development across the intelligence community properly exploiting domestic and international partners. (survey respondent 73)

Several respondents also raised a number of counter-intelligence challenges IC leaders face in managing ICT capabilities. In particular, there were several observations made about both the security and encryption of ICT systems and devices of interest to ICs. On the security perspective, one respondent said: the 'increased proliferation of smart devices in the internet of things and industrial internet constructs will lead to increases in cyber-attacks that will impact (IC) operations' (survey respondent 56). Additionally, as noted earlier, the greater use of encryption and the move to block chain technology will also provide secure and deceptive opportunities for threat actors that require capable IC leaders to manage (Ibid).

On the technological advantages of various freely available ICT (both social media and secure/encrypted devices), another respondent argued that this was due in part to:

risk aversion and poor investment in developing secure inter (IC) agency communications. The fact that the average person now has secure communications (WhatsApp, Signal etc) and instant ability to search across open source domains limits the competitive advantage intelligence agencies have in addressing threats. (survey respondent 34)

Other survey respondents also noted the demands on IC leaders to manage adeptly the need to 'disseminate secure information on phone tablets and other smart devices; while simultaneously overseeing capabilities to obtain information from similar encrypted devices' (survey respondent 46). Still others mentioned the impact of fake news and foreign interference on ICT systems used by ICs (survey respondent 37).

In addition to the technical and counter-intelligence issues raised, other survey respondents suggested that the main ICT governance issues IC leaders will face are not technical, but legislative. As mentioned in the explanation of the effective intelligence framework outlined in Chapter 2 (Intelligence and Leadership), 'legislation' is one of the five key enabling activities in the framework. This is because legislation enables the activities of all ICs, including what information agencies can share. One IC leader suggested that while there is a technical ability often to share information:

unfortunately, the understanding of some intelligence leaders around what they are legally able to share is lacking. The biggest challenge is not ICT but legislative—what are we allowed to share legally and ensuring that intelligence leaders are across the legislation that enables and limits their work. (survey respondent 55)

An IC leader from Canada also highlighted how legislative challenges will impact on the development and maintenance of ICT systems.

> I think the continuing challenge we will confront in Canada will be the absence of the appropriate legislative basis to deal with many of the information, communication and technology challenges. While we may, in some cases, find 'work-arounds,' others will not be resolved and will lead to intelligence gaps. (survey respondent 82)

Another critical intelligence governance issue related to ICT, which came out of the survey results—but was not discussed in Chapter 6—is that some IC leaders still felt intelligence sharing remains a core challenge for ICs. Survey comments suggested that this was again a technical issue, i.e. ICs needing to find better platforms to facilitate sharing internally and across the 'Five Eyes' countries (survey respondent 67). However, others suggested that it was also an organisational cultural issue. One respondent argued, for example, that there was still continued siloing and dissociation of agencies between those traditional/original agencies within Australia's intelligence community and those that have more recently joined. They argued this dissociation was 'beyond what is actually required for security purposes and is self-defeating' (survey respondent 5). Survey respondent 5 went on to add: 'the need for effective synergistic integration and inter-operation is paramount. This does not require combination of two or more agencies into one, but an appreciation of where such opportunities exist and a willingness to act on them. This needs to happen before we can integrate sophisticated AI platforms.'

A final noteworthy observation made by one survey respondent that I think will remain a critical ICT governance challenge is how IC leaders can invest in organisational IT capabilities in ways that can also help attract and retain Gen Y/ millennials, Gen Z, and beyond who have higher expectations about technology in the workplace than older leaders (survey respondent 64).

HR governance issues

In Chapter 7 (Human Resources), we had a normative discussion about what IC leaders needed to consider in promoting effective workforce planning of analysts (and others) in the future. This discussion was informed by an assessment of the workforce literature and identifying broad attributes and better practice evidence-based processes that need to be considered in order to improve IC HR outcomes. Several themes were identified from the literature, such as diversity, inter-generational factors, training, and education. It seems from a number of survey respondent's comments that the relevance of these themes to managing human resource issues well are also shared by current and former IC leaders. For example, one said:

> If I learned one thing in my time as director, it was that human resource issues were amongst the most important issues for which I was responsible. Because

of the immediacy of the consequences of an operation gone bad it is easy to be swept into worrying about operational issues, but it is human resource issues broadly writ that, if not well managed, can make an operational failure inevitable or, in and of themselves, damage an agency. (survey respondent 104)

Given space is limited, it is not possible to provide a detailed analysis of all comments provided by survey respondents as they related to the governance challenges in HR. Instead I will just mention briefly some key themes identified from the survey—many of which are aligned to themes raised in Chapter 7 (HR). However, before getting to a brief outline of those themes, it is worth prefacing that discussion with one interesting cluster of survey comments, which referred to the variation in the levels of authority some IC leaders had across the national security, military, and law enforcement sectors. In this context, survey respondents made the point that 'authority' is relative and can impact on the extent that some leaders can initiate meaningful HR reforms in the workforce. Two respondents—one from a military and the other from a law enforcement background—made the point that seniority of IC leaders in some of their working environments stops at a certain point and other more senior leaders not necessarily with any intelligence expertise make the decisions about overcoming HR governance issues (survey respondent 65). These insights remind us that in some cases, critical HR workforce decisions in some IC contexts could be made with little or no input or expertise from senior intelligence staff members.

Arguably, one overarching HR governance theme arising from the analysis of survey results was an even greater focus on strategic workforce planning capabilities (survey respondent 108). However, on other more specific themes, there were a number of comments raised expressing concern that the pool of intelligence professionals was still relatively small on an agency basis and that HR governance challenges such as recruitment and training and education needed a greater community-wide rather than agency response (survey respondent 6). Additionally, there were several insights about skill sets, training competencies, and specialisations analysts needed and the challenges of employing sufficient generalists vs subject matter experts (survey respondent 51). Much of this discussion is aligned to points made previously in Chapter 7 (HR). Some IC leaders surveyed provided examples of areas of specialisations, which they argued were critical workforce shortages including CBRN, region, country specialists, and cyber (survey respondents 7, 20, 21). Unsurprisingly, diversity and recruitment practices and the challenges associated there were also identified by a number of respondents. One said 'diversity. Simple as that. Standing in front of intelligence forums, looking out at all those white arts graduates scares me sometimes' (survey respondent 41). Another suggested we still seem 'to be recruiting to obtain a clearance and not for diversity' (survey respondent 42).

A final cluster of HR governance challenges identified related to recruitment and retention practices. Again, many of the survey comments were aligned to issues raised in Chapter 7 (HR). A number of survey respondents made observations about the validity and reliability of existing IC recruitment practices to attract and retain the next generation of analysts and other workers needed to meet the challenges of the volatile security environment. These comments expressed concern about not only whether current practices were reliable or 'fit for purpose,' but some also argued that the continuing outsourcing of IC HR (including recruitment) was likely not to improve recruitment outcomes. One said 'a one size fits all cookie cutter approach to the types of people we need will not serve the community well into the future' (survey respondent 48). On the recruitment process of analysts and diversity, one IC leader said:

> the latest trend is to outsource recruiting; to hire third party companies to 'test' candidates via ill-formatted online questionnaires (testing analytical ability using traditional find the pattern questions, etc.). This is a cost cutting measure that also destroys the potential diversity of the team and community. Diversity must be increased. Currently, diversity is defined as diversity in gender, ethnicity, age, and similar physical attributes. Diversity of background, education, and cognitive ability is needed—it is this diversity that HR practices effectively destroy. (survey respondent 30)

In addition to several insights about the challenges related to recruitment, several IC leaders made comments about the difficulties in retaining and growing a skilled IC workforce. On the inter-generational factors that impact on effective retention discussed in Chapter 7 (HR), the following quote from one IC leader encapsulates well the many challenges associated with the changing nature of the workforce.

> there is an assumption of a need for pathways, of career development, and of long-term association with the discipline. Intelligence professionals might not jump across employment sectors as much as some other professionals but there is no reason to suppose that the transient nature of the workforce will recede. We need to recognise that people might now work in intelligence for much shorter periods than their predecessors and, with that, comes the loss of knowledge, the loss of investment, and indeed the risks to sensitive information being known across a greater number of people. But that is the nature of employment today and probably tomorrow. An associated issue is the need to step away from rigid public service classifications for remuneration: if intelligence agencies need talent, they might have to start paying for it at competitive rates. Again, cue government and adequate funding. (survey respondent 12)

Addressing intelligence governance challenges

In this second section, we shift the focus from summarising the big intelligence governance challenges IC leaders are confronting towards how these may be addressed in the future. As with the previous section, the objective here is not to provide a specific and detailed menu of options for IC leaders to adopt. Rather, the goal is to synthesise some of the analysis provided in earlier chapters and insights from IC leaders who responded to the survey about potential initiatives that may improve IC performance against the various governance challenges identified. Accordingly, the points raised here should not be seen as either fully comprehensive or sufficiently detailed enough to offer solutions to the many challenges identified above and throughout the book. In many cases, time-bounded solutions to governance issues such as organisational structure, cultural or technological challenges don't exist. They are either in some cases no definite solutions, or if an ultimate resolution of the governance challenge exists, it is likely a longer-term prospect if a number of external and internal variables can be aligned. The dynamic nature of the security environment also suggests that IC leaders will need to constantly work to improve incrementally a number of large governance challenges over time. Incremental and consistent improvement may have more value than revolutionary transformations that overpromise and under-deliver. And any improvements made today will need to be re-examined regularly as events will likely render them ineffective and potentially harmful to IC missions in shorter periods of time in the future. This section uses the same sub-headings as the one above—only this time the focus is on how IC leaders address the key governance challenges identified above.

Tasking, coordination, and integration

The one governance challenge we are going to discuss here is organisational structure. As mentioned in Chapter 3, structure is critically important in all aspects of the intelligence enterprise, but particularly so in the tasking, coordination, and integration of intelligence products and processes. IC leaders do have influence within the constraints of legislation and funding on how their organisations are structured to respond to nationally set intelligence priorities. For example, we have seen how after 9/11 there has been a growth in fusion centres, mission intelligence officers, and other inter-departmental taskforces to allow IC agencies to better coordinate and integrate on mission tasking, collection, and analysis. Such initiatives, however, are often added onto existing larger IC organisational structures without necessarily greater reflection on whether any of these structural responses are aligned sufficiently well enough to mission outcomes. What we have also seen is that attempts to improve tasking, coordination, and integration through new organisational structural arrangements (e.g. fusion centres) have not always brought about what they were intended to do—but rather some have added to inefficiencies, duplication, and poor information sharing (Walsh 2015). There is likely no completely optimal organisational structure IC leaders could engineer to comprehensively manage challenges related to tasking, coordination, and integration. But in the future, and as noted earlier, IC leaders will preside over increasingly volatile security environments in periods where significant funding increases are likely to be the exception than the rule. So IC leaders will need to move more explicitly than in the past in developing metrics that can assess whether organisational alignment within teams, branches, agencies, and across the entire community are fit for purpose. Set and forget organisational structures will no longer serve IC mission performance into the future as more agile institutional responses will be required.

As indicated earlier, a range of vulnerabilities (e.g. resource limitations, technical, and cultural constraints) can impact on organisational performance, particularly how intelligence is tasked, coordinated, and integrated. Some 'Five Eyes' ICs, particularly those that have developed formalised centralised agencies (e.g. ODNI in US and ONI in Australia) to examine tasking, coordination, and mission integration, have made progress in 'measuring' organisational performance, but there is still a lot of room for improving on existing initiatives.

Improving agency and community-wide metrics around organisational (structural) performance will require IC leaders to adopt a systems-wide approach that can monitor and evaluate how intelligence is tasked, coordinated, and integrated at strategic, operational, and tactical levels in real time. IC leaders should consider investing in or strengthening existing organisational performance teams that can evaluate the interdependence of requirements, priorities, and agency/IC response to these. As a general approach, performance teams should measure organisational/structural alignment to mission priorities of key decision-makers, which may change close to real time—rather than solely and slavishly sticking to annual checking off bureaucratic and mechanistic exercises to determine whether enduring collection and assessment priorities have been met.

A real-time monitoring capability will help identify and remedy more quickly problems with tasking, integration, and coordination, and whether there are either capability gaps or changes required in the organisational response of a structural nature. IC leaders are likely to gain increased awareness of whether organisational structure is fit for mission by investing in organisational monitoring teams that can examine work flow allocation in both short and longer-term priorities and how resources are being allocated within their own and other agencies in the IC. Research from social network analysis might provide some clues on how to inform the work of these teams, particularly how resources and collaboration (or the lack thereof) are brought together on priorities, outcomes, and outputs. IC leaders will need to align their own organisational performance team's work with any centrally coordinated initiative monitoring overall tasking, coordination, and integration efforts by the entire community. In short, IC leaders will increasingly need to demonstrate that performance stays focused on priorities and reduces duplication of effort. One IC leader summed up nicely the responsibilities of such a performance team:

1) Priorities must be set according to organisational/legislated key performance indicators. All priorities must link to key performance indicators (KPIs).
2) Resources and activities must be tasked according to the KPIs. If it counts, it should be measured.
3) Outputs must contribute to outcomes.
4) Proper governance requires the identification of trends and issues affecting different intelligence capabilities (survey respondent 29).

Collection

As noted above, there are a number of collection related governance challenges IC leaders will continually need to negotiate in the future. Reflecting back to Chapter 4 (Collection) and the analysis here of the survey data, in many ways the kinds of challenges are not new. They relate to sourcing better information, managing the role of technology that supports collection platforms, and handling the increasing 'data asphyxiation' that has been the reality for most ICs for several decades now. Similar to organisational performance measures discussed above, IC leaders in different agencies will likely have to address specific aspects of these collection challenges as they relate to their own particular operational environment. But the way IC leaders initiate measures to improve collection challenges clearly needs to be in concert with other agencies and must be a 'whole of community approach.' Importantly as well and reflecting back to Chapter 4 (Collection), you may recall one IC leader surveyed made the simple point that dealing with collection challenges must be about 'being future focused, not thinking about current collection but what will we need in 5 years' time' (survey respondent 60). From my perspective, this simple statement is a logical yet important point to make in terms of how IC leaders begin to address the many challenges associated with intelligence collection now and in the future.

IC leaders need a conceptual and strategic framework to think more systematically about collection challenges rather than trying to respond to every single difficulty when they arise. This is akin to trying to putting out spot-fires as an even larger fire is just over the horizon. In some contexts, such as tactical intelligence that supports counter-terrorism or military deployment, IC leaders may frequently be asked to resolve problems quickly associated with insufficient collection, legislative restrictions, or technological and capability constraints. However, the type of conceptual and strategic framework I am proposing here would seek to provide a more global understanding of particular governance challenges at all levels: tactical, operational, and strategic. In the discussion earlier, several critical governance issues for collection were identified. However, for the sake of brevity many of these can be broadly categorised into two areas: *knowledge management* and *counter-intelligence*. IC leaders in agencies and at whole of community level should focus on the most pressing issues in both areas in their conceptual and strategic frameworks. Knowledge management challenges include a number of issues that are inter-related and cannot be effectively addressed in isolation. They include regularly auditing information sources and actively managing data overload both technically and culturally. Reviewing knowledge management challenges includes introducing management processes that help IC staff work smarter with what they have, while at the same time being quicker to identify other and often external sources. As mentioned, resolving collection issues is often as much about managing cultural attitudes towards collection sources and methodologies as it is a technical capability issue. Indeed, in the context of improving collection capabilities, any conceptual and strategic framework will need to articulate actions IC leaders can take to affect organisational cultural change that allows new ways of thinking about collection and addresses biases staff may have about the relative value of different information sources. On this matter, one IC leader underscored, albeit a bit bluntly, the cultural barriers in some IC environments that work against effectively improving collection/knowledge management. They said: 'don't be arrogant. Do not assume that anyone/company/group that does not have a TS SCI clearance has less information, expertise, insights, ideas about how to use innovative methods to collect information' (survey respondent 78).

While cultural issues impact on effective collection/knowledge management measures, collection governance issues as mentioned above and in earlier chapters also need to be informed by a greater focus on research and industry collaboration for identifying new collection technologies and techniques. Outreach should not just be on the STEM side (e.g. AI), but also critically needs to include tapping social-behavioural sciences that can help ICs better understand how threat actors interact socially and with technology. So enhancing the leveraging of industry and academia as noted already will be critical to all facets of improving knowledge management in the collection context. The optimal utilisation of industry and academia will of course be dependent on IC leaders implementing comprehensive innovation strategies as part of the conceptual and strategic collection framework discussed above. This is not to suggest that ICs are not currently engaging industry and academic in effective ways—clearly they are. However, a comprehensive innovation strategy would mean IC leaders develop a much more holistic understanding of their entire capability ecosystem to identify gaps and through regular fora identify an even broader array of industry and academic providers that can be engaged consistently to address capability gaps beyond the often usual suspects (providers) that win IC contracts.

Finally, from a counter-intelligence perspective, any conceptual and strategic collection framework will need to address how the increasing availability of external sources to help close difficult collection/knowledge gaps may also raise CI concerns. As noted in Chapter 4 (Collection) and other survey comments made earlier in this chapter, embracing OSINT and social media and academic engagement will be even more vital collection sources for ICs in the future. However, the rise in fake news, deception, and foreign interference in open sources will require more detailed CI risk management than is currently the case in many 'Five Eyes' ICs. Ironically, though, it may likely be experts in the private and academic sector that are best placed to advise ICs on CI risks in using open source collection platforms.

Analysis governance issues

As mentioned in Chapter 5 (Analysis), since 9/11 all 'Five Eyes' ICs to varying degrees have increased their investments in enhancing analytical practice. For example, there has been an increased focus on training analysts in structured analytical techniques than seen pre-9/11, and some agencies have instituted virtual and physical collaboration initiatives to help analysts develop communities of practice aimed at improving assessments. However, it's less clear how such capability investments have improved the reliability and validity of analytical judgements—points made more recently by several scholars (Dhami 2018; Chang and Tetlock 2016). With this background in mind, the key analysis governance challenge as discussed above is how ICs know whether capability investments in analytical innovations are good practice and make a demonstrable positive impact on analysis. While IC leaders should seek the expert counsel of analysts in what capability investments are made, it's clear that analysis is linked to other core intelligence processes (tasking and coordination and collection) as well as key enabling activities (ICT and HR). This means decisions made about how best to improve and innovate analytical practice impacts on these other areas and vice versa. In short, IC leaders need to both drive and support future analytical innovation initiatives because investments made impact on all aspects of organisational performance in ICs. IC leaders if sufficiently engaged should have a 360 degree view of the interdependencies between investing in analytical innovation and how this may then require investments or capability reviews in other areas such as collection or ICT and vice versa.

I do not want to imply that thinking about analytical innovation means necessarily immediate or radical change to every analytical principle ICs have been using for generations. As noted in Chapter 5 (Analysis), there are a number of normative principles that under-gird all analysis, such as critical thinking, research, and writing skills, which will always govern good analysis. Yet given the growing volatility in the security environment, IC leaders will need to prioritise analytical innovation strategies that can improve the validity and reliability of judgements decision-makers use. As discussed, fake news and foreign interference are just two growing areas of concern that will increasingly impact on the analysis of a range of complex security threats. While some IC leaders are thinking about how best to garner analytical innovation, it's clear a more consistent and enhanced conceptualisation of what analytical innovation means within and across ICs is needed. Indeed, given limited resources, the 'Five Eyes' IC network provides an ideal environment to foster enhanced analytical innovation that benefits all members. As one IC leader surveyed put it:

> there is already a strong body of knowledge and decades of Five Eyes collaboration that can be leveraged. Integrating these into a common, continuously improving 'canon of intelligence analysis' would allow them to be enriched and adapted over time—similar to practices among the scientific communities (survey respondent 69).

In summary, to address key analytical governance challenges, IC leaders will need to implement an analytical innovation strategy that can identify opportunities for capability investments in this area. The strategy should also include mechanisms for assessing organisational learning by sponsoring research programs that can evaluate the evidence for the value in implementing analytical innovations over time. Analytical innovation strategies at an operational level will likely mean different things across the diverse 'Five Eyes' agencies. For an assessment agency, it may mean investing in a particularly emerging subject matter area, in another it could be building up analysts' abilities to exploit AI data-driven technologies. The operational detail will need to be decided by IC leaders in their own particular context, but ideally leaders should also aim to achieve an IC-wide vision of key priority areas for an analytical innovation strategy and what agencies should take the lead on certain measures. The resilience and relevance of any strategy will also naturally rely on the ability of IC leaders to engage their analytical work-force in its implementation. A strategy should not be something imposed on the analytical cadre, rather it is something that analysts would be included in as key stakeholders and collaborators—in order to harness their expertise and build trust in the workforce. As correctly noted by another survey respondent: 'leaders need to be able to take their analysts on a journey. Analysts need to trust that their lead-ers will treat them with respect and give them support which means analysts are prepared to go the extra mile' (survey respondent 52).

ICT

Several ICT governance challenges were identified above and IC leaders will play a central role in addressing all of them. Given that space is limited, however, I focus on the implementation of AI capabilities in ICs. Chapter 6 (ICT) outlined in detail the many dimensions to integrating AI capabilities within ICs. These include several factors such as addressing technical issues, managing counter-intelligence, social-ethical issues, legislative, workforce, and organisational cul-tural issues. Also, as we saw earlier, one additional governance challenge in the AI area is the opinion of some survey respondents that there may not be sufficient competence amongst IC leadership ranks to steer the development of further AI capabilities across 'Five Eyes' ICs. It's important to avoid hyperbole around the promise of AI in the IC context. But nonetheless for many IC agencies its incorpo-ration is likely (eventually) to result in significant changes to the way intelligence is collected and assessed. And so there remains a concern about whether IC lead-ers are prepared for the coming change. As one IC leader said:

> AI and quantum computing will change the reality of security and intelligence at a global level. Leaders must begin investing in the research and develop-ment of practices that assume that reality will take hold within the next five years. Most agencies are ill prepared for the future in this regard and there is an element of ignorance and misunderstanding on how this will reshape the security and intelligence landscape. While much discussion and effort is placed on better improving current practices, very little attention is being paid to how the intelligence community will be forever altered with the intro-duction of game changing and society changing technology. Unfortunately, countries like the PRC and Russia are taking progressive and leading-edge approaches to this new paradigm, while the West continues to reinforce cur-rent practices and make superficial changes with limited outcomes. (survey respondent 34)

Again, there are no simple, glib prescriptions for remedying a lack of prepared-ness by some IC leaders to manage change brought by the adoption of AI tech-nologies. However, as noted in Chapter 6 (ICT), it's clear from the many survey comments that some progress is being made by IC leaders in considering the multi-dimensional impacts AI will have on ICs. For example, there has been some consideration of technical and counter-intelligence issues. But what so far seems to be missing at the time of writing is a complete IC AI strategy that considers all the organisational variables that will be influenced by the incorporation of AI and how to maximise the benefits while minimising the risks.

Some 'Five Eyes' militaries and governments have adopted national AI strate-gies, but these do not seem to address IC enterprise issues in any detail. IC leaders should develop national IC AI strategies that can coherently identify how such emerging technologies, practices, and processes will be integrated into core intel-ligence processes and key enabling activities. Within any national IC AI strategy, leaders will need to pay close attention to developing strategic and operational KPIs around many areas of AI technical development, particularly in areas of surveillance, robotics, space assets, and quantum computing. But the clear articu-lation of KPIs will also be required to track performance of these technologies against hostile AI that could promote 'deception, disruption, fake news or algo-rithmic training data being manipulated' (survey respondent 13). An IC AI strat-egy will also need to, as mentioned earlier (Chapter 6 ICT), set objectives on how social and ethical challenges will be addressed to ensure the efficacy of new tech-nologies and practices within ICs—whilst at the same time promote transparency and legitimacy in liberal democratic states. Finally, as noted in Chapter 6 (ICT) and 7 (HR), IC leaders will also need to include KPIs on resolving workforce implications of AI integration into existing processes.

HR

In the earlier section on HR governance challenges, a number of issues were iden-tified relating to promoting diversity, inter-generational change, and workforce planning. All of these and others discussed in more detail in Chapter 7 (HR) are subsets in a larger mission of IC strategic workforce planning. Again, as noted earlier, since 9/11 progress has been made on a number of workforce issues, but the increasingly complex security environment will demand IC leaders develop further holistic and integrated strategic workforce planning. Each IC will have their own approach, but again, as hard as it might be there needs to also be a 'whole of IC framework' adopted for workforce planning as well that can pro-mote better HR standards and identify vulnerabilities. Much of the issues that need to be addressed by IC leaders in strategic workforce planning has already been mentioned in Chapter 7 (HR) and again summarised above in this chapter. Accordingly there is no need to repeat that detail here.

But it is worth making a few observations about what should inform an IC stra-tegic workforce plan. First, it's important to simply note that trying to plan both for the current and the workforce of the future will always be difficult. Leaving aside the very real resource constraints many ICs operate under, how the security environment will evolve—and therefore what kind of workforce is required—cannot be estimated accurately. It is possible, however, for ICs to develop better research and foresight analysis capabilities to frame more holistic, evidence-based and integrated approaches to workforce planning. Such knowledge could be used to inform KPIs for diversity, inter-generational change, recruitment, training, retention, and other HR objectives to better pivot human capabilities to the changing mission.

A second observation is that designing workforce planning, if it is not just to be a cosmetic process, will require IC leaders accumulate better evidence in which to make investment decisions in HR. Where should this evidence come from? Again, IC leaders will need to adopt a best practice approach to gather evidence, which will increasingly mean in the future looking outside their agency to benchmark better HR practices. Doing this hard work does not necessarily mean IC leaders turn to the 'usual suspects' (e.g. large accounting or defence contracting or consulting firms) to provide advice on HR workforce issues. Arguably, ICs paying substantial sums of money for cookie-cutter approaches to workforce strategies may be a bad investment in the future. The research gathered for this study suggests other external sources such as more targeted engagement with academia and researchers would be useful and possibly cheaper in exploring how to evaluate what works better in improving diversity, recruitment, training, and retention. Again in Chapter 7 (HR) there were a number of examples given on how a multi-disciplinary research approach to a number of workforce challenges could generate solutions. Of course IC leaders in designing better strategic workforce planning frameworks will as in the past confront technical, resourcing, cultural, and human constraints to actioning such plans. Perhaps the greatest challenges may lay in attracting and retaining Generation Y, Z, and beyond to ICs in ways that reliably address capability gaps into the future. How can IC leaders, for example, better align the values and missions of their agencies with the values, ethics, and professional aspirations of an increasingly young and diverse recruitment pool who may not see themselves devoting their entire work life to the IC? As succinctly put by one IC leader:

> people want flexible careers and we should accommodate that. People may not want a 30 year career in one organization. People also want to lead modern lives and do not want to have to isolate themselves in a vault just to do their work. (survey respondent 102)

Given this reality, what are the common value denominators that ICs can use that will have real resonance for the next generations as they consider employment in ICs? This remains a difficult question to answer. IC leaders can look to other industries such as finance, medicine, law, and IT to see how HR departments are tapping into next-generation values and expectations. But after reflecting on trends in other industries, they will have to implement initiatives, which still make sense in the relatively closed IC workplace. What could such initiatives be? Perhaps greater flexibility will be key rather than a dogmatic full time (9–5) approach to filling roles. Could IC leaders adopt strategic workforce initiatives that offer more flexibility to work arrangements yet still benefit the IC? For example, a part-time role either in the private or academic sector as well as the IC could be of mutual benefit. For recruiting next-generation employees, could IC leaders set up HR arrangements that provide intern positions at lower levels as part of a recruitment strategy—a kind of 'try before you buy' approach for young workers? Internships could be temporary and offered at lower levels of security classification in some work environments. Interns who have the right skill sets and see their values aligned to IC missions could be offered ongoing employment. A strategic workforce planning framework would also need to promote greater workforce flexibility and professional development opportunities for mid and senior career staff. This could be 'more opportunities and career time dedicated to 'sabbatical training,' when experts can update and expand their knowledge and learn new approaches to analysis (and other areas) without the pressure to produce operational materials on a constant basis. Time out to refresh and to think' (survey respondent 65).

Leadership attributes

This last section shifts the focus away from IC governance challenges at the organisational level back to the personal attributes of leaders themselves. Now that we know a bit more about what kind of governance challenges leaders will face; this section explores whether it is possible to know what kind of individual leadership attributes are more likely to have a positive impact on the challenges identified. Following this discussion, Chapter 9 (Leadership Development) will then reflect on all aspects of IC leadership explored in the study and provide some tentative conclusions about how to conceptualise future IC leadership development programs that foster both the individual leadership attributes and knowledge required to negotiate the many governance challenges identified.

In simple terms, what kind of personal attributes do IC leaders need to steer and adapt their teams, branches, agencies, or entire communities to the increasingly complex security environment? In this section we reflect back on key points made in Chapter 2 about IC leadership from historical, organisational, psychological, and individual perspectives; and connect it with what former and current IC leaders surveyed believe are critical leadership attributes. The objective is to progress knowledge about leadership in the IC context by bringing together theoretical perspectives from the more established leadership field with insights from both former and current experienced IC leaders. Can a broader synthesis of traditional leadership theorising discussed in Chapter 2 and insights gathered in the IC leadership survey advance both theoretical and practitioner knowledge about how one can best produce the next cadre of effective IC leaders? It's important to build on the theory, but better theorising can also help inform strategies for the developing future generation of IC leaders—the topic of Chapter 9 (Leadership Development).

You will recall in Chapter 2 several leadership theories and their associated research agendas were discussed (e.g. neo-charismatic/transformational and follower-centric). With all types of leadership theories, several characteristics have been identified by researchers and attempts made to test empirically how they inform leadership behaviour in a range of industries. For example, in Chapter 2 transformational leadership was described as someone who can transform or change basic values, beliefs, and attitudes so followers are willing to perform beyond the minimum levels. Transformational leadership characteristics such as the ability to change basic values and beliefs could, for example, be useful for an increased understanding of the motivations, drivers, and behaviours of the changing inter-generational workforce discussed in Chapter 7 (HR). But just how applicable are transformational leadership theoretical approaches to understanding leadership in the IC context? Having charisma and influence are considered important attributes in transformational leadership theories. But do leaders need to be charismatic to have effective influence within ICs?

Question 8 (of the IC leadership survey) asked respondents to select from a range of options what attributes they thought are most important for current and future leaders of our ICs. On the matter of charismatic attributes, 87.6 per cent of respondents (n = 128) indicated that charismatic qualities are either somewhat important, important, or a very important attribute for an IC leader to have. Yet interestingly, only 2.74 per cent (n=4) thought that it was essential for IC leaders to be charismatic to shift followers values. Why did most IC leaders surveyed believe it was important to very important, but not essential for leaders to be charismatic? Some survey respondents provided insights into why they believe being charismatic is important. One respondent said being charismatic 'excites followers, shows you are interested in the field enough to energize others, and are visibly interested in leadership' (survey respondent 2). Others respondents also commented that it was somewhat important to be charismatic though not necessarily essential 'so that you can engage and relate to the team and the executive as well as those outside your immediate sphere of influence' (survey respondent 3). Yet other comments suggested the extent that being 'charismatic' is important was likely contextual to different IC agencies or even within agencies. Such comments seem to challenge the critical importance of the single, all, and mighty omnipotent charismatic leader. The following comment from survey respondent 1 encapsulates well some of these views:

> I believe that leadership attribute requirements can be different at different stages of an organisation's development. A stable well-functioning agency might not have the same requirements for charismatic leadership as might a new agency that is setting up relationships with other agencies, still developing its budget base, etc. Additionally, it can also be a question of the overall skill mix of the leadership team rather just of individual leaders.

It's not possible to expand on all insights collected in the survey relating to charismatic leadership attributes. But a closely connected attribute is transformational leadership, which as discussed in Chapter 2 has been the most empirically tested theoretical approach in leadership studies. Similar to charisma being seen as important/very important, 70.95 per cent of respondents (n=105) also thought it was important for leaders to exhibit transformational leadership behaviours in the IC context. Of interest and in contrast to the low number (2.74 per cent) that thought it essential for leaders to be charismatic, however, 24.32 per cent (n=36) of participants believed that IC leaders should be able to demonstrate transformational attributes. What accounts for the slight increase in the essential ranking for transformational leadership attributes? At this point there is no clear answer to explain the rating differences between charismatic and transformational leadership. The low ranking (2.74 per cent) of respondents indicating the importance of being charismatic as 'essential'—yet the higher level (24.32 per cent) of others suggesting being transforming as 'essential' at least in the survey context suggest IC leaders see being able to transform people's values and behaviours as most important. So if this is true and an IC leader need not necessarily display charismatic qualities, what other behavioural characteristics will allow transformative change?

A number of comments from respondents suggested that IC leaders must have basic values that underpin any transformational behaviours in ICs. One respondent encapsulated this point well, adding 'one cannot lead if one does not understand what is guiding and motivating those working beneath them.' 'More important, one must have a strong set of personal values and standards that guide how best such a transformation process can be implemented without sacrificing integrity' (survey respondent 78). Others also raised the importance of leaders having values and beliefs that are in themselves 'transformative' that can challenge the conservatism of IC cultures, which are often resistant to change (survey respondent 85).

These comments indicate some participants link the importance of leaders having a strong set of personal values to being transformational leaders in the IC context, yet do not specify what the values should be. However, other insights provide clues of what specific values might promote transformational leadership including trust, ethical behaviour, transparency, and authenticity (survey respondents 15, 208). Other behaviours were also listed as being important, such as mentoring.

What the survey results show is that it remains unclear how useful charismatic/transformational leadership theorising is to developing current and future IC leaders. The survey sample size (n=208) is obviously not representative of all possible leadership perspectives from either former or current IC leaders across the 'Five Eyes' countries. A more extensive collection of IC leader's views on various leadership attributes is required before accurate assessments can be made about the relative weightings given to various attributes and why. It should also be pointed out that survey question 8 was not designed to elucidate respondent's understanding of a particular leadership theory. It is possible that if the question provided specific definitions of leadership theories respondents may have weighted levels of attribute importance differently.

Two factors influenced the more exploratory rather than empirical approach adopted in the survey to garner insights about leadership attributes from IC leaders. First, given the contestability and overlap in many leadership theories about what attributes are most important, it made sense to allow IC leaders to demonstrate their own understanding of leadership characteristics rather than require them to respond through a particular theoretical prism. Second, due to the absence of any substantial theorising currently on leadership in IC contexts, I took the view that designing survey questions should be influenced by a grounded theory approach that would allow them to express their own values, beliefs, and practitioner perspectives on leadership. This would allow a comparing and contrasting of insights with other non-IC leadership research (in Chapter 2) yet at the same time help develop much needed leadership theorising in the IC context.

The final two leadership attributes we are going to focus on here are ethical behaviour and self-awareness by IC leaders. Out of all the nine leadership attributes survey respondents were asked to rate the relative importance of (from not at all important to essential), 72.67 per cent (n = 109) believe IC leaders having ethical attributes is essential. Or in total by adding those that stated it 'essential' to those that rated it either 'somewhat important,' 'important,' and 'very important,' 99 per cent (n = 140) stated that it was important for IC leaders to be ethical. As mentioned in Chapter 2, ethical leadership attributes are seen as important to a range of follower-centric leadership theorists, particularly the research perspectives of authentic, ethical, and servant leadership. Ethical attributes are linked to both ethical and authentic leadership perspectives. Ethical leadership is concerned with how IC leaders may negotiate the many ethical dilemmas they face in running intelligence agencies. In several chapters we explored how ethical issues have historically intersected with intelligence leadership practice and the impact this has on privacy, transparency, and accountability in liberal democracies such as the 'Five Eyes' countries. Several comments from IC leaders surveyed underscore the core role ethics plays in IC leadership. Simply put, one said ethics is 'fundamental to the profession and practice of intelligence' (survey respondent 21).

Briefly, the second follower-centric perspective—ethical leadership—is concerned with how the leader's actions result (or not) in ethical outcomes and how these impact on the organisation they lead. This strand of follower-centric leadership is clearly relevant to many other issues explored in this study given most have an ethical dimension to the decisions leaders need to take. Additionally, another respondent referred to the importance of being an ethical leader particularly as the environment for collection and analysis becomes more difficult:

> Being an ethical leader is essential as we all try and navigate a changing world view and environment. Understanding that all is not what it seems, that 'facts' are fluid and that sources may have their own agendas are important. It is only through being ethical, having integrity in how we conduct ourselves and present our findings that we can try and provide useful information to

stakeholders and not adversely contribute to the already difficult operating environment. (survey respondent 26)

Several survey comments indicated the importance of ethical leadership in the context of negotiating the integration of new technology into ICs (see Chapter 6 ICT). Of interest, one respondent highlighted the problems associated with the intersection of new technology and technology and ethics as well as what other leadership behaviours might strengthen ethical leadership. One said: 'as technology advances, intelligence practices may be 'extra-legal.' Ethical intelligence practices compliment other attributes like being 'transparent and authentic' (survey respondent 27). This quote raises a critical point as IC leaders will continually be called upon to understand not only the legal powers they can operate in, but also how to ethically risk manage an increasingly complex and technologically enabled operating environment.

It is likely that IC leaders will increasingly be faced both with a legislative permissive operating environment and/or one which does not keep up with technologically enabled threats or collection methodologies. So referring back to survey respondent 27's comment, being able to assess the 'extra-legal' risks in operating in such an environment will be a crucial leadership attribute and skill. Finally, in the context of ethical attributes several IC leaders link this attribute to transparency in directing the mission and the leading and mentoring of others (survey respondents 23, 60, 69).

Transparency as mentioned in Chapter 2 is also a key attribute of authentic leadership. It remains difficult, however, to define this kind of leadership. In 2003, Luthans and Avolio defined authentic leadership as 'a process that draws from both positive psychological capacities and a highly developed organisational context, which results in greater self-awareness and self-regulated positive behaviours on the part of leaders and associates, fostering self-development' (Luthans and Avolio 2003: 243). Authentic leadership scholars argue that a leader's positive values, beliefs, ethics, and their ability to develop transparency amongst other characteristics impact on whether followers are more likely to adopt such qualities—resulting in a better organisation (Walsh 2017: 444).

Another attribute of authentic leadership theory which scored highly in the IC leadership survey was the need for the leader to be self-aware. Out of 150 respondents who answered question 8 (about leadership attributes), 54.67 per cent (n=82) thought that it was essential for IC leaders to have self-awareness. Overall, 100 per cent (n=150) stated that it was somewhat important, important, very important, or essential for IC leaders to have self-awareness. But what does it mean to 'have self-awareness' in the IC leadership context?

Four themes were discernible from the survey comments that provided some clues about what self-aware leadership could mean in ICs. The first theme was about being able to make evidence based and ethical decisions that allowed the leader to know (to the extent that this is possible) they have made the right call. Secondly, self-awareness was linked to the ability by leaders to promote a team (less hierarchical) environment in order to navigate the increasingly complex security environment. Third, being self-aware was associated with effective inter-personal skills and being positive and optimistic. Finally, several survey respond-ents associated being self-aware to the leader knowing their own strengths and weaknesses in order to better mentor others. Space does not allow a full detailing of the various comments made by IC leaders surveyed about the importance of self-awareness. However, the following two comments encapsulate the types of sentiments expressed by several survey participants. On the theme of being able to make evidence-based decisions, a point made now several times in this study, one participant said a leader needs:

> to be able to make decisions based on evidence and experience, which may not always be held by the one person. Therefore one needs to be self-aware, promote a team environment with the ability to gain a cross section of infor-mation, making evidence-based ethical choices and mentoring others to do the same. (survey respondent 7)

On the theme of knowing one's own strengths and weaknesses, another respond-ent said:

> A leader who is not self-aware will usually fail to perform as a strong leader. To be self-aware one must actively seek out constructive critique and respond faithfully to what is received. Very good leaders actually develop a network of sensors within their organization who can provide honest feedback on how well they are performing and how they are being perceived. (survey respond-ent 88)

In summary, 150 survey respondents addressed question 8, which asked them to rate the relative importance of nine leadership attributes. Out of 150, 96 respondents provided detailed textual responses that generated further insights into why they weighted the importance of some leadership attributes over others. Regrettably, space does not allow a detailed discussion here of all their insights. But in general, it is pleasing that many IC leaders have reflected extensively on their own experiences about what they think are important leadership attributes. Many have also provided insightful comments, which underscore why they believe some attributes are more important. It is also clear that many of the com-ments, while not necessarily explicitly linked to various mainstream leadership theoretical perspectives, can be associated with the different research agendas discussed in Chapter 2.

However, it is also clear that the sample of data collected for question 8 (lead-ership attributes) is very small (n = 150) and is no way representative of the larger number of former or current IC leaders across the 'Five Eyes.' Additionally, the results cannot at this point accurately rate which leadership attributes are the most important and why. Larger sample sizes collected within and across IC agencies would allow for more valid and reliable analytical generalisations on the relative importance of various leadership attributes. This would be an important first step before ICs spent valuable resources investing in more elaborate programs (if they were so inclined), such as empirical leadership testing regimes (e.g. multifactor questionnaires or authentic leadership questionnaires) to assess behavioural characteristics of IC leaders. Indeed, the next step in gaining further empirical evidence for what leadership attributes the next generation of leaders should embody is not elaborate workplace 'testing' of the influence of various leadership behavioural attributes. Rather, a more achievable first step would be for ICs to engage with trusted external researchers (not generic business consultants) who can through a Delphi process help agencies to come to 'a whole of IC view' on how to define attributes and then agree on which ones are the most important for leadership developmental programs.

What the results for questions 8 and 9 and indeed more broadly the insights gathered from the entire survey (23 questions) suggest is we are still a long way from any grand theories that allow an understanding of how to improve leadership in the IC context. Nonetheless, the analysis of all the data collected for this study does allow more scaffolding in which to build larger studies that will progress our theorising—but also more importantly the transfer of knowledge into designing better leadership development programs in the IC workplace.

Conclusion

This chapter assessed the significance of three significant and inter-related issues as they relate to leadership in the IC context. First, it summarised the key governance challenges that will continue to occupy the minds of likely generations of IC leaders. Secondly, the chapter—while avoiding offering glib 'silver bullet' solutions to the many governance challenges—provides strategic road maps so they could start to be addressed in more systematic ways. Finally, Chapter 8 moved away from the organisational governance issues and back to the individual IC leader. It brought together the traditional leadership theorising discussed in Chapter 2 with the insights gathered from IC leaders surveyed. The hope here is to generate deeper conversations both in the IC workplace and with researchers about what leadership attributes are important to improving outcomes across the 'Five Eyes' IC. Using the insights gained about governance challenges and the significance of various leadership attributes, Chapter 9 (Leadership Development) briefly explores what principles could inform a leadership development framework for 'Five Eyes' ICs.

Note

1 Thomas Fingar was the first Deputy Director of National Intelligence for Analysis and a Chairman of the National Intelligence Council.

References

Chang, W., & Tetlock, P. E. (2016). Rethinking the training of intelligence analysts. *Intelligence and National Security*, *31*(6), 903–920.

Dhami, M. K. (2018). Towards an evidence-based approach to communicating uncertainty in intelligence analysis. *Intelligence and National Security, 33*(2), 257–272. doi: 10.1080/02684527.2017.1394252

Lim, K. (2016). Big data and strategic intelligence. *Intelligence and National Security, 31*(4), 619–635. doi: 10.1080/02684527.2015.1062321

Luthans, F., & Avolio, B. (2003). Authentic leadership development. In K. Cameron, J. Dutton & R. Quinn (Eds.), *Positive organizational leadership* (pp. 241–258). San Francisco, CA: Berrett-Koehler.

Walsh, P. F. (2011). *Intelligence and intelligence analysis*. Abingdon: UK: Routledge.

Walsh, P. F. (2015). Building better intelligence frameworks through effective governance. *International Journal of Intelligence and Counterintelligence, 28*(1), 123–142. doi: 10.1080/08850607.2014.924816

Walsh, P. F. (2017). Making future leaders in the US intelligence community: challenges and opportunities. *Intelligence and National Security, 32*(4), 441–459. doi: 10.1080/02684527.2016.1253920

9 Leadership development

Introduction

In this final chapter, based on the synthesis of all the data including insights gathered from the 208 former and current IC leaders who participated in the study's survey, I explore what leadership principles are potentially most germane to the implementation of IC leadership development programs. A second objective is to use these principles in order to provide the reader with a broad leadership development framework. The hope is that the framework offered here will help inform leadership development programs for 'Five Eyes' ICs and others across similar liberal democracies.

Neither the discussion below on leadership development principles nor the framework, however, should be construed as either exhaustive or immutable. Indeed, I would welcome hearing from scholars and IC leaders on how this framework can be built upon further to better inform leadership development programs in ICs. In short, the framework should be seen as a catalyst for further research and discussion, not an endpoint in itself.

Leadership development

As mentioned in the introduction (Chapter 1), I deliberately choose a very broad definition of IC leaders (from team level up to executive heads of agencies or communities). Given such diversity, one should expect to see a cross spectrum of opinions about the attributes, skills, and competencies IC leaders need to develop—depending on one's own professional journey and levels of seniority. I did wonder when analysing the data whether it would have been better to have pitched the relevant survey questions on leadership development to a particular career stage (early, mid, or senior). This could have provided a more focused set of suggestions—perhaps on what a certain level of IC leader requires developmentally. It would be useful in a subsequent study to focus on one particular level of IC management—for example head of agency or middle-management—to identify more granularity in leadership development frameworks relevant to these levels.

Nonetheless, as a starting point, and given there still is an absence at least publicly on what kinds of attributes, skills, and competencies should inform IC leadership development, I argue having a broader, diverse set of views from different levels of seniority captures important information about both what senior leaders expect of themselves as much as what lower level leaders expect of themselves and vice versa. Putting a leadership development framework forward, however tentative, will hopefully generate discussion on how development should be sequenced through the advancement of current and future IC leaders' careers. The hope is that a working framework can also provide a taxonomy of principles to guide more in-depth empirical reflection on what works best in developing our leaders and why.

Before getting into detail about what the development framework might include, it's worth briefly mentioning two additional survey questions included in the study—the results of which though requiring further analysis could influence how ICs conceptualise leadership development programs. The first question (question 20) posed a series of five sub-questions about leadership background, experience, and training. The first sub-question posed a negatively worded question: that IC leaders *did not need* a background in intelligence to be an effective leader. A total of 71 per cent (n=71 out of a total of 91 respondents) either strongly disagreed or disagreed with this statement. This implies that most respondents believed IC leaders did need an IC background to be effective leaders in this context. Question 20 also asked IC respondents to rate the importance of length of experience (five years or more), as well as if a leader from a relevant national security/law enforcement policy area would be just as effective being an IC leader than those who climbed through the ranks. On length of experience, 66.6 per cent (n=66) stated they thought at least five years (and more) was a reasonable time frame for IC leaders to develop leadership expertise. Regarding the question whether a senior leader from a policy background (e.g. national security or law enforcement) will more than likely be an effective IC leader—44 per cent (n=44) strongly disagreed/disagreed with this statement. The results were more mixed. A large proportion of respondents (32.32 per cent n=32) were neutral on the question, and only 22.22 per cent agreed that a leader from a policy area could be an IC leader. I would have thought that there would have been a closer association between the 71 per cent who argued that leaders should have a background in the IC versus the 44 per cent who disagreed that someone with a policy background would be an effective IC leader. I would have expected the latter to be higher in line with those who overall rated the necessity for IC leaders to have an intelligence background.

The relatively high number of respondents (32.32 per cent) or around one-third of the total 99 responses who clicked 'neutral' for whether leaders from policy backgrounds would be effective IC leaders could be interpreted as a belief overall that effective IC leaders should come from the community, but there remains a lack of clarity based on the survey results of whether those from policy backgrounds could make effective IC leaders with only 22.22 per cent (n=22) agreeing that they would be good leaders. At this point, it's unclear what is behind the discrepancies in some of question 20 responses. A larger sample response may help explain further IC beliefs in regards to IC vs policy background for future

IC leaders. Additional targeted interviews of all IC leaders who completed the survey might have also helped resolve these different views. However, in reality, we know that across the 'Five Eyes' IC leaders often come from policy roles and vice versa, so the more instructive question might be the length of experience a leader can accrue within the IC in addition to any other professional experience they bring to the role. The fifth and final sub-question (for question 20) asked whether respondents agreed with the statement that there was insufficient training for aspiring leaders in ICs. A total of 81.81 per cent of 99 respondents (n = 81) either strongly agreed or agreed with this statement with only 3 per cent agreeing that there was sufficient training for our future IC leaders.

Again to emphasise, this is a very small sample size of all potential IC leaders who may have an opinion one way or the other on this matter. Further sampling and targeted interviewing would be the next step to fully assess how reliable this view was for the greater population—particularly lower level IC leaders. It is clear there are a number of diverse and even conflicting views about whether IC leaders had sufficient training—or indeed even needed any training. For example, two respondents believed that IC leaders didn't need any type of training—yet then suggested they receive training in management, research, and government experience beyond the IC (survey respondents 10 and 113). It is likely that 'training' and 'experience' mean different things to people and how IC leaders understand and use terminology in the context of leadership development also requires further investigation. Nonetheless, the results discussed above underscore at least some belief amongst the IC leadership cadre that currently training initiatives are lacking across the broader IC.

IC leadership development principles

Out of the over 80 per cent who believe there is insufficient leadership training opportunities for IC leaders, what knowledge, skills, and competencies do they think should inform developmental programs? Using NVIVO—a qualitative analytical software package—I coded 138 detailed textual references to issues related to leadership training. This was the second highest number of texts related to one theme after 'governance challenges,' which had 197 references. This was a pleasing result because it was clear many respondents care sufficiently about leadership training and how it can be improved to draft in many cases paragraph responses to the relevant survey question.

The rich textual detail provides an additional tranche of insights in addition to analysis from earlier chapters to provide the IC leadership development framework outlined below. Within the 138 textual responses to the issue of leadership training, several themes emerged. I grouped these into six broad thematic and inter-related areas: *individual behavioural attributes, technical training, strategic and business planning, mentoring, evaluation,* and lastly *training and education strategies.* In the remaining space, I briefly illustrate some of the issues IC leaders raised under each of these six themes before presenting a summary of the analysis in the form of the IC leadership development framework.

Individual behavioural attributes

Many of the behavioural attributes mentioned by respondents in the context of leadership development are similar to the various leadership attributes discussed in Chapter 8 (The Future IC Leader and Intelligence Governance) so there is no need to repeat them here. Suffice it to say though, strategies to promote ethical behaviour, self-awareness, authenticity, and team-based work were mentioned by a number of respondents (e.g. survey respondents 43, 60) in the context of leadership development. Interesting too, there were a few comments about the importance of mindfulness and EQ (survey respondent 43). But how do you foster in development programs the more positive behavioural attributes discussed in this study? How do aspiring leaders become more authentic or ethical leaders? It is after all difficult to change one's behaviours, which are often linked to enduring values, personal beliefs, and organisational culture. Improving leadership capabilities, which rely on, for example, greater awareness of ethical dilemmas working in ICs or being more authentic and team based cannot be recalibrated overnight. Addressing personal behavioural attributes that may be reducing a leader's capabilities to effectively influence IC outcomes for the better will be for any aspiring leader a gradual process. It is difficult to generalise about the types of specific training strategies that could be employed across all 'Five Eyes' ICs given the different operating contexts.

This study has not been able to take a 'deep dive' into the various leadership attribute training initiatives that might currently be operating across all ICs. There are likely some leadership strategies such as 360 degree feedback tools and competency frameworks that aspiring leaders across both the broader public and private sectors—not just those working in IC—may be able to use to manage and lead self, others, and organisations. It is also difficult to know for sure what types of specific self-awareness analytical tools are being already used in ICs. But reflecting on the survey data collected, the interviews conducted, and the analysis of other secondary sources, it seems true enough to suggest one key principle of any IC leadership training development framework should be a greater focus on leadership attribute training. How this is achieved might be IC-wide or agency specific, but the focus needs to promote three broad strategies to identify and modify (where necessary) behavioural changes in the IC leader. These strategies are self-reflection, team reflection, and external feedback and support. Of greatest importance will be opportunities for current and aspiring IC leaders to be given formal and informal mentoring opportunities to self-reflect fundamentally on who they are and why they want to be in a leadership role in the IC. In his now-famous 2009 TED talk and first book *Start with Why*, Simon Sinek asks people to be clear about what makes them fulfilled. This is a more fundamental question than asking how we do something and what we do (Sinek, Mead and Docker 2017: 12–13). Leaders need to know personally 'their why' before they can articulate the why, what, and how of their teams. Managers might ask the 'what' and 'how' but leaders always need to know the 'why' and the latter might change significantly in their careers as different governance challenges arise because of the increasingly complex security environment.

Similarly, on being more aware of the ethical dimensions associated with managing both the core intelligence and key enabling activities within ICs, IC leaders need additional opportunities (e.g. workshops and scenarios) to discuss various ethical scenarios arising from an increasingly complex operating environment. As raised in previous chapters, particularly in the management of AI-enabled collection and analytical capabilities, IC leaders will need to understand and respond to actual or potential ethical dilemmas that inevitably arise. Joint IC and academic workshops run in collaboration with trusted applied ethicists will assist in helping IC leaders identify practical ethical decision-making options. As noted earlier, some colleagues and I are currently progressing an Australian Research Council research project that is investigating whether ethical guidelines for use by ICs can be identified in security intelligence collection. This kind of research could be used to inform ethical decision-making workshops run in collaboration with ICs.

One final area of leadership attribute training that is worth pointing out is emotional intelligence awareness. The importance of emotional intelligence (EI or EQ) in leadership theory and practice has grown in the last 30 years (Goleman 1998; Bar-On 1997; Mayer and Salovey 1997: 3-31; Cooper and Sawaff 1998; Petrides *et al.* 2007:151-166; Petrides and Furnham 2001, 2003). There remains, however, conflicting definitions of EI and EQ models—as well as less certainty how EQ impacts on organisational outcomes across industries. A leader who has a high EQ has highly developed self-awareness, self-regulation, social awareness, empathy levels, and motivation. The literature suggests there is a close link between emotionally intelligent leadership and employee performance and satisfaction. This is why understanding EQ is important for IC leaders because if they can identify emotional information (good and bad) and how it impacts on other leadership attributes, they can progress in more positive ways their own emotional regulation and that of their teams in productive ways. There are several EQ assessment tools such as MSCEIT and Genos which could also be included as part of the self, team, and external reflection and feedback activities in a leadership development framework.[1]

Technical training

Not surprisingly, several IC leaders surveyed for the study suggested a range of technical issues current and aspiring leaders needed 'training' in. There were diverging views on what this training should consist of and how it should be delivered. Some comments were also vague and offered little details such as 'IC leaders needed to stay current and take time out for training' (survey respondent 70), though at times there were comments that were a lot more granular and provided specific areas where IC leaders thought knowledge, skill, and capabilities were lacking. Again, there was no surprise given earlier comments made about the importance of AI that several respondents highlighted the need for greater understanding about AI, but also in the context of IC leaders being more competent in STEM subjects. Greater investment in specialised in-house training combined with higher education was mentioned frequently by respondents as ways to help improve STEM capability gaps. In addition to AI, several STEM areas were also listed that IC leadership training programs could consider incorporating, including but not limited to big data, biometrics, encryption, and the dark net (survey respondent 70). In the social-behavioural sciences (political sciences/international relations, sociology, psychology, and criminology), some respondents suggested that in addition to 'on the job experience' IC leaders should be given opportunities to complete an MA or even a PhD in a relevant area study (survey respondent 23). However, there was less detail provided in what areas of study are more critical over others.

Mentoring

Mentoring is linked to the first theme above (individual behavioural attributes). First, in order for leaders to be able to reflect deeply on their behaviours, self-mission, and be able to clarify values, there needs to be as part of this process opportunities to receive mentoring from more senior leaders. Learning from others' experience has to varying degrees of intensity been done within ICs. However, in addition to receiving mentoring from other more senior IC leaders, I would suggest further opportunities be considered outside the agency—potentially in another agency/industry or someone in academia to expand their thinking on how to promote more helpful leadership styles and how these impact their staff. There may be the need for some background vetting of external mentors, but I think ICs could risk manage such exercises in ways that allow an aspiring leader opportunities to reflect generally and non-operationally on leadership identity and challenges yet at the same time not breaking any secrecy laws. The importance of mentoring in any IC leadership development framework was well underscored by two IC leaders: 'mentor the most promising people and provide opportunities for cross organisational assignments to broaden a future senior manager's perspective. For senior analysts put them in close contact with their clients and customers so that they learn their needs and constraints' (survey respondent 79). 'Every intelligence organisation I have served with is a team. Mentorship is how we build the next generation' (survey respondent 122). This later quote from survey respondent 122 sums up well the importance of IC leaders learning to mentor staff not as a perfunctory bureaucratic exercise, but in ways that can actually impact positively on the personal professional growth of individuals and their organisations.

Strategic and business planning

As far as strategic business planning is concerned, there are several knowledge, skills, and competencies that could be considered for inclusion on an IC leadership development framework. A full audit of current strategic and business planning development opportunities already available within the IC and broader government service is a necessary first step prior to designing targeted development programs. This is because it is not uncommon for both public and private sector agencies to have access to several learning programs broadly related to strategic and business planning issues including environmental and business planning, risk management, and workforce/capital development. Such generic programs may be more suitable in training programs for lower levels to provide an initial knowledge of management principles in the IC context—before they rise to middle ranking and beyond leadership roles. However, although some generic public sector management principles would be useful for early career leaders to take advantage of, it's critical for IC leadership development planners to ensure they continually do the 'fit for purpose' test for any basic training. Can the training, for example, be sufficiently contextualised to allow IC leaders to see how learning outcomes could be applied in their context as much as a policy or private sector environment?

Based on the analysis of the research gathered for this study, however, I argue that just sending IC leaders off to generic leadership training programs is not sufficient and careful thought needs to be given on how to supplement generic management training with IC contextually relevant cases and examples. It's clear that differences in strategic priority setting processes, operational activity, legislative, and other technical issues more peculiar to ICs rather than other public and private sector agencies will need to be considered and injected into early, mid-career, and senior generic leadership training programs. Nonetheless, there is likely to be a range of leadership and management knowledge areas practiced in the private sector such as strategic stakeholder management, marketing, communication, and influence, which can also provide IC leaders with new ways to improve their practice in such areas.

One key deliverable in any strategic and business planning will be improving the skills, knowledge, and competencies of mid-career, but also senior executive IC leaders to improve their understanding of workforce planning in the volatile security environment. Workforce planning challenges as illustrated in both Chapters 6 (ICT) and 7 (Human Resources) will remain difficult and enduring governance challenges for IC leaders to manage. They include recruitment, diversity, continuous professional development pathways, retention and attrition, and how to strategically manage them.

The final important area that needs considering when exploring strategic and business planning skills, knowledge, and competencies required in an IC leadership development program is intelligence governance. As noted in Chapter 2 in the explanation of the effective intelligence framework, intelligence governance is the most important key enabling activity because it is fundamentally about how leaders lead by coordinating laws, rules, processes, and organisational culture in ways that hopefully improve core intelligence processes and other key enabling activities. As theorists remind us, governance both in theory and practice is about how IC leaders make collective decisions (2008: 3). There is always 'a leader' at the apex of an IC agency who formally 'makes a decision.' However, in reality, even final executive decisions come about through a broader, collective decision-making process. This fact will become even more the norm in the more volatile and less uncertain security environment. The several complex governance challenges raised in previous chapters will rely on future leaders who understand what effective intelligence governance means in their context and more broadly across the entire IC enterprise. I first started using the term 'intelligence governance' in 2011 in the context of developing the 'effective intelligence framework' outlined in Chapter 2. But governance has broader multi-disciplinary origins—and each discipline has its own definitional perspectives (e.g. political science, the law, and the corporate sector) on what 'governance' means. Leaving aside the multiple ways it can be defined, most theorists at least agree that governance implies both a formal and informal set of rules and conventions about how decisions are made (Pierre and Peters 2000: 7; Hyden *et al.* 2004; Kaufmann and Kraay 2007). There may eventually be a set of normative theoretical perspectives that future IC leaders can rely on to help them identify what good intelligence governance is. Further theorising and practitioner reflection may help us get there, which is one reason I embarked on this study. But in reality, applying good governance solutions will be more messy affairs rather than neat formulations—frequently changing as the political (external governance) and institutional IC (internal governance) actors attempt to adapt to the ever dynamic and uncertain security environment. In particular, major existential changes such as the COVID-19 pandemic, but also less impactful new and emerging threats, underscore the importance of developing good IC leaders that can identify solutions to the myriad of governance issues raised in this book. We are only at the beginning of understanding how to improve intelligence governance across ICs in ways that create transparency, value, flexibility, sustainability, and institutional adaptedness.

Future IC leaders will need to understand how to improve collective decision-making in ways that are flexible to the operating conditions. Better decision-making will be even more informed by IC leaders' ability to tap into institutional, individual, and group strengths—yet at the same time checking the influence of cultural pathologies. Achieving good intelligence governance will not just be about considering ways group decision-making ownership can drive long-lasting reform at the agency level, but also how governance challenges can be addressed at the whole of enterprise and across the 'Five Eyes' levels. Likely a critical metric for good intelligence governance in the future will be how IC leaders as a matter of habit, not of sporadic exception, build institutional arrangements that foster a larger volume and variety of external expertise to assist in addressing the number of governance challenges identified in previous chapters. There will not be one way to develop intelligence governance skills of the next leadership cadre. Agency and IC context as always will inform specific development strategies, but a combination of in-house seminars, industry placements, and higher-degree learning that focuses on governance theory/practice and working through scenarios relevant to the IC context would be worth exploring further.

Evaluation

Somewhat expectantly there were a number of comments from IC leaders surveyed about the need for leaders to improve their own skills, knowledge, and the capabilities of their agencies in measuring what is working and what isn't. This was encouraging as a critical point that has emerged throughout this study is that IC leaders can only solve the many governance challenges identified by evaluating evidence for what works in ameliorating them. In terms of evaluating one core part of the IC business, for example, the 'effectiveness' of analytical products, several respondents described the need for products to be timely, objective, useable, ready, complete, and accurate (survey respondent 43). Such measures as listed here are of course largely subjective—meaning different things to the various ICs and decision-makers who use the various products. While the crude 'tick and flick' product evaluation forms that used to be attached to most intelligence products have gone the way of the dodo bird, IC leaders will still need to oversee the implementation of less course qualitative metrics to evaluate intelligence products in the future and adjust format and style—but not of course analytical rigour. More recently we have seen how the distillation of text products into infographics or shorter dot points delivered on iPads is partly due to decision-maker feedback, but it is also the result of decisions taken by IC leaders to improve products based on internal evaluation. Another IC leader raised a further qualitative metric 'value' for evaluating product—though again it remains difficult to define uniformly, their answer did suggest ways IC leaders could further define 'value' for decision-makers.

> A leader must seek out value promoting data and information to always be consolidating their team efforts and products. Where possible tasking products with the additional benefits of risk reduction, cost effectiveness, loss prevention, for example. Utilising various industries methodology to value tangible and intangible benefits. For example, identifying that failures may cost lives, property, ongoing health issues, lost revenue, disruption to commerce, political support loss, and reputational loss. As much as being an "incident" without included costs (survey respondent 38).

Being able to provide products, however, that allow for enhanced empirical and qualitative analytical judgements that better estimate harms or identify opportunities for intervention will require IC leaders to, as noted in Chapters 5 (Analysis) and 7 (Human Resources), invest in analysts who can do this as well. In addition, IC leaders as noted earlier should expand academic outreach programs that can help bolster evidence-based analytical approaches. Of course, as some survey respondents remarked, not everything can be quantified (survey respondent 70), nonetheless the evolving security environment will demand that IC leaders in the broader institutional sense (not just in products) can demonstrate value add and value for money invested. Hence, IC leader development programs should include modules on various multi-disciplinary approaches to evaluating performance of core intelligence processes and key enabling activities. Mid-career leaders, for example, would likely benefit from having some literacy in evaluation research principles and how they have been applied in other fields (e.g. policing, health, and corporate settings). IC leaders should learn both internally from their strategic, policy, and governance units and from academic researchers how to construct meaningful KPIs for different aspects of strategic, operational, and tactical activities, particularly as they relate to the various governance challenges identified. Evaluation planning learning modules should also include foresight analysis that helps IC leaders map likely capability investments that are five years away and how well they are progressing toward these requirements bi-annually. Finally, no evaluation skills, knowledge, and competencies module would be complete without inclusion of material, which can get IC leaders to reflect on current communications/stakeholder influencing strategies and how they can improve value to decision-makers in more agile ways.

Training and education strategies

The fifth and final leadership development theme that arose from surveying IC leaders was not what leaders should be trained in but how. As shown below in Table 9.1, I make suggestions on how the various leadership development content discussed above could be delivered. As some respondents suggested, military command training including with intelligence provides some structure for IC leadership development programs, but it may not suit other civilian-based agencies given differences in mission and organisational culture. Others referred to training and education as being something that should be conducted jointly with other agencies to create a good understanding of where the intelligence function sits within the whole process. For example, one said: 'some of the training should be "immersive" and all should be duly assessed to enable personal development' (survey respondent 56), though the respondent did not mention what training in particular could be immersive. Other respondents emphasised the need for formal higher education pathways in international relations or management (survey respondents 23, 3). But in short there were few details provided by survey respondents on how training and education could be delivered.

Since 9/11, there have been some efforts to establish internal IC leadership programs such as the NIU Certificate in Leadership and Management of the IC established in 2011 by (at the time ODNI Chair) Dr Barry A Zalauf, who is currently the IC Analytic Ombudsman at the ODNI. The certificate Zalauf created is a four-week program consisting of four courses: leadership and intelligence, intelligence and national security policy, national security law and ethics, and organisational management (pers comms Zaluf 2020: 25 April). The Certificate combines a series of business, management, and organisational principles with contemporary IC challenges that the students learn. Guest presenters and IC staff deliver course content. Assessment includes experiential activities, case studies, personal reflection, and facilitated group discussion. DNI Jim Clapper during his tenure described the Certificate as 'the gold standards of leadership education in the IC' (Ibid), though it seems more recently that the NIU is running fewer Certificate courses, which is concerning given the program is the only US IC enterprise-wide leadership development program available.

Table 9.1 IC leadership development framework

Mid-Career Leadership Program (min 5 years' experience)	Skills, knowledge and competencies	Delivered by and additional comments
Leadership attribute training	1. Self and team reflection (360 degree and EQ testing, and evaluating resilience) 2. Ethical risk management principles 3. Contemporary IC issues 4. Leadership theory and practice in IC and non-IC contexts	IC and external facilitation (1 to 4) IC and external experts (1 to 4) (case studies, and crisis exercises to be used for 2 and 3 and 4)
Strategic business planning	1. Strategic planning principles 2. Team building 3. Analytical methods and writing 4. Governance knowledge 5. Workforce planning 6. Stakeholder engagement and influence 7. Crisis management 8. Academic and research engagement strategies	IC and external collaboration with leadership higher education provider (1 to 8) IC and external social psychology provider (2,4,7) Senior analysts (3) Seminars, case studies, cross agency placement, and post-graduate study (2, 4, 5–8) IC-wide approach, foresight analysis, collaborate with higher-education provider (5) IC, marketing, and PR experts (6) IC and multi-disciplinary inputs including running crises scenario exercises from relevant external SMEs, collaborating and overseeing IC-related research projects (7 and 8)
Mentoring	1. Mentoring early career staff 2. Mid-career mentoring	IC and external training provider (1) Senior leadership mentoring mid-career leaders (2) External placements (2)
Technical training— STEM	For example: AI, cyber, biotechnology, WMD, forensics, research collaboration, counter-intelligence	Candidate specific planning Basic to advanced training in IC and via higher learning depending on job role and likely future career placements. Knowledge/competencies to be assessed in the workplace by SMEs

(Continued)

Table 9.1 (Continued)

Mid-Career Leadership Program (min 5 years' experience)	Skills, knowledge and competencies	Delivered by and additional comments
Technical training—SBS	Social psychology, anthropology, IR/security studies, area specialisation, (country, region, transnational), languages	Candidate specific planning Basic to advanced training depending on supervisory role and likely future career placement. Knowledge/ competencies to be assessed in the workplace
Evaluation	Project management, cross-disciplinary evaluation knowledge from research fields, engineering, and organisational theory about evaluating outputs and outcomes in the IC context	IC internal programs, plus cross-disciplinary workshops on promoting evidence-based governance measures

At the time of writing, Australia's Office of National Intelligence (ONI) is also developing a mid-career leadership program, but at this point its content is unknown. I have not been able to find out whether other 'Five Eyes' countries have established enterprise-wide leadership development programs. It is likely that many have their own internal (agency only) programs, but I suspect most of these may be focused on management rather than leadership development. However, regardless of the exact number and nature of IC leadership development programs that may be in existence, responses from survey respondents suggest ICs are not doing enough and need to invest more resources and expertise into such programs. Externally, in higher places of learning there does not seem to be (with a few exceptions) many courses and subjects offered in aspects of IC leadership. In Australia, Charles Sturt University offers an intelligence management subject as part of its MA (Intelligence Analysis) and the Australian National University also offers short executive courses to mid and higher-ranking IC staff. Executive courses have also been offered in a range of other 'Five Eyes' countries such as the Canadian Security and Intelligence Leadership Program at the University of Ottawa. Again, this is not an exhaustive list. There may likely be a few more programs, but I suspect many offer generic leadership/management courses that IC staff can enrol in as any other student can do so. Such programs at business schools are no doubt potentially useful in nurturing future IC leaders, but they are not focused on the intersection of leadership theory and managing the types of governance challenges discussed in this study.

Reflecting now on all the IC leadership issues raised in this study, and as a point for further discussion, I offer a framework below that includes the types of topics that may be considered in conceptualising IC leadership development programs in the future. Table 9.1 depicts elements for an IC leadership development pitched at IC staff with a minimum of five years with some supervisory experience. Based on the analysis of all the data collected for the study, I believe it is at the mid-ranking management level, where the greatest need is for further development. Five years of overall service may be long by some people's perspectives given post-baby boomers tend to spend less at one place of employment. But by focusing on those that have stayed in long enough, but are not towards the end of their careers—you are hopefully investing in the next generation of leaders who via the development program and other professional experience will be equipped with the attributes, skills, knowledge, and competencies to navigate the array of intelligence governance issues discussed. Above all, the framework is underpinned by a philosophy that an effective mid-career development program should be an enterprise-wide IC initiative in order to promote diversity and challenge potential organisational cultural pathologies. While officially the IC would manage the program, the overall approach should be a hybrid model. This means some content such as simulating a crisis situation might be delivered using classified material; other modules such as leadership attribute learning could be taught using unclassified learning material. Hybrid also means that teaching on the program should be a mixture of IC and non-IC experts.

The framework below is not meant to be concise or exhaustive and again will need to be contextualised to the particular operating environment. More than anything the framework is designed to spark further debates about how to develop better IC training development programs and curricula for our future IC leaders. As I wrote back in 2017 in the context of analyst's training, designing rigorous training and education can be difficult and is labour intensive. To do it well requires trainers, educators, and the ICs themselves to engage actively in a range of important and interrelated aspects including curriculum, accreditation, continuous professional development strategies, teaching and learning, and content and assessment (Walsh 2017b: 1005–1021). The brief framework is only a first step in conceptualising potential content for leadership development courses. Much larger, challenging, but nonetheless critical discussions need to occur about curriculum, delivery, accreditation, and how programs fit into a wider continuous professional development for IC leaders.

Conclusion

This chapter provided a synthesis of all the analyses presented in previous chapters in order to identify leadership principles that should inform an IC leadership development framework. It is hoped that the IC leadership development framework presented in Table 9.1 will be used to generate further theorising about leadership development in the IC context. However, even more importantly, it is hoped that the framework can help inform discussions within ICs about designing much needed leadership development programs. In Chapter 10 (Conclusion), I summarise the key findings of the study and suggest some next steps for scholars and practitioners who are interested in advancing the next generation of IC leaders.

Note

1 The MSCEIT (the Mayer-Salovey-Caruso EI Test) measures reasoning ability of an individual given emotional information and series of problems and assesses their solving competencies based on emotions or problems that require the use of emotions to be solved. Genos is an emotional intelligence testing instrument that examines a set of emotionally intelligence competencies that according to its creator are measurable and observable. The six core emotional intelligence competencies to be assessed are: self-awareness, awareness of others, authenticity, emotional reasoning, self-management, and positive influence.

References

Bar-On, R. (1997). *BarOn emotional quotient inventory*. Multi-Health Systems.

Chhotray, V., & Stoker, G. (2008). *Governance theory and practice: A cross-disciplinary approach*. London, United Kingdom: Palgrave Macmillan UK.

Cooper, R. K., & Sawaf, A. (1998). *Executive EQ: Emotional intelligence in leadership and organizations*. London: Penguin.

Goleman, D. (1998). The emotional intelligence of leaders. *Leader to Leader, 10*(10), 20–26. doi: 10.1002/ltl.40619981008

Hyden, G., Court, J., & Meae, K. Eds. (2004). *Making sense of governance: Empirical evaluation from 16 countries*. Boulder and London: Lynne Rienner Publishers.

Kaufmann, D., & Kraay, A. (2007). Governance indicators. Where are *We*, where *We* should *We* be going. *Policy Research Wing*. Washington DC: World Bank, Paper 4730.

Mayer, J. D., Salovey, P., Salovey, P., & Sluyter, D. (Eds.) (1997). Emotional development and emotional intelligence: Implications for educators. In *What Is Emotional Intelligence* (pp. 3–31). New York: Basic Book.

Petrides, K. V., & Furnham, A. (2000). On the dimensional structure of emotional intelligence. *Personality and Individual Differences, 29*(2), 313–320. doi: 10.1016/S0191-8869(99)00195-6

Petrides, K., Furnham, A., & Mavroveli, S. (2007). Trait emotional intelligence: Moving forward in the field of EI. *Emotional Intelligence: Knowns and Unknowns, 4*, 151–166.

Pierre, J., & Peters, B. (2000). *Governance, politics and the state*. Basingstoke: Palgrave Macmillan.

Sinek, S., Mead, D., & Docker, P. (2017). *Find your why*. In Penguin. New York, NY: Portfolio.

Walsh, P. F. (2017b). Teaching intelligence in the twenty-first century: Towards an evidence-based approach for curriculum design. *Intelligence and National Security, 32*(7), 1005–1021. doi: 10.1080/02684527.2017.1328852

10 Conclusion

Introduction

As noted in Chapter 1 (Introduction), this book had four research questions:

1. What is leadership in the contemporary IC context?
2. Is 'intelligence governance' a useful theoretical construct to understand IC leadership, and what are the key governance challenges IC leaders will need to navigate through?
3. How can IC leaders address intelligence governance challenges to improve organisational effectiveness and adaptation?
4. What individual attributes, skills, and capabilities are critical for the next generation of IC leaders to develop, and what principles could underpin leadership development programs?

The preceding chapters went some way to addressing the four questions. However, as noted several times in different chapters, it is difficult to answer them fully. The knowledge gained from both the primary and secondary sources has moved the needle slightly in the direction of understanding different aspects of IC leadership. But the questions are complex and largely open ended. To be fully answered, it will take a concerted effort by researchers and the ICs themselves to address the still significant knowledge gaps related to all four questions. In this final chapter, I provide a summary of key outputs and show how they have addressed aspects of the four research questions. The final section (future IC leadership practice) then provides a short summary of how scholars and ICs can continue to build on the research laid out in this book.

With regards to the first research question, (what is leadership in the contemporary IC context)—several chapters provided insights into this. Chapter 2 (Intelligence and Leadership) went a long way to addressing the question by adopting a multi-disciplinary approach to understanding IC leadership. By using five multi-disciplinary knowledge areas (historical analysis, leadership theory, organisational theory, leadership psychology, and the effective intelligence framework), the chapter argued for a broader approach to understanding leadership in the IC context rather than through the lens of just one discipline. This approach is important because at this stage contemporary IC leadership is significantly under-theorised and a multi-disciplinary approach to studying it will bring richer perspectives—beyond a narrow intelligence studies perspective. Additionally, Chapters 8 (The Future IC Leader and Governance Challenges) and 9 (Leadership Development) provided further insights into both individual and organisational aspects of IC leadership. In particular, significant insights about 'what is leadership in the IC'? was gathered from the 208 IC leaders who responded to the survey. The thematic analysis (facilitated through the qualitative software NVIVO) did show a number of leadership attributes leaders thought were important. Many of these were aligned with attributes traditional leadership theorists also view as critical to various leadership styles and research agendas (e.g. transformational and authentic leadership), though the relevant survey questions did not ask respondents whether they thought a particular leadership theoretical perspective was important. This question was avoided in the survey because even in mainstream leadership theory there remains significant contestability about what attributes constitute different theories and how they impact on followers. The objective, therefore, was not to provide respondents with a pre-ordained theory upon which they had to weigh in on its significance or not. Had I asked respondents which leadership theory is most important and why, I suspect I would have gotten fewer richer insights from IC leaders about what attributes they thought most important—particularly from those who may not have formally studied leadership theory.

The second research question asked whether 'intelligence governance' is a useful construction to understanding IC leadership, and what are the key governance challenges IC leaders will need to navigate through. As noted earlier, 'intelligence governance' was a term I began using in 2011 in the context of the effective intelligence framework (see Chapter 2 Intelligence and Leadership). The framework was first published in my book *Intelligence and Intelligence Analysis*, and a key conclusion I came to at that time was 'intelligence governance' was a useful construct to think about how leaders coordinate core intelligence processes and key enabling activities to ensure IC effectiveness and adaptability over time. This means that to be a good leader you also have to understand intelligence governance. Without a good grasp of 'intelligence governance' it seems less likely that IC leaders are able to make effective collective decisions, which consider the inter-connectedness of both core intelligence processes and key enabling activities.

In this study, I have been able to build further on this concept of 'intelligence governance' by asking surveyed IC leaders about whether they thought this concept was relevant to understanding IC leadership and its organisational impact. Question 15 asked four sub-questions. The first was stated negatively—that developing good intelligence governance of an intelligence organisation or function was not related to having a good leader in charge. Combined, 75.35 per cent (n = 79) indicated they either strongly disagreed or disagreed with this statement—suggesting that most respondents believe good governance was linked to having an effective leader in place. The second sub-question asked respondents whether they believed that 'intelligence governance' was the most critical element in bringing effective coordination, cooperation, and integration of intelligence processes. Of the 106 who provided an answer, 70.1 per cent said they either strongly agreed or agreed that intelligence governance was the most critical element in bringing many of the key core intelligence processes together, particularly those mentioned in Chapter 3 (Tasking and Coordination), Chapter 4 (Collection), and Chapter 5 (Analysis). The third sub-question sought to discover whether IC leaders surveyed also thought if leaders who gained skills and attributes would result in effective intelligence governance. Out of 106 responses, 67 per cent either strongly agreed or agreed that if IC leaders had relevant skills, experience, and attributes this would result in effective intelligence governance in their workplace. This is an important validation of the link between improving leadership skills and effective intelligence governance—one which was developed further in both Chapters 8 (The Future IC Leader and Governance Challenges) and 9 (Leadership Development). The final sub-question on intelligence governance asked whether IC leaders thought political leaders rather than themselves had more impact on intelligence governance outcomes. Out of 106 respondents, 43 per cent disagreed with the statement, but a similar amount agreed with it. It's clear this last sub-question does not provide any meaningful result. In Chapter 2 (Intelligence and Leadership) and 3 (Tasking and Coordination), we did note the powerful influences of external governance actors (political leaders) on IC operations and reform. But it was also pointed out that IC leaders still have significant leeway in directing internal governance in their ICs. In summary, the survey results on the importance of intelligence governance to IC leadership suggest most IC leaders (who participated in the survey) believed it was critical to improving various organisational outcomes—and that having good governance meant having good leaders in place.

Turning now to the second part of research question 2 (what are the key governance challenges IC leaders will need to navigate), Chapters 2–9 explored several that will consume the attention of leaders well into the future. In each chapter, specific governance challenges were clustered around several themes including, but not limited to, organisational structure and culture, collaboration, information sharing, technological innovation, ethics and efficacy, and workforce planning.

Chapter 8 (The Future IC Leader and Governance Challenges) provided a summary of governance challenges detailed in earlier chapters and assessed how they are related. More importantly, Chapter 8 suggests several strategic initiatives IC leaders could consider to begin tackling the governance challenges identified. I will not repeat the complete list of strategic initiatives listed in Chapter 8—but they ranged across the full set of key governance challenges in tasking and coordination, collection, analysis, ICT, and human resources. In brief, they included initiatives from implementing performance teams that can evaluate the interdependence of requirements, priorities, and agency/IC response (for tasking and coordination)—to analytical innovation strategies (analysis)—and also to IC AI and workplace strategic planning (ICT and human resources).

The fourth and final research question asked what individual attributes, skills, and capabilities are critical for the next generation of IC leaders to develop, and what principles could underpin leadership development programs. This question was partly addressed in the last section of Chapter 8 (The Future IC Leader and Governance Challenges), but more significantly dealt with in Chapter 9 (Leadership Development). As noted in Chapter 8, respondents were asked what leadership attributes they think are most important and why. The two standout attributes IC leaders rated most highly were ethics and self-awareness, though several other attributes were also identified and rated by respondents as also being important, such as the ability to embody key values that allow a leader to transform an organisation.

The analysed survey data on leadership attributes in some ways aligned to various leadership theoretical and research agendas discussed in Chapter 2 (Intelligence and Leadership). But as noted earlier, the results do not indicate whether IC leaders were rating attributes based on prior knowledge of any traditional leadership theories outside of the IC context. Regardless, what the survey results do provide is a foundation upon which to build larger studies about what ICs think are the most important leadership attributes to develop in the next generation of leaders. The Future IC Leader and Governance Challenges, Chapter 8's discussion of leadership attributes, then informed analysis in Chapter 9 (Leadership Development) about what principles could be included in a leadership development framework for future leaders. As noted, the principles are *individual behavioural attributes*, *technical training, strategic and business planning, mentoring, evaluation*, and lastly *training and education strategies*.

Future IC leadership practice

With the key outcomes of the study now summarised, in this final section I want to provide some 'next steps' suggestions for ICs and researchers who are interested in leadership development. As noted in Chapter 1 (Introduction), this book is a clarion call to ICs and intelligence studies researchers to focus more on IC leadership development. The book does not pretend to have all—indeed any of the answers—but hopefully it will spark more informed discussions on this topic. Therefore, the 'suggestions' that follow are just that— 'suggestions'—on how to progress this work beyond this point.

I see two broad agendas (an internal IC leadership development and an academic research agenda) that will likely provide useful places to start progressing theory and practice in IC leadership. Both the internal IC and external academic research agendas should be ideally linked. But it is the 'Five Eyes' ICs themselves who will substantially need to steer efforts in leadership development. In crisis situations such as the current COVID-19 pandemic, real reform, particularly in areas such as improving capabilities, like leadership can be seen by some as less of operational importance. IC can always make the claim that other priorities and resources need to be directed elsewhere. But as noted several times in previous chapters, the increasing complexity of the security environment will require ICs to bite the bullet sooner than later and begin to make a longer-term, strategic investment in IC leadership capabilities. While a post-COVID-19 world may see less resources from governments to all public sector agencies (with perhaps the exception of health authorities), ICs can nonetheless do a lot to progress IC leadership development that doesn't rely on large outlays or hiring expensive external consultants. The key will be to decide how to make a start in improving IC leadership development in ways that are consistent, modest, incremental, and doable for the foreseeable future. In terms of internal capability development, ICs could do two things in the short to medium term. First, they could use the IC leadership survey designed for this study to improve their own understanding of what staff think are the more important leadership attributes and governance challenges future IC leaders will need to address. If the survey, or a variation of it, could be used across all 'Five Eyes' ICs, it would provide a rich amount of data to help them understand leadership in order to address broader capability issues and develop leadership development programs.

Second, 'Five Eyes' ICs could consider using the IC leadership development framework outlined in Chapter 9 (Leadership Development) to identify comprehensive ways to build evidence-based and fit for purpose leadership development programs. The framework hopefully can steer discussions about curriculum development, learning, and assessment and teaching strategies. It promotes a hybrid approach to leadership development that engages the best of the internal IC to deliver such courses with targeted, relevant, and trusted external providers.

In addition to what ICs should do internally to progress knowledge about IC leadership issues externally, I hope the book will expand interest from intelligence studies scholars to increase their research focus on contemporary IC leadership issues. At this point, it seems that there are only a few scholars doing work in this area. In particular, it is hoped that the book provides a foundation where cross-disciplinary teams of scholars can begin to expand knowledge about the range of topics discussed here.

Index

Page numbers in *italics* represent figures, while page numbers in **bold** represent tables.